LOST CAUSES

DEEPAK LAL
LOST CAUSES

THE RETREAT FROM CLASSICAL LIBERALISM

Biteback Publishing

First published in Great Britain in 2012 by
Biteback Publishing Ltd
Westminster Tower
3 Albert Embankment
London
SE1 7SP
Copyright © Deepak Lal 2012

ISBN 978-1-84954-288-3

10 9 8 7 6 5 4 3 2 1

A CIP catalogue record for this book is available from the
British Library.

Set in Adobe Garamond Pro
Printed and bound in Great Britain by
CPI Group (UK) Ltd, Croydon, CR0 4YY

CONTENTS

INTRODUCTION

For most of my professional career since the early 1960s, as an Indian development economist teaching at Oxford and University College London till the early 1990s, I have worked in and on Third World countries. But after living in Britain for nearly thirty years, it seemed time to become a naturalised citizen of the country in which I had spent most of my life, and where my children were born and bred. Having become a British citizen in 1987 it seemed appropriate to take an interest in the public policy debates in the country. I wrote a number of pamphlets for various UK think tanks from the late 1980s, which are collected in this volume.

It may seem vainglorious to put together a collection of one's past scribblings. But, as many of the issues the pamphlets raised are still part of the ongoing public policy debate in the UK, a new audience may find them of interest. Moreover, they were written from the classical liberal perspective, a perspective at least rhetorically espoused by the Thatcher government, which adopted some of its principles, leading to Britain's economic renaissance and improved standing in the world from the middle of the 1980s.[1]

I had planned to put them together in 2009, as an indictment of the failures of the long 'socialist' winter since Labour's second term. But with the new coalition government elected in 2010, it seemed they would rectify many of these failings from the viewpoint of classical liberalism, which many in the government claimed to advocate. But these hopes were soon belied. So, sadly, these pamphlets still remain relevant.

But, even during the Thatcher years, the dirigiste impulse had not been quelled, and the earliest pamphlet included in this collection (Chapter 3) was written for the Centre for Policy Studies (CPS) she and Sir Keith Joseph had founded, attacking the nationalisation of Britain's universities by Kenneth Baker and Robert Jackson. Jackson threatened to sue me, which led to him being lampooned in a cartoon in *The Times* Higher Education Supplement. But of course my pamphlet had little effect on policy. John Major furthered the destruction of one of the best higher education systems in the world, by converting the numerous polytechnics – which provided an excellent route to vocational technical education to those lacking an academic aptitude – into second-rate universities, with all the academic pretensions and claims of a parity of esteem (in terms of pay and prestige) with the ancient universities. Worse, this *de facto* Tory nationalisation of what was an independent though state-financed higher education system provided the means for the subsequent

Labour governments to their *de jure* nationalisation, and use for dirigiste social engineering, leading to their ensuing decline. This was the first of my lost causes.

The continuing desire of all political parties to use the older universities to ensure 'access' by the disadvantaged has been prompted by the dismal performance of the pupils in state secondary schools. This in turn was due to the abolition of grammar schools by Shirley Williams and the socialist ideologue Tony Crosland, which the Iron Lady did nothing to reverse. Grammar schools had provided the essential ladder of opportunity for poor academic children to get the first-class education that their richer peers from public schools continue to obtain. A major error of David Cameron and his band of 'modernisers' is their reneging on the earlier Conservative pledge to expand grammar schools. Michael Gove's push for 'academies' as a substitute, though laudable in many ways, is nothing more than a souped-up version of the plans introduced by Tony Blair. Meanwhile, the vast majority of Britain's youth continue to be short-changed by an education system which fails to empower them for a globalised world, where their prospects depend increasingly upon brains, not brawn.

Similarly, it was Lady Thatcher, having been converted by Sir Crispin Tickell, who began Britain's public adoption of the Green agenda on global warming. She opened the floodgates for public funding of the scientists espousing the theory of man-made global warming by setting up the Hadley Centre and the environmental unit at the University of East Anglia, which has lately been in the news for its purported academic malpractices to further its beliefs. My first foray into this minefield was accidental. In 1989 I had been asked by Ralph Harris to give the Wincott lecture.[2] I chose as my theme an attack on the international macroeconomic and exchange rate co-ordination embodied in the Plaza agreement, based on correcting international 'pecuniary externalities'. As these are merely a sign of market interdependence and not of 'market failure' they do not require any public action. To be balanced, I thought I would also include a section on international 'technological externalities', which if present would require international public action. The emerging threat of global warming seemed to fit the bill.

I asked my old friend Julian Simon, who had spent a lifetime studying environmental problems, for a reading list on the topic. I was appalled to find the fragility of the scientific evidence and the climate forecasting models on which the draconian polices to curb CO_2 were based. My lecture on *The Limits of International Cooperation* became an attack on both the flawed arguments for international macroeconomic and environmental dirigisme. Though the former cause has not as yet been undermined, the second remains 'lost', as the West has unanimously embraced this call for an International Green Economic Order. All the political parties in the UK are committed to the most draconian cuts in CO_2 emissions, which if implemented would return Britain to the Stone Age. Chapter 9 (which is culled from my monthly op-ed columns for India's *Business Standard*) discusses this widespread Western collective madness. But this too remains a lost cause.

With the advent of New Labour's thirteen-year rule in 1997, while the economic liberal policies of the Thatcher era were preserved in its first term, their slow erosion began with the growing public expenditures on an unreformed National Health Service (NHS). Having moved to the University of California (UCLA) from University College London (UCL) in 1991, I was impressed by the excellent health care provided by the US private insurance system for those who were lucky enough to be employed by UCLA. Looking at the total monthly cost (to me and UCLA) of this comprehensive coverage for my whole family, I found that it was about the same in 2000 as the per capita cost of the dysfunctional NHS. I produced a pamphlet for *Politiea* on the subject (Chapter 3), arguing for the NHS to be replaced by a tax-funded national health insurance system.

This had some political resonance, with some reformers in the Liberal Party even endorsing it in their *Orange Book*, and some Tory politicians accepting that it was an elegant solution. But, public support for the NHS is clearly a religious movement in the UK (rather like the environment and the BBC), as I found when I gave a talk on my scheme at the Reform Club. Not surprisingly, the Tories have joined Labour as being the arch defenders of the largest remaining nationalised industry in the world, which at vast expense continues to serve producer rather than consumer interests. Every party is committed to throwing ever more money into this dysfunctional institution. Yet another lost cause.

One of the largely economic essays in the book is a lecture I gave at *Politiea* on the Economic and Monetary Union (EMU) and which they brought out as a pamphlet in 1999. This emphasised how this was a misguided project as the eurozone was not a natural 'optimum currency area' and that, without a fiscal-cum-political union, a monetary union was unsustainable. A judgement being increasingly borne out by the current travails of the euro, with the highly indebted Club Med economies hoist on the petard of the euro. I had argued that its future depended on a contest between the 'dinosaurs', who saw the euro as a means to maintain the unreformed labour markets and generous welfare states of the 'social market economy', and the 'modernisers' who saw the need to create flexible labour markets and to curb the excesses of their burgeoning welfare states. Germany turned out, *par excellence*, to be a moderniser; the Club Med countries continued to be dinosaurs.

With the worldwide boom, and its reformed labour markets, Germany's real wage fell relative to those in the Club Med countries. Denied their traditional route of devaluation to regain competiveness because of the single currency, they ran trade deficits financed by the growing trade surpluses of Germany. This inflow of capital in turn fuelled a boom in non-traded services – particularly housing and banking – (as their *real* exchange rates rose), and allowed their 'entitlement economies' to flourish. With the global financial crisis of 2008, the unsustainability of the public and private debt (which was foolishly converted into public debt – as in Ireland) accumulated during the earlier boom became manifest. The Club Med countries have found themselves in an actual or incipient sovereign debt crisis. There is little hope that they can grow themselves out of the crisis even if the private and public holders of their debt take sufficient 'haircuts', as without a devaluation they cannot attain competiveness. The alternative they have been forced to accept, to keep the euro project alive, is an *internal* devaluation through massive and prolonged deflation to lower their real wages below those of their northern European peers, particularly Germany. This seems politically unviable as the riots in Greece attest, and the breakup of the eurozone is imminent unless the Germans and the other northern Europeans are willing to continually subsidise their southern neighbours – an equally unlikely prospect.

In the mid-1960s when I was a lecturer at Christ Church, Oxford, my senior PPE colleague was Roy Harrod. At lunch, after giving the last lecture before retirement of his 'Currency and Credit' course, he told us that he had spent the entire lecture attacking Britain's desire to join the European Economic Community (EEC). He saw the European project as a disguised attempt by Germany to establish the European hegemony it had failed to achieve through two World Wars. He asked rhetorically, how he would be able to look upon the graves of all his many friends and colleagues who had tried to prevent this outcome during the two World Wars.

But, with the eurozone moving towards some form of quasi-fiscal union to deal with the sovereign debt crises facing its southern periphery, this outcome is now likely. It would imply Germany accepting the continuous subsidisation of its southern neighbours for the political end of achieving a united Europe, with Germany as the hegemon and the Club Med countries as its vassal client regions. This is the outcome that George Osborne (a professed Eurosceptic) has now seemingly accepted. But, it is equally likely that southern nationalism will derail this project, as they realise their loss of fiscal sovereignty and become like Italy's Mezzogiorno – increasingly dependent on handouts. This could lead to the destruction of the euro or an exit by the northern Germanic currencies around a new 'hard' deutschmark (or perhaps a new 'bismarck' as a recent correspondent in the *FT* has suggested), leaving a southern-Med-eurozone, which could maintain the undervalued euro they need to regain competitiveness and thus growth.

Thus, the ideal underlying the belief I had (like much of the British electorate) that, when voting for Britain joining the EEC in the 1970s, we were voting for Britain to be part of a competitive and integrated European common market of sovereign nation states seems to be a lost cause. This is particularly ironic given David Cameron and other coalition glitterati's recent trips to India and South Africa to whip up business for Britain. They seem to have implicitly recognised a fatal mistake that post-imperial Britain made in the 1960s. It chose to break its long cultural, commercial and familial links with its ex-colonies grouped in the Commonwealth, seduced by the seeming economic and geopolitical advantages Europe seemed to offer. Now, with economic growth in the countries of the Commonwealth since 1991 far out-passing that in a sclerotic and 'inward-looking' Europe, this economic choice can be seen to have been a serious mistake.

Equally, the geo-political calculation that Britain could 'punch above its weight' because of its 'special relationship' with the American superpower, acting as a bridge between it and Europe, has misfired since the collapse of the evil Empire.

In the post-1991 world a largely pacifist European Union (apart from Britain and France) has shown little will or ability to even deal with civil wars in its own neighbourhood (*pace* Yugoslavia, and now Libya), let alone being able to join the US in the unenviable task of maintaining global order. It is members of the Commonwealth who have, instead, often joined the 'coalitions of the willing', which the US has had to assemble, for good or ill, to fight its wars to maintain order. If, instead of throwing in its lot with Europe, Britain had strengthened its ties with the Commonwealth, with even the hope that the US prodigal son might eventually return to the fold, both Britain's economic and geopolitical standing might have been better than it is currently.

Apart from these continuing economic policy issues, the most disturbing development over the last two decades has been the growing intrusions in the hitherto protected private sphere, with the growth of the nanny state. So J. S. Mill's principle of liberty, which had hitherto seemed sacrosanct in the country of his birth, is increasingly being debauched, most heinously by dirigistes who claim to be following the principle in the area of personal health. Nowhere is this more apparent than the spurious arguments based on the evil effects of second-hand smoke and the purported *akrasia* of the smoker's divided self, to justify the ban on smoking. My pamphlet for the South African Free Market Foundation argues against this illiberal policy. (Chapter 5)

Equally disturbing is the vast expansion of the surveillance state in Britain, with its millions of CCTV cameras and the granting of myriad powers to various local and national bodies to search an Englishman's home – which is no longer his castle. The terrorist attacks by Islamist jihadists (as well as the 'yob' culture of the burgeoning 'underclass' created by the entitlement economy) have provided the justification for this move towards Big Brother. But, for a country that dealt stoically with the even worse terror unleashed by the IRA for over four decades, this is puzzling. As I argue in Chapter 6, written soon after the terrorist attack on the World Trade Center in New York on 9/11, the social costs of terrorism are greatly exaggerated, and have allowed the state to exact mounting personal costs (with one having to virtually strip before boarding an airline) which far outweigh any of the purported benefits from most counter-terrorist measures.

Even more illiberal and a source of global disorder has been the nearly century-old War on Drugs. Ironically, as I argue in Chapter 7, the ongoing War on Terror in Afghanistan against the Taliban and Al-Qaeda is being undermined by the War on Drugs. Moreover, the hope that foreign aid could turn a tribally torn Afghanistan into a Western-style liberal democracy is being increasingly belied.

One of my continuing surprises is how British governments of every hue still fail to accept Peter Bauer's trenchant critique of foreign aid – despite the fact that he was ennobled by Mrs Thatcher (as she then was) for his pains. After the various plans to 'Save Africa' promoted by the recent Labour government, the new coalition government has not only ring-fenced foreign aid against the cuts in public spending, but also pledged to increase it to achieve the UN target of 0.7 per cent of GDP. This is economic madness, when seemingly there is not enough money to maintain Britain's defence forces, and in particular, as I argue in Chapter 8, there is incontrovertible evidence that foreign aid has failed to achieve any of its purported purposes. Yet another lost cause.

How does one explain this continuing seeming irrationality of public policy? In the 1980s, while I was the research administrator at the World Bank in Washington,

I was exposed to the public choice theories of Jim Buchanan and Gordon Tullock. In a large multi-country comparative study I directed at the bank on the political economy of poverty, equity and growth,[3] I became aware of the systematic nature of the predation which led to policies that seemed so misguided from an economic viewpoint. As most government interventions are equivalent to implicit or explicit subsidies to favoured groups, paid for by implicit or explicit taxes on the rest, one needed to understand the incentives and disincentives facing predatory states (whether autocratic/authoritarian or democratic) to maximise either their discretionary net revenue or the size of the bureaucracy.

I applied this theory of the predatory state to fiscal policy in the UK, in a pamphlet for the newly established Social Market Foundation in 1990.[4] Much later I refurbished this in a lecture at *Politiea* which was issued as a pamphlet. This is the first chapter in this book, for it sets out the reasons why, irrespective of the party in power, the predatory dirigiste impulse is ever present even in seemingly liberal democracies. For the prey, an understanding of this impulse, particularly in the area of taxes and subsidies, is important if they are to limit the predation of their peers. It also shows why globalisation is so important in limiting the amount of predation through the implicit and explicit tax competition it promotes. The recent assault on so called 'tax havens' and the desire for a global harmonisation of taxes is nothing else but the creation of a cartel of predatory nation states seeking to maximise their takings from their various national prey.

The last essay in the book (Chapter 10) is the most recent and deals with the causes and consequences of the global financial crisis (GFC). In September 2008 in Tokyo, at its bi-annual general meeting, I became the President of the Mont Pelerin Society (MPS) – the academy for classical liberals founded by Friedrich Hayek after the Second World War. On returning to Los Angeles via China, I was on a trip to Suzhou with economist Steven Cheung, who was constantly on the phone to his stockbroker. He got a phone call on a late September afternoon that Lehman had gone belly up. The GFC had begun. With talk of the end of globalising capitalism rampant, I organised a special meeting of the MPS in New York in March 2009 to discuss the GFC from a classical liberal perspective. For most of the current prognostications and analyses were based on various forms of Keynesianism, and most observers had forgotten Keynes's main protagonist in the 1930s – Hayek. In a presidential address to the meeting based on a series of columns for the *Business Standard*, and in the annual lecture of the Adam Smith Institute in June 2009,[5] I set out my own diagnosis of the crisis, as a Hayekian recession with Fisherian consequences. The subsequent course of the crisis and the muddled attempts to contain it only confirmed the Hayekian analysis, as I documented in a lecture I gave at the Centro Einaudi in Turin in September 2010. The published version is Chapter 10. Its main argument is that the ultimate cause of the sovereign debt crises that are now threatening the West in the aftermath of the GFC is the crisis of the entitlement economies that have been created since the Second World War. Britain has bitten the bullet by attempting to roll back the entitlement economy, and many eurozone countries are being forced to do the same. But, the US still remains in denial. The West remains near the economic precipice.

I hope this brief introduction whets the reader's appetite to read the more detailed discussion of these policy issues in the chapters that follow. To show that most of these issues are longstanding, I have not attempted to edit the essays to remove the references to the context and time when they were written. But I do commend these lost causes, as the wealth and welfare of my adopted country continue to depend upon their redemption.

London, August 2011

CHAPTER ONE

TACKLING THE
PREDATORY STATE

INTRODUCTION: FROM HIGH TAX DIRIGISME TO A NEW LIBERALISM

Gordon Brown, when Chancellor of the Exchequer, set a trap on public spending and higher taxation – and all three political parties fell into it, showing no desire to challenge him on health and education spending. Even before the financial crisis the Conservatives had ruled out immediate tax cuts.

All the political parties have embraced the status quo of a large, unreformed welfare state with high levels of tax and spending. The position is like that of Butskellism. This post-war economic ideology dominated until questioned by Keith Joseph in the 1970s and repudiated by the Thatcher governments in the 1980s. Since then the parties have been changing their clothes: Tony Blair stole the Conservatives' clothes and David Cameron is stealing New Labour's. All three parties seem prepared to spend over 40 per cent of our money on a range of activities including 'public services'. Neither opposition party questions whether health and education should in the main continue to be publicly provided and/or financed services, as at present; or, indeed, why public funds are spent on a local and central government bureaucracy designed to address 'social exclusion'. The fiscal reforms which dramatically reduced public spending from 45 per cent of GDP in 1983 to 37.5 per cent in 1989, leaving it at 39.2 per cent when New Labour came to power, have no current appeal in the party that pioneered them. The upshot is that there is now little to choose between the three parties when it comes to tax and spending.

The Tories, like their Swedish counterparts, appear to suggest they should be elected because the (overgrown) welfare state is safe in their hands and they can run it more efficiently than their competitors. They have been intimidated by their 'progressive' opponents. They are mindful of the fact that nearly 50 per cent of the electorate has been made direct or indirect wards of the state. Any attack on the welfare state will, therefore, be opposed by a majority of dependants when they vote. As a result power will depend on accepting the new political reality and joining the 'progressive' social democratic tide.

Though the Swedish model is offered to prove that high levels of social security can be paid for from the cradle to the grave without damaging economic performance, the claim is false. The Swedish economy, between 1870 and 1950, grew faster on average than any other industrialised economy, and the country became technologically one of the most advanced and richest in the world. From the 1950s Swedish economic growth slowed relative to other industrialised countries. This was due to the expansion of the welfare state and the growth of public – at the expense of private – employment.[6] After the Second World War the working population increased by about one million: public employment accounted for c.770,000, private accounted for only 155,000. The crowding out by an inefficient public sector of the efficient private sector has characterised Sweden for nearly half a century.[7] From being the fourth richest country in the Organisation for Economic Co-operation and Development (OECD) in 1970, it has fallen to fourteenth place. Only in France and New Zealand has there been a larger fall in relative wealth. By contrast Ireland, with economic reform and a low tax regime, improved its ranking from twenty-first place to fourth. Yet all the political parties in Britain now want to emulate the fabled Swedish model. David Hume and Adam Smith would not have been surprised.

This pamphlet will consider why this has happened. Why, on tax and spending, has political paralysis set in, other than a belated and vague acknowledgement that some cuts will have to be made? What has happened to the classical liberal principles and how has the collectivist impulse been channelled into a 'new dirigisme'? The new dirigisme must be countered by classical liberals as the first, essential, step towards the lower taxes and better public services the electorate as a whole wants.

THE PREDATORY STATE: FROM MONARCH TO MIDDLE CLASSES

The power to tax is the 'power to take'. The state has this monopoly of coercion over its citizens. When absolute monarchs ruled, the interests of the people required that the 'power to take' should be restricted (as happened in the tax revolt which cost Charles I his head). Those who controlled the state were recognised, both in their origin and actions, to be self-interested predators. The monopoly of coercion provided the controllers of the state with the means to extract revenue from their prey. The state was in effect the equivalent of a Mafiosi protection racket. It is always inherently predatory and the interests of predators and their prey are not wholly divorced from each other. Predators to some extent are interested in the welfare of the prey which provides their own food supply. Similarly, self-interested predatory controllers of states have an interest in the welfare of their prey.

The prey needs the state for protection against external and internal aggression and to settle disputes between individuals. These ends – the classical public goods – prompt them to give the state the monopoly power of coercion and to finance itself from their earnings. But, once transferred to the sovereign, this power should not be used to extract more than necessary to finance public goods.

For the predatory state the 'power to take' allows it to extract from its prey when it can; or it allows a rival (external or internal) to provide the public goods at lower cost and contest its monopoly of coercion within the state. This is the dilemma of politics. How can the prey tie down an inherently predatory state to take only what is needed to provide the classical public goods?

When the state consisted of monarchs who took for themselves (for mistresses, palaces, armies and other paraphernalia of power) more than was needed to provide protection or other public goods, the dilemma was clear. At first the absolute monarch's 'power to take' was restricted by representative legislatures. But with the rise of majoritarian democracies, 'we' become the state if not the predator – and democratic governments also seek to maximise public revenue exercising discretionary power over its disposal.

Political parties, in two-party democratic systems, tend to serve the interest of the median voter, the 'power to take' having passed from absolute monarchs to the 'middle classes'. Why? Both parties in a two-party system will appeal to the interests of the median voter by occupying the middle ground. As much of democratic politics is redistributive, politicians serve the median voter by taking from those who are both richer and poorer through the welfare state tax-benefit systems of today's democracies. This is a form of transfer state. The US failure – by any party – to tackle middle-class entitlements to social security, or the UK's to get the middle classes to pay for their children's higher education, illustrate the phenomenon. Gordon Brown's success in making the 'median' voter a ward of the state has now been embraced by David Cameron who recognises the reluctance of such voters to allow state handouts to be taken away.

Politicians do not just promote the interests of the median voter: they resemble the monopolistic revenue-maximising absolute monarchs of yore. Suppose two parties announce their platforms successively.[8] The party to announce policy last can, by taxing some minority and transferring some of the revenue to a new majority, keep the rest for discretionary use and win. (One illustration of this is Gordon Brown's pledge to find savings from the current 'waste' in public services, to use it for his own purposes of 'investing' it – as he puts it – in public services).

Contemporary ethics do not, in most Western democracies, permit the direct transfer of the discretionary 'surplus' to politicians themselves. Instead, it buys future votes, provides favours to 'friendly' interest groups, or – where close 'social' links exist between the politicians and bureaucrats – allows for an expanding bureaucracy. (One example is the former polytechnic lecturers who crowded the New Labour benches and social workers in local councils.) There is then a continued interest in expanding the size of their 'bureaux' and budgets: to establish, maintain or expand monopoly of public provision of goods and services (including those which competitive private producers could provide more efficiently). Expanding the public sector leads to lucrative tenured jobs at the base of the bureaucratic pyramid and improves the future 'life chances' of bureaucrats in income, perquisites and power.

Though direct income transfers to government ministers are not now permitted in Western democracies, they are advocated for alleviating poverty. However, public servants do not favour direct non-discretionary monetary transfers to the 'poor', which give them little advantage. They prefer indirect and discretionary transfers which require the larger 'welfare bureaucracy', characteristic of the welfare state. With declining poverty in most industrial countries, new 'welfare' needs are discovered, for example that of 'social exclusion' (discussed later). This in turn leads to a further expansion of the welfare bureaucracy.[9]

Just as the interventions of self-interested politicians and bureaucrats affect public finances, so too do the pressure groups into which individuals organise themselves. Election results will therefore reflect the interests of the most successful interest groups. Public policy will, as a result, be determined

by competition amongst pressure groups, the most successful of which will be small and concentrated. As the income
taken from the majority is spread over their members, the
per capita costs to the 'losers' will be small and will rarely
lead to the majority forming an opposing pressure group.
Foreign trade protection advocated by producer interests,
though contrary to consumer interests, can be explained
in this way. One example is that of the protection offered
to agricultural producers in the EU through the Common
Agricultural Policy (CAP).

A further difficulty in checking the inherent predation
of the state is the move from representative to participatory democracy. The increasing use of opinion polling in
the political process in the United Kingdom and United
States has led to this. With the median voters now seen
as holding the key to electoral success, politicians need to
know their opinions and interests to design the 'bribes'
to be offered for votes; they also need to train the spin
doctors to win the rest of the electorate (through the altru-
istic rhetoric in which such self-seeking can be clothed).

The slide to participatory democracy is contrary to
the Western notion of liberal democracy based on the
representative principle. From the founding fathers of
the American Republic to liberal thinkers like Immanuel
Kant, direct or participatory democracy on the model of
the Greek city-states has been held to be deeply illiberal.
Subject to populist pressures and the changing passions of
the majority, it can oppress minorities. By contrast, in a
representative democracy, people choose their representatives for a legislature which legislates. The people do not
themselves write or pass legislation. The representatives
judge legislation on the merits of the case, moved ideally

by reason. Edmund Burke's summary is as apt today as it was in 1774:

> Your representative owes you, not his industry only, but his judgment: and he betrays it instead of serving you if he sacrifices it to your opinion. You choose a member indeed; but when you choose him, he is not a member of Bristol, but he is a Member of Parliament.[10]

The move towards direct participatory democracy has nonetheless taken place gradually in the US and UK. With the rise of the pollsters, and the weakening of party loyalties, politicians – particularly those of the 'third way' – have come to rely increasingly upon 'focus groups' to discover and pander to public opinion, the practice decried by Burke. By opening up the legislative process to greater scrutiny and accountability the system paradoxically becomes more open to influence by pressure groups and the phenomenon of *demosclerosis*,[11] where well-funded interest groups hijack domestic politics. Changes designed to democratise the system or to make it easier 'to listen to the people' have too often led to well-organised interest groups forcing governments to bend to their will. It is, as Zakaria put it, now clear that reforms 'designed to produce majority rule have produced minority rule',[12] as the people have neither the time nor the inclination to monitor the legislators' laws on a daily basis. As a result, instead of rational consideration of alternative policies by the people's representatives, referenda determine the outcomes, often the consequence of 'spin' and emotion.

It might therefore seem quixotic to champion classical

liberal principles for public finance. But even predatory political processes around the world have at various times yielded liberal reform.[13] The solution may lie in the theory of 'crisis and reform'.[14] A serious economic crisis, caused by the prey seeking through evasion, avoidance or flight to escape predation must occur so as to force the state to disgorge. Ideas help, but ultimately it is the interest of the state in overcoming the disorder its predation has bred that leads it to reverse direction.

Has the United Kingdom reached such a crisis in its social policies, with the NHS, schools and universities increasingly in disarray? Only time will tell. But when the crisis does arise and the median voter sees that the prey fleeing predation on this scale can no longer continue, the nature of reform must be clear. As numerous examples from around the world attest, the window of opportunity for reform is likely to be very small.

STATE, ECONOMY AND SOCIETY: RIGHTS AND WRONGS

The aim of political economy is to find how the state can provide the essential public goods at the least cost in terms of taxation. The classical liberals recognised the aim, and laissez-faire economics provided a realistic approach where predatory governments were seen to put revenue maximisation above the social welfare maximisation of Platonic guardians. The classical policy prescriptions have been misrepresented.[15] The classical liberals were neither hostile to the state nor of the view that the role of governments in economic life was minor. Their view of the state was positive; and indeed[16] Adam Smith's view is almost identical to that of Keynes, who argued that 'the important thing for government is not to do things which individuals are doing already, but to do those things which at present are not done at all'.[17]

The state's three functions were recognised as (i) to protect society from foreign invaders, (ii) to protect each member from oppression and injustice by others, and (iii) to provide and maintain the public works and institutions which provided public goods.[18] The principles of economic liberalism were set out in J. S. Mill's *Principles*, and their clearest modern reformulation is to be found in Friedrich Hayek's *The Constitution of Liberty*. In fact, the current 'Washington Consensus' on economic policy is essentially a classical liberal policy package.[19]

Classical liberals from Smith to Hayek to Milton Friedman have agreed that equality may be in conflict with liberty, and the liberal is not an egalitarian.[20] Classical liberals advocate public transfers when private transfers are not available or sufficient to help the 'deserving poor'[21] and, since Mill, they have also advocated the public *financing* but not *provision* of merit goods such as health and education for those unable to afford them.[22] Though the programme promoted by social democrats increasingly resembles the classical liberal prescriptions, the exception is merit goods. In eschewing egalitarianism in taxation and by welfare state reform designed to concentrate the benefits to the 'deserving poor', both the New Democrats under Clinton in the United States and New Labour under Blair in the United Kingdom were closer to the classical liberal viewpoint than they imagine. The main difference is over the merit goods of health and education, for which they believe that planned public provision should replace the operation of the market and that bureaucracy should be expanded to enforce various forms of political correctness. This is an enterprise view of

the state as distinct from the state viewed as a civil association by classical liberals. These two views of the state – that
of civil association with no purposes of its own and that
of an enterprise seeking to legislate some vision of perfect-
ibility – have been the two dominant voices in Western
political thought and action: one going back to the Greeks,
the other being part of the Judaeo-Christian tradition.

The 'New Dirigisme': The rise of the 'enterprise' voice
of socialism towards the end of the nineteenth century
led to 'the end of laissez-faire'.[23] The erosion of the classical liberal 'civil association' view of the state had begun
in Europe with Bismarck's social insurance scheme in
Germany and the liberal welfare reforms in Britain of
1906–14. It spread to the United States during the Great
Depression and Roosevelt's New Deal. The dominant
ideology which was to follow – 'embedded liberalism' or
'social democracy'[24] – was encouraged by the economists;
and by the Second World War the nineteenth-century
classical liberalism had been replaced by the dirigiste dogma,
especially pronounced in the Communist countries. With
their demise after the Berlin Wall fell, the socialist impulse
has been transformed. Rather than seeking to replace
capitalism, it wishes to create 'capitalism with a human
face'. Moreover, the notion of freedom has been used to
promote the 'enterprise' views of the state under cover of
an implied view of the state as a 'civil' association by using
the distinction between negative and positive freedom, and
by arguing that the promotion of 'positive freedoms' is no
different from the promotion of negative freedom, which
classical liberals value.[25]

'Freedom' and 'liberty': The economist-philosopher
Anthony de Jasay has provided classical liberals with

an escape from this dirigiste trap. De Jasay jettisons the
notion of freedom as being central to classical liberalism.
The most basic reason for not relying on the concept of
freedom to justify a classical liberal society and polity is
that freedom in ordinary speech involves ensuring that
deliberate obstacles are not being placed in the way of
individuals' actions. This immediately leads to the slippery
slope, where 'being *free* to do something and being *able* to
do it' are elided. The discourse of freedom then degener-
ates into one in which freedom means the general avail-
ability to all of the good things of life. This allows various
policies forming part of the socialist enterprise view of the
world to be smuggled in as being part of freedom.[26]

Instead de Jasay, relying on the English common
law tradition, defines the rules which the state as a civil
association should uphold. These are Mill's principles of
liberty: a person can undertake any *feasible* action which
does not harm others or break an obligation.[27] The
burden of proof lies on someone who wants to prohibit
an individual's actions. This process is equivalent to the
presumed innocence of the accused unless found guilty
by due process. In contrast to this common law tradition
of justice there is an alternative which may be called the
continental system of justice, or 'public law' as de Jasay
calls it. Under this, individuals are forbidden from feasible actions unless they are expressly *permitted* by various
'rights' granted under constitutional provisions.

Of the two alternative legal traditions, the common
law based on a list of *prohibited* actions is more readily
verifiable than the public law tradition based on a list of
permitted actions. For feasible actions are limitless, and
listing what we must not do is less onerous than listing

what we are permitted to do.[28] If the 'liberty' norm of the common law tradition based on prohibitions of feasible actions is more sound (being verifiable) than the continental tradition based on permissions, what of 'property rights' and 'human rights'?[29]

Property rights: Property rights are mistakenly called rights. If an individual is free to do something which is not wrong, this liberty must include the freedom to do what he likes with his property. *Liberties are different from rights.* While the property owner has the *liberty* to use his property, the non-owner has to get the *right* to use it which is provided by the lease. Thus, whereas liberties are not conferred by anyone, rights require someone else to have agreed to fulfil some obligation.

Ownership is often acquired through the proceeds of work, through exchange (e.g. like that of assets) or from gifts and inheritance. These means of acquiring property meet the requirements of justice; they involve exercising a liberty without transgressing any obligation or causing harm to others.

Conquest and seizure have been equally important in acquiring land. The means are morally unjust and calls for restitution would be justified. This is at the heart of the controversy about the Palestinians' 'right to return' in the Arab–Israeli dispute. But, though the claim may be morally just, it is not expedient. For most societies throughout history have recognised the chaos that would be caused by seeking to redress every fault in the historical descent of every current title to property, no matter how far back the chain of transfers stretches. They have, therefore, (correctly) applied some form of statute of limitations – if for no other reason than recognising that the sins of the fathers should not be visited upon their grandchildren and great-grandchildren.

Human rights: What of 'human rights?' Rights (as already mentioned) arise from contracts – actual or implicit – which give rise to obligations that have been accepted by someone else. Thus 'every right of one person has the *agreement* of another as its source, cause and evidence'.[30] Agreement is crucial in generating rights and the corresponding obligations. Thus social rights are not rights but *entitlements*. The right of the unemployed to unemployment insurance or the poor to welfare are not rights, but entitlements created by the state, which can be changed or repudiated because they are not based on contract. By contrast a genuine right arising from a contract cannot be limited or withdrawn without the right holder giving his consent. These rights are sometimes called *specific* rights.

In addition the claim is made for 'human rights' – a *general* right – which arise from the assumption that being *human* justifies certain rights which go beyond specific rights. They are the descendants of 'natural rights'.[31] They arise from the general right, namely 'the equal right of all men to be free',[32] including the right to free speech, free worship, to walk about, to breathe. However such a 'right' is redundant in the common law tradition where one is free to act provided it does not infringe one's obligations (the specific rights of others) or cause others harm.[33] Only in the public law tradition do these 'rights' need to be specified where all feasible actions require *permission,* including these 'human rights' to breathe, to be able to speak freely, to walk around etc.[34] Individual freedom of action is much better protected by the common law tradition, where one is free to take any feasible action subject to the constraints of harm and specific obligations (rights).

Capitalism with a human face: Many of capitalism's opponents use the concept of freedom to imply an 'enterprise' view of the state, yet appear also to subscribe to the classical liberal view of the state as a 'civil' association. They aim to justify redistributive measures. Their position is one of denying that distribution of property based on contract, transfers and first possession can be just. Instead they view property as arising from the mutual gains provided by social cooperation.

The claim is that much existing wealth is the result of social cooperation going back to Adam and Eve. It is a social inheritance and belongs to the whole of society. But, largely for reasons of efficiency, it is inexpedient to rule out some private appropriation of this social wealth. Hence, some social wealth can be converted into private property, on the terms and conditions specified by the co-owner society. This can be done provided social exclusion from this social wealth – of those disadvantaged by lack of talent, luck or who are unable to share in the benefits of social cooperation – is prevented. The state as the co-owner of this social wealth should use its powers to coerce some to give up part of their property or income to the disadvantaged.

The false premise is that individual contributions to past and present social cooperation and wealth are impossible to trace and all wealth is seen as that generated by society as a whole.

But, though social cooperation has generated the wealth in the world, it is false to claim that no trace of the individual contributions is available. Everyone who has contributed through work has been paid in voluntary exchanges. Some payments were consumed, some saved and invested and the resulting assets have the contributors' title to them. To coerce them to give away what is theirs – and which they are at liberty to use as they see fit – would be unjust. Though over the millennia everyone has contributed to the generation and accumulation of a society's wealth, this does not mean that everything is owed to society. '*Nothing is owed*', de Jasay rightly notes, 'everything has been paid for, one way or another, in a manner and to an extent sufficient to call forth the contribution. There is no further common-pool claim overhanging the lot, for no payment must be made twice. He who sees an overhanging claim in favour of 'society' is seeing a mirage, or the wishful image of one.'[35]

In the same way it is false to claim that, because social cooperation is needed for gains in a business or corporation, everyone is a *stakeholder*, to be consulted and if necessary assuaged. A corporation consists of a series of voluntary exchanges based on a contract where the worker is obliged to perform certain tasks in payment for the agreed remuneration. The obligation to consult may be given by the employer to the worker as part of the contract and in this way a specific right is granted matching the voluntarily agreed obligation.[36] But there can be no general right to consult 'stake-holders', unless one believes that the sharing of the fruits of cooperation cannot be assigned by voluntary contract, and hence this social product has to be shared by continual negotiation or mediation by the co-owner of society's capital – the state. For the dirigistes, the employer's capital has been leased to him from society's capital owned by the state on its behalf. The claim is false. The employer has justly acquired capital from past savings and can do with them what he pleases. There is nothing which belongs to society which has been leased out to the employer.

Another illegitimate claim is that the economic power wielded by employers and corporations is coercive and forces the weak to give into the demands of the strong. That confuses the *actual options* open to the weaker party (where they can act freely on the offer of the employer) with their *hopes* for a better deal.[37] However, it would be unjust to use the coercive power of the state to enforce this hope of the weak and violate the stronger party's liberty to use their endowments as they wish.

In the same way, other state coercion to take a person's justly acquired property to give it to anyone else would also be ruled out where the state is seen as a civil association. Inheritance taxes would be ruled out; other redistributive taxes would be unjust. Would public transfers to the destitute be ruled out? Most societies have made provision for the destitute: those incapable of making any living. The safety net has usually been provided through private transfers from other family members or public charity. With the fraying of families in the West these private social safety nets have also become frayed. Public charity remains the only alternative. Therefore, where private charity can no longer be relied on to alleviate destitution some form of public transfers may be forthcoming.[38]

WHAT KIND OF TAX FOR THE GLOBAL ECONOMY?
How then can the fiscal exactions of democratic, predatory states be controlled? How can the fiscal privileges inherent in the government's power to take and give to whom it

chooses be limited? Two different answers are given, both from Nobel Prize winners. The first is that of the 'optimum tax theory', for which James Mirrlees won the Nobel Prize, but which goes back to the Cambridge mathematician Frank Ramsey in the 1920s. The idea is that the optimum pattern of taxation to raise a given revenue is higher taxes levied on goods for which the price elasticity of demand (which measures the sensitivity of the quantity of the good consumed to its price) is low (e.g. cigarettes and alcohol). It assumes (falsely) a benevolent government.[39]

But suppose, if instead of a benevolent government seeking to raise a *given* revenue, we have a predatory government which wants to raise the *maximum* revenue it can, what set of taxes will it choose? These are Ramsey's optimal taxes which a consumer (e.g. an addicted smoker facing a tax on cigarettes) finds inescapable.[40]

The only taxes which citizens should grant to a predatory state, says the other Nobel Prize winner, James Buchanan and others, are those from which people can escape – those for goods with elastic demand. In the same way for providing local public goods there should be local sales taxes in a decentralised fiscal system, with tax competition between localities limiting their predation, not taxes on property or wealth. All sides agree, however, that the base of the tax system should, ideally, be consumption and not income.

Recent proposals for flat taxes to limit the fiscal predation of governments should be considered in this context. A flat tax, in its pure version, replaces multiple marginal rates with a single marginal rate; it also abolishes the complex systems of allowances and reliefs used by governments to buy votes or for social engineering. A high personal tax-free allowance allows the poor to be taken out of the tax net and imparts progressivity to the system. All taxes – corporate, personal income and commodity taxes (e.g. VAT) – are set at the same rate, amounting in effect to a consumption tax which abolishes any double taxation (such as that of dividends). The flat tax has the advantage of simplicity and transparency (which lead to greater tax compliance and increased tax revenues), faster economic growth (due to greater incentives to work) and the removal of disincentives and distortions in existing tax systems. The main costs in the short run could be a loss of revenue with the reduction in rates and the increased income tax threshold to help low earners. The UK Treasury, in its uncensored version of the flat tax, found support for many of these beneficial effects to the UK economy from a flat tax.[41]

The major advantage from a classical liberal viewpoint is that the flat tax prevents governments from politically inspired redistribution. But whereas the East European countries which adopted the flat tax were replacing defunct tax regimes, in developed countries mature tax systems are based on such a redistribution game over many generations. The likely losers would be the middle classes, the former beneficiaries who would resist the flat tax. So, even though a number of developed countries, including the UK, Germany, Spain, Greece and Italy are considering a flat tax, it is unlikely to be of the pure form. According to George Osborne, the shadow Chancellor and a British supporter, that also would probably be the case in the UK. If, however, a flat tax could be implemented, it would, on account of its transparency and simplicity, make it more difficult for governments to increase predatory public expenditure. *All* taxpayers would know it implied a rise in the flat tax they would have to pay. This should aid the tax resistance of all the prey who can no longer be played off one against another by the predatory state.

The signs are that developed countries like the UK may adopt the classical liberal principles on tax and spending on account of the growing tax competition from the new economies of Asia and Eastern Europe. Many of the emerging economies are, because of their own economic reforms, low tax and spend economies. Based on classical liberal principles China has undertaken the largest unilateral trade liberalisation since the UK's repeal of the Corn Laws in the nineteenth century. If they can resist the siren pressures for the European 'social model', they will increasingly provide a more congenial environment for footloose capital from around the world. As their per capita incomes rise and they attract home their 'best and the brightest', the United States and United Kingdom will find it increasingly difficult to use the present 'brain drain' from Asia to reverse the damage done to their indigenous human capital formation by failed public education systems. Perhaps this will lead to the crisis of the welfare state, which alone will persuade the median voter in these countries to abandon continuing dirigisme and adopt the classical liberal principles they still, at least, rhetorically espouse.

THE CATALYST FOR CHANGE: COMPETITION

As the global economic picture changes, new and successful economies are poised to challenge the survival of older high tax and spending countries. Western politicians must therefore grapple anew with one of the oldest economic problems: How can lower taxes and better public services become the natural order? How can the state, by nature predatory and with monopoly power of coercion, be forced only to extract what is needed for the basic classical public goods – defence, law and order – financing merit goods (for those unable to afford them) and alleviating destitution? Today the problem has come full circle, as the concept of 'freedom', which provided a basis for controlling the predator, is used to justify the predatory state.

Whereas the classical liberals recommended laissez-faire as the best way of tying down the state, their socialist successors promoted the dogma of state enterprise, central control and dirigisme. Even after socialism's demise, the dirigisme – the way in which the state fulfils its inherently predatory instincts – was not reversed. Rather, the socialist impulse found a new voice advocating a 'new dirigisme'. It appropriated the (classical liberal) ideal of freedom and championed predatory dirigiste policies in the name of 'positive' freedom. New Labour's legacy is a burgeoning nanny state based on moral and social paternalism, and an intricate web of stealth taxes which has considerably raised the state's 'take' to finance unreformed public services. The upshot is that in the UK today, government and opposition parties all seem to want to imitate Sweden's tax and spend policies. But just as Sweden has slipped in the growth league because of its overextended welfare state, the UK's previous economic boom – largely due to the Thatcher reforms – has been dramatically stifled by this new dirigisme.

What then does the future hold? How can the UK ensure economic prosperity with a fiercely competitive global market? At a theoretical level, the new dirigisme (in the name of 'positive freedom') can be curbed by distinguishing 'freedom' from 'liberty' as enshrined in the common law tradition. If economic as well as social policy is once again based on classical liberal principles it will serve the interests of the prey who want lower taxes and better public services. In particular the UK must address two developments.

First, the growing economic competition from the emerging economies of Asia and Europe with its potentially serious implications for the UK's economic future must be understood and met. These new and successful economies have relatively low spending and tax, where the UK's by contrast is high. As a result these new economies may attract both footloose capital and (given time) their bright and able nationals who currently work abroad. That would lead to the flight of much needed capital for investment from the UK and it would reverse the brain drain, now seen as helping to sustain an increasingly unsustainable dirigiste economy in the United Kingdom. So the United Kingdom must change course if it is to maintain its prosperity.

Second, the ever increasing appetite by the state for funds to feed unreformable public health and educational systems could lead to a crisis. Just as in the 1970s national-ised industries eventually compelled reform, so now these nationalised public services may do likewise. When that happens, the (classical liberal) principles that have already shaped reform – that of tax and spending reform and that of moribund industries – may once again provide the solution to the crisis. The state must then denationalise and allow the winds of competition and freedom to blow.

First published as 'Taxing Matters', Policy Studies No. 56, Politiea, *London 2007.*

CHAPTER TWO

FROM THE NHS TO A NATIONAL HEALTH INSURANCE SYSTEM

INTRODUCTION: THE NHS IN COLLAPSE

The National Health Service (NHS), one of the world's last and largest nationalised industries, remains a sacred cow. For the conditions of care in the NHS are now so bad that, as one consultant in a recent *Panorama* programme put it, 'if animals were treated in this way they would rightly be condemned for animal rights violations'. This documentary showed in graphic detail the perils now facing anyone who has to be treated in an NHS hospital.

The documentary showed patients first in trolleys waiting in the Accident and Emergency (A&E) corridors. Then to meet the government's targets for waiting time on trolleys they are merely transferred to beds in the same corridors. If they need to use a bedpan, someone is wheeled out of a regular ward and the unfortunate patient waiting for a regular bed is wheeled in temporarily, till, ablutions done, they are wheeled out – albeit on a bed – back into the A&E corridor. The documentary showed the postponed operations after an interminable wait to see a consultant, followed by the wait to have an operation, followed by the wait to get a surgical bed before the operation can be performed. Once it is completed, the horror does not cease, for there is high danger of picking up a life-threatening infection because of the generally filthy conditions and the grossly overstretched nursing services, and, of course if you are of a certain age, there is the further danger of meeting Dr Shipman. And yet the great British public consider the NHS to be 'a national treasure', so that any reformers touch it at their peril.

The New Labour government is now attempting to refurbish this Old Labour inheritance in Old Labour style by announcing more cash tied to a national plan for the NHS. But this is a panacea to deal with non-performing nationalised industries that I have seen offered again and again in country after country during my thirty-year professional career as a development economist. More cash, tied to moral crusades, managerial rearrangements and 'crash' programmes is – as with the NHS Plan – the usual medicine offered. It invariably fails for well-known reasons concerning the incentives and information required for maintaining productive efficiency.

This is sometimes referred to as the 'soft budget constraint' faced by public enterprises. With no bankruptcy or danger of takeovers facing the managers of public monopolies and, with their finances being determined by the political process, there is no incentive for public enterprise managers to achieve any given objective in a cost minimising manner. Target setting leads to perverse incentives. Thus, as the National Audit Office has recently confirmed, setting targets for waiting lists has meant that hospitals have been treating patients with ingrown toenails earlier than those with life-threatening cancers to meet the waiting list target. This is reminiscent of those Soviet factories which produced either left or right shoes to meet their total shoe targets!

Moreover, given the unavoidable division of knowledge in any real world economy, as Hayek has emphasised, the planners will never have the requisite information available to either devise an 'optimal' plan or to monitor managerial performance. Inevitably, therefore, public monopolies are run in the interests of the producers who, with little danger of any competitive supply, and in democratic societies any fear of the Gulag, can extract what they will to do from what they think is best. Tony Blair is about to learn this universal lesson about nationalised monopolies personally and painfully – unfortunately at the expense of the hapless British taxpayer.

REPLACING THE NHS BY A NATIONAL HEALTH INSURANCE SCHEME: THE PRINCIPLES

So, given the British electorate's reluctance to give up this collectivist jewel of 'a universal service for all based on clinical need, not ability to pay', as the first core principle of the NHS Plan states, what can be done? As it turns out, Gordon Brown's latest munificence with taxpayers' money might provide an alternative which accepts this political reality while creating a system that provides incentives for the efficient production of health care.

The starting point in thinking about public policy about the so-called 'merit goods' of health and education, is Mill's distinction in his essay *On Liberty* between the public provision and public financing of these merit goods. As he, and later Hayek (in his *The Constitution of Liberty*), rightly maintained, while there may be a case for the public financing of these merit goods there was none for their public provision. As Mill put it for education:

> If the country contains a sufficient number of persons qualified to provide education under government auspices, the same persons would be able and willing to give an equally good education on the voluntary principle, under the assurance of remuneration offered by a law rendering education compulsory, combined with state aid to those unable to defray the expense.[42]

Nor was this standard view of nineteenth-century economists confined to classical liberals. Here is another well-known nineteenth-century economist's view on state education:

> Elementary education by the state is altogether objectionable. Defining by a general law the financial means of the elementary schools, the qualifications of the teachers, the branches of instruction etc., and ... supervising the fulfilment of these specifications by state inspectors, is a very different thing from appointing the state as the educator of the people! Government and church should rather be equally excluded from any influence on the school.[43]

The same principles apply to the 'merit good' of health with, moreover, no need for a law to make its consumption compulsory! But this classical nineteenth-century view conjures up the 'means testing' and 'two-tier' demons of contemporary political discourse. This pamphlet proposes to convert the NHS into a National Health Insurance Scheme (NHIS) which can exorcise them while adhering to these nineteenth-century classical principles.

REPLACING THE NHS BY A NATIONAL HEALTH INSURANCE SCHEME: THE PROPOSAL

The proposal is very simple. It was suggested by considering the amount Gordon Brown promised in last year's budget on health spending till 2004. The Tories agreed to match this expenditure if elected. The sum promised was £69 billion by 2004. With a population of sixty million, this implies £1,150 per man, woman and child will be spent on the NHS. The University of California (UC) – a large public university – munificently buys employees and their families excellent private health insurance as a benefit. This can be topped up if the employee wants. I teach at the Los Angeles Campus of UC (UCLA): looking at my April 2000 pay stub I found that it costs the University $475 per month or $5,700 per year to insure the four members of my family. Converting this at an exchange rate of $1.6 = £1.0, yields a premium of £890 per family member,[44] which is less than the £1,150 per capita proposed to be spent in 2004 and slightly more than the £816 per capita that was proposed to be spent in the current financial year (2000/01) on the NHS. Moreover, the same insurance continues even after retirement, so that UC retirees do not have to rely entirely on the flawed public Medicaid scheme. UC employees thus have completely free medical care of high quality from their entry to their grave, covering all illnesses including long-term ones and those of old age.

This presents the magnificent opportunity for the UK government to purchase for every single man, woman and child a private health insurance policy at least as good as the UC provides its employees – and judging from personal experience there can be no question of the incomparable superiority of the health care we get in the US to that in the UK. This UC system provides complete and unlimited free lifetime coverage (with no account of medical preconditions on entering the scheme) through a health maintenance organisation (HMO) much like the GP based system in the NHS. For those wanting even more choice, the basic insurance can be topped up, as we do ourselves as we live part of the year in London. For a top-up policy which allows us to see any doctor of our choice anywhere in the world we pay $54, which surmounts to £33 per month, with some deductions.

What is more, there are a number of different insurance companies we can choose from each year – an essential feature of the scheme, as it provides the necessary incentives for these companies not to attempt to cheat on their promises, and to monitor the doctors and hospitals providing their insured benefits. This power to exit gives the consumers of health care the necessary means to ensure that the insurance companies and their agents – the medical practitioners – in fact meet patient needs in a timely, cost-efficient and consumer friendly manner.

The UK government can now do what UC does on a much larger scale. It can pay from general taxation for a basic health insurance policy – the NHI – negotiated on behalf of the sixty million inhabitants of these isles, which provides complete and free health care, with a number of private insurance companies from which individuals and households can choose and switch. Given the larger pool of people it will be insuring, the UK government would have even greater monopsonistic power than UC in negotiating good terms for this basic universal policy. Each citizen would get a private insurance policy from the company of their choice, paid for by the state. Each year they would receive a piece of plastic for all members of their family, which would be used to purchase health care, with the bill being paid by the insurance company financed by the premiums the government pays on behalf of every citizen to them. Every citizen would have the same health benefits as do the 'toffs' today with their private health insurance.

It may also be advisable to earmark revenues from general taxation for the NHIS, as this will probably make it politically easier to raise further revenues for the NHIS if the costs of health care rise in the future – as people can readily see this as a rise in the premium the government is paying on their behalf. Though, as the sad experience of the Dome might be a warning, even earmarking revenues cannot tie the hands of a predatory government. The electoral consequences of raiding the earmarked revenues for an NHIS are likely to be more drastic as this can then be directly linked to the resulting diminution in the level and quality of health-care provision.

Most important of all, with this proposal, the government would be able to get completely out of the business of providing hospitals, doctors and nurses – and the continual angst that this has caused politicians of all stripes. These would all become private agents competing with each other and monitored by the private insurance companies to whom they sell their services. Like most other private industries there would be no need for any government involvement in these activities of providing health care. Moreover, as the example of privatised industries has shown, the ensuing competition between health providers will be the sufficient spur for efficiency. There will be no more need for 'health authorities', the myriad of quangos or the new Cabinet committee announced by the Prime Minister. The efficiency they seek will be provided by the market, whose abiding superiority over any system of centralised planning is that it provides the necessary incentives and information (at virtually no cost) for maintaining productive efficiency. The government's role will be to negotiate the terms, and pay the premiums for an NHIS policy, which provides the free universal health care promised but not delivered or deliverable by a nationalised industry – the NHS.

How would the scheme affect the current providers of health care? As currently, GPs and consultants are at least notionally private agents contracting with the NHS, they would merely switch their employer – from the government to the private insurance companies. They could either choose to practise independently as private providers or, as is more likely, many of them could – as they do now – join a joint practice which could become the equivalent of a US-style health maintenance organisation (HMO). But as this would be a private entity and not part of some government health authority as at present, the assets, including the goodwill of the practice would belong to them, which they could, if they wished, sell to those wanting to join the practice. This would give them a market driven incentive not only to invest in their practice but also to provide customer satisfaction on which the goodwill depends. This would be a more effective and efficient way of providing incentives for good GP care than all the targets being laid down for GPs in Mr Blair's NHS Plan.

The various NHS hospitals can be privatised in a number of different ways – from non-profit trusts to commercially owned entities with stockholders – and new hospitals depending upon local preferences, which could include the resurrection of cottage hospitals, would also emerge. For, as in most other areas of economic activity, unlike a Planning Commission legislating its views, however technocratically and altruistically derived, the market is in Hayek's felicitous phrase 'a discovery process'. The final market driven outcome would be determined truly by consumer preferences and not as in the current centrally planned system by planners' preferences – the 'gentlemen in Whitehall who know best', in Douglas Jay's immortal phrase.

Moreover, as with the privatisation of other nationalised industries, immediate efficiency gains would arise through eliminating the various layers of bureaucracy which are necessary in any command and control system where the usual market indices of profit and loss are absent. With the diversity of forms of hospital there would also be a diversity in the types of management. No planner can know what these are, and hence the constant attempt in every nationalised industry for constant rearrangements and reorganisations to determine the holy grail of the ideal management structure – which of course turns out to be a mirage. The only thing we know with certainty is that these extra-market arrangements will never be as efficient as those driven by the market and, moreover, that the main beneficiaries of Gordon Brown's munificence – following Parkinson's law – are not likely to be the patients but the burgeoning number of bureaucrats in a nationalised hospital system.

POSSIBLE OBJECTIONS TO THE NHIS

What are the possible objections to such a scheme? Four were outlined by John Appleby of the King's Fund in a letter to the *Financial Times*[45] after my *FT* article proposed this scheme.[46] The first two concerning coverage were that, as the University of California employees are likely to be healthier than the UK population, there are differences in the risk pool and that the premium UC pays on my behalf does not cover the coverage of poorer and older people's health care, which is paid for through taxes. My answer[47] was that the UC health benefits system covers all employees including dustmen, cleaners and all the other staff besides the dons, and their dependents – including dependent-aged parents! The students being younger might have been a better risk pool, but they have their own separate health-care system. Thus there is no reason to believe the UC employee health system has a pool of healthier people than the UK population. Many of those covered – for example our domestic cleaner from El Salvador, who got a job as a cleaner at the university – are poor, and as the scheme covers retirees and aged dependents it also covers the old.

It is thus a universal system for employees, who are a cross section of the Californian population. Given the larger numbers to be covered in the whole UK population, the risk pool should even be better for my proposed scheme, and the negotiated premiums even lower. But see below for an explicit comparison of costs between the NHS and costs to match the UK's age and socio-economic profile for Kaiser Permanente, a Californian HMO insurance company whose HMO plan is offered as one of those fully paid for by UC and whose per capita costs, therefore, form the basis of the employer contribution to the UC health insurance plans.

The third objection Appleby makes is that 'US experience of contract setting and monitoring by private insurers is littered with failed attempts to control costs and ensure efficient use of health care. The losers in this system have been the millions of uninsured and under-insured people.' Two points need to be made on this. First, I am not sure what is meant by the 'efficient use of health care'. There is the dirigiste, health economist's view, which seeks to lay down efficient outcomes in terms of some theoretical norm. But just as this is irrelevant in judging the relative efficiency of a market economy, so is any such technocratic norm for health care.[48] Ultimately, there is no reason to treat health any differently from any other consumer good, where consumer satisfaction provided at low cost is as good a test of real-world efficiency as any other. Given that the costs of providing UC health care are less per capita than planned for the NHS, the only real test is with relative consumer satisfaction. In a recent survey, the satisfaction of consumers with their UC health-care plans varied from 85–93 per cent. Leave alone the currently dismal level of consumer satisfaction with the NHS as detailed in the NHS Plan, it is difficult to believe that Gordon Brown's billions will change the picture markedly, for the reasons noted above about the tendency of public monopolies to absorb the money made available to serve producer rather than consumer interests.

The second point about the purported inefficiency of

the US health system conflates two separate issues: the fact that many people in the US are under or uninsured, and the efficiency of health care for the insured in good health-care systems like the University of California. There are historical reasons for the large number of uninsured persons in the US, but that is not germane to this argument as my proposed scheme would cover the whole population.[49] For those who are insured in the US there is no question, from my own personal experience with the US and UK health-care systems, about which is more efficient in delivering quality health care (also see the following on the comparison of the NHS with Kaiser Permanente).

The final objection Appleby makes is that: 'the proposal relies on government negotiating and monitoring a contract with the insurers that guarantees the outcomes we all want. But if the government is failing to do this through its own "in-house" health authorities, why should it be able to do it with private purchasers?' The answer is simple. Just as with other nationalised industries, for example the natural monopolies such as water and electricity, replacing them with competing providers enables the government to monitor and ensure desired outcomes through regulatory regimes that rely on the only incentives that work: profit and loss.

There is no reason why this alternative should be any more expensive for health than for water and electricity. Continuing to rely on political command and control mechanisms – like the 'health authorities' – as demonstrated by the history around the world of attempts to reform nationalised industries while maintaining them as public monopolies, will always end in tears.

THE FEASIBILITY OF A NATIONAL HEALTH INSURANCE SCHEME: THE KAISER PERMANENTE STUDY

More can now be said about the feasibility and desirability of my proposed NHIS, as a result of a recent comparative study of the costs and benefits of one of the major insurers of health in California (Kaiser Permanente, whose HMO is one of those offered as part of the UC health plan) with the NHS by Professor Richard Feachem, Director of the Institute of Global Health at the University of California, San Francisco and Berkeley (and a former Dean of the London School of Hygiene and Tropical Medicine) and his associates.[50]

Kaiser Permanente is a non-profit fully integrated HMO set up in 1945 – about the same time as the NHS – by various trade unions. Its total enrolment is now eight million (about the same population as Austria's) and six million of these are in California. It employs its own doctors (who are salaried employees) and owns and operates its own ambulatory and inpatient facilities. So it is rather like the NHS – except it has to compete for customers!

There are differences in the risk pool of the people covered by Kaiser Permanente and the NHS. Thus 10 per cent of Kaiser's population is over sixty-five as compared with 16 per cent in the NHS. As the Kaiser system was set up as a 'working-class system' it includes all socio-economic tiers, including the indigent, who are covered by the public insurance scheme Medicaid (who are 3.5 per cent of those served by Kaiser), but it obviously does not include the unemployed.

Given these differences, particularly in the age profile, Feachem et al. made adjustments for the differences in age and socio-economic status of the Kaiser from the NHS population. They find that the same age profile as the NHS would increase Kaiser's costs by 13 per cent, and the socio-economic profile by 5 per cent. After making these adjustments and adjusting for purchasing power parity (PPP) they find that the adjusted per capita costs for Kaiser would be $2,392 as compared with the NHS of $2,186 (in PPP dollars), that is the Kaiser per capita costs would be 9 per cent more than the NHS. Given the necessarily uncertain nature of the calculations, this suggests that there is not likely to be much difference in the costs of the NHS and a Kaiser system with the same coverage as the UK population.

But there would be a marked difference in the relative benefits. The average time spent with a primary care doctor would rise from 8.8 minutes in the NHS to sixteen minutes in Kaiser, and the waiting time to see a specialist, which is seven weeks on average in the NHS (and over six months for 7 per cent of the patients), would fall to twelve days under Kaiser. Nor would they have to perambulate to some other facility for their laboratory, imaging or pharmacy needs for, unlike the UK where only about 25 per cent of primary care providers have these onsite, 100 per cent of those in the Kaiser system have them. The clinical outcomes under Kaiser would be similar to those for the insured US population, which are much better than under the NHS, for instance in cancer survival rates, where in the UK only 5 per cent of patients with stomach cancer can hope to survive for more than five years as compared with over 40 per cent in the US.

Clearly the Kaiser insurance system provides a more timely, responsive and efficient health-care system at roughly the same per capita cost as the NHS. The essential difference is that unlike the NHS, Kaiser and its doctors and hospital employees have to compete for business with other insurers in the US system, and even though they are non-profit they have to manage their costs and generate sufficient revenues to cover not only the running but also the capital costs (like those of hospitals and equipment) to stay solvent. Here we have an insurance-based system which meets the NHS objectives – universal (given the age and socio-economic adjustments to the actual Kaiser figures) and free at the point of use, and based on need, not income (as the insurance premiums, as in the UC system, are provided by employers). It moreover delivers a quality of health care which is still beyond the moon for most in the UK at a per capita cost that is about the same as the NHS.

CONCLUSIONS

So, I offer my humble proposal to any political party that seeks to keep the promise of universal provision so beloved by the British public, while getting off the hook, which every government running the NHS has faced and that is faced by any nationalised industry: it cannot, given the problems of incentives and information, ever satisfy consumers, no matter how much money is thrown into the pot. It is time to convert the NHS into the NHIS, which, by separating the issues of public production and public financing, could provide the efficient provision of health care, free at the point of timely delivery to all – a goal that has not been and cannot be achieved by the NHS. As the example of the UC health-care system and Kaiser Permanente shows, it is feasible to deliver the objectives of the NHS with current levels of spending but only if the shibboleth of a nationalised monopoly as the provider of health services is given up, and substituted by public financing of universal access to privately provided health care.

First published as 'A Premium on Health', Policy Series No. 27, Politea, *London 2001.*

CHAPTER THREE

PRIVATISING UNIVERSITIES

INTRODUCTION

In July 1988 Mr Kenneth Baker, so it seemed, *nationalised* Britain's universities, contravening the principles professed by the government which he serves. For is not this government committed to enlarging freedom and developing a free-market economy?[51] This is not to deny that there is a powerful case for the state financing of students. Mr Baker may demur that the university clauses in his Great Education Reform Act are no more than a culmination of the steps towards central direction of higher education, which began with the institution of the University Grants Commission in 1919. Such central planning has subsequently been advocated by many commissions composed of leaders of the academic community (most notably by the Croham and Jarratt Committees). So Mr Baker can plausibly cloak himself in the pragmatic garb of a traditional Tory who has followed post-war dirigisme to its tidy conclusion. But it should be noted that Thatcherism (at least as proclaimed) is based on defending a set of principles whose objective is the demise of socialism, while Mr Baker's nationalisation of universities must go beyond the wildest dream of any socialist if only they could regain power![52]

Of course, Mr Baker can claim that in principle he is as ardent a Thatcherite as any member of his party, but that as a politician he has to translate these principles into a popular programme by reconciling a number of conflicting political pressures. Amongst these are:

i) the government's desire to control public expenditure on higher education, as part of its general programme to reduce the public pre-emption of national resources;

ii) its desire not to alienate its middle-class constituency which, through the system of mandatory awards and free tuition, at present is entitled to a subsidy from the public at large of virtually the full cost of their progeny's higher education;

iii) the desire of university academics and vice chancellors to maintain the 'parity of esteem' which they have fought for, as a basis of a uniform system with common salary scales and type and structure of courses – so that to the casual observer there is an interchangeability with the 'old' universities of Oxford, Cambridge and London;[53] and

iv) their desire to increase access to higher education to a larger proportion of school leavers.

Only a centrally planned high-education system, Mr Baker can claim in his defence, can reconcile the impossible, or at least seem to do so. Any alternative to nationalisation will obviously have to deal with these political realities.

Recently, however, reports have been published in the

press that both Mr Baker and the Minister for Higher Education, Mr Robert Jackson, are having second thoughts about their 'nationalisation' of British universities. Commenting on Mr Baker's speech to the Committee of Vice Chancellors and Principles at Oxford in October 1988, Michael Prowse in the *Financial Times* parodied the drift of his thinking thus:

> I made a ghastly mistake. The provisions on universities in my recently enacted Education Reform Bill will do nothing to increase choice or efficiency. Indeed, I now see that the creation of the Universities Funding Council (UFC) represents strengthening of central planning and bureaucratic direction that is without parallel elsewhere in the economy. I have instructed my civil servants to consider new market-based mechanisms for financing higher education. In the meantime, please accept my apologies for wasting everybody's time.

More recently, Mr Baker is on record extolling the virtues of the market mechanism in higher education in an even more marked fashion. In January 1989, he told a conference that

> the diversity and flexibility, so evident across the Atlantic, represents the future towards which we in Britain ... will want to move ... universities will have to go out and market what they have to offer, rather than wait for applications to roll in.[54]

Moreover, Mr Baker has already taken some small steps towards balancing the new mechanism for central planning with a more market-oriented approach toward universities. A scheme for top-up loans – to cover maintenance but not tuition – has been proposed; and it has been made clear that universities will be left free to set tuition fees in excess of the fees element paid by the LEAs.

After examining and rejecting the arguments for central control, this pamphlet proposes a thorough-going new scheme. These recommendations go well beyond the government's present proposals which offer top-up loans for students' maintenance only; and represent a scheme whereby on the one hand universities can charge full cost fees at their discretion, and on the other the government provides qualified students with finance (some in the form of grants, some in the form of loans, some in the form of means-tested scholarships) which will cover the entire costs of their higher education.

THE PLANNERS' HUBRIS

The first question of principle to be asked is what, if any, role should the state have in higher education? Here a crucial distinction needs to be made between the state provision and direction of higher education, (or any other level of education for that matter) and the financing of students who for whatever reason may not be able or willing to pay for their education.

J. S. Mill set out the argument clearly in his essay *On Liberty* while discussing general (i.e. non-university) education, but it applies with even greater force to higher education:

> Unless, indeed when society in general is in so backward a
> state that it could not or would not provide for itself any

proper institutions of education unless the government undertook the task: then, indeed, the government may, as the less of two great evils, take upon itself the business of schools and universities, as it may that of joint stock companies, when private enterprise in a shape fitted for undertaking great works of industry does not exist in the country. But in general, if the country contains a sufficient number of persons qualified to provide education under government auspices, the same persons would be able and willing to give an equally good education on the voluntary principle, under the assurance of remuneration afforded by a law rendering education compulsory, combined with state aid to those unable to defray the expense.[55]

At a time when the government, by privatising industry, is turning its back on decades of dirigisme it is ironic that it should appear to be doing the reverse in respect of universities.

Mr Baker's white paper, *Higher Education: Meeting the Challenge*, argues, however, that there is a place for some overall state direction and planning of higher education, through guidance by quangos such as the Universities Grants Commission (UGC), or its successor the University Funding Council (UFC). This is essentially an argument of social utility, of which the government is assumed to be the best judge. Thus the white paper states:

In higher education itself there is a need to pursue reforms, both in the management and funding of the system and in the monitoring of the quality of its work, so that we can build on areas of excellence in the arts and sciences. But above all *there is an urgent need, in the interests of the nation as a whole*, and therefore of universities, polytechnics and colleges themselves, *for higher education to take increasing account of the economic requirements of the country.* Meeting the needs of the economy is not the sole purpose of higher education; nor can higher education alone achieve what is needed. But this aim, with its implications for the scale and quality of higher education must be vigorously pursued.[56] [emphasis added]

This passage is riddled with intellectual muddles and unsubstantiated assertions. Two are crucial. First consider the assertion about the presumed link between higher education and economic performance (in the italicised passages). This may be part of today's conventional wisdom (due to repeated assertion by journalists and politicians), but the evidence for a direct link between economic performance and education is at best weak and at worst non-existent. Thus Maddison[57] summarised the available historical evidence on the link between education and productivity as follows:

It is sometimes argued that the productivity performance of economies is highly dependent on the state of 'educational capital' embodied in the labour force. The relationship of education to economic performance is obviously a rather subtle matter of both cause and effect, complicated by variations in the quality of education, and by the fact that the roles of intelligence and education are difficult to disentangle... All countries have increased the educational qualifications of their populations significantly since 1950, but the economic significance of this is probably no greater than the changes that occurred from 1870 to 1950. In 1976 the average stock of formal education per person in these countries was 9.7 years; in 1950 it was 8.2 years. The evidence available for a few countries suggest that in 1870 the average stock of education per person in these countries was about three to four years, with substantial sections of the population illiterate and with very little higher education at all.

It does not seem, therefore, that the post war acceleration of productivity growth was matched by an acceleration in the growth of educational capital. Similarly, it is clear that the slackening in productivity growth since 1973 is in no way due to a slowing down in the pace of growth of educational capital. Indeed, the evidence available shows more rapid growth in the educational stock in the 1970s than in the 1960s or 1950s.

Second, the idea that specific educational needs of an economy can be specified by an external authority, which universities should seek to meet, reflects the cast of mind of the manpower planner. But the arguments against planning of manpower are the same as those against the planning of output beloved by socialists.[58] Manpower planning assumes that fixed inputs of different skills are required to produce national output: skills produced through fixed inputs of different types of education. In practice, however, opportunities are virtually limitless, except in the very short run, for substituting different skills in producing national output (which moreover does not, as the planners predicate, consist of a set of goods and services produced in some given and fixed proportions). Nor do fixed inputs of schooling yield such definable skills.

Finally, and most importantly, even if such fixed

coefficients did prevail, planners would be able to forecast future 'needs' of different skills only if they were
omniscient prophets, and knew the future composition
of national output for which these different skills were
required. There is no basis whatever for this assumption
which underlies all beliefs in central planning. Given our
unavoidable ignorance about the composition of future
output, a central forecast of educational needs imposed by
Mr Baker's officials could lead to the nemesis visited upon
many developing countries addicted to planning. Thus,
Indian planners persuaded by utilitarian arguments similar to those advanced in the white paper sought to increase
the supply of engineers which they deemed essential for
India's future economic prosperity. As there is no realistic
basis for any central forecasts of future manpower needs,
the only effect of this policy was to create a vast pool of
unemployed engineers.[59]

MR JACKSON'S JUSTIFICATIONS

The Higher Education Minister, Mr Robert Jackson,
has recently adumbrated a more nebulous interest of the
state in higher education. In a talk at Churchill College,
Cambridge, in March 1988, he defined the government's
interest in higher education in the following terms:

> Why does higher education matter? It matters because
> in modern dynamic, progressive societies and cultures
> you need to have organised centres for creativity and for
> criticism – intellectual creativity and criticism... In the
> knowledge society, there is enormously rapid change...
> This is constantly raising the standards of intellectual
> sophistication that are required to do business, to conduct

politics, to manage affairs and so institutions which are dedicated to creativity, to criticism, to keeping abreast with what is happening all around the world, to contributing to it, to taking it forward, are actually of almost primordial importance in modern societies... The fact of the matter is that the government's interest in higher education – while it embraces that concept, the pursuit of knowledge for its own sake – also has a stronger, more dynamic element in it which is this sense of the way in which higher education is important in the functioning of a modern society... There is another implication of the government's vision of higher education as a source of intellectual dynamism in society and that is that the higher education institutions should indeed be intellectually dynamic... It isn't so much – because government doesn't have the capacity or the desire to pronounce upon or intervene in it – the content of what is being taught and the research that is being done. Government is concerned – and is quite legitimately concerned – with another set of questions which bear on quality and that is the question of process. We are not concerned about the content of what is done but we do ask questions like 'how good are the arrangements in higher education for making quality decisions about content?'[60]

From this verbatim transcript Mr Jackson goes on to justify the paraphernalia of the planners' ways of control – various monitors of performance, a system of contracts, abolition of tenure etc. – which the quangos established before will administer.

The questions, however, arise: even if we accept Mr Jackson's argument that the government has some general interest in maintaining the 'intellectual dynamism' and hence the quality of universities: (a) is there any reason to believe that the present quality of British higher education is suspect? (b) even if it were, are the government's proposed remedies – through central direction – likely to be efficacious?

In his eloquent pamphlet *Diamonds into Glass*[61] Professor Elie Kedourie has answered 'no' to both questions. Neither the current quality of British higher education, nor the management of their resources by universities is reprehensible. At least the government has produced no evidence which could support these charges.

The belief in the efficacy of dirigiste monitoring of the 'quality' of higher education is built on sand. True, just as the government may legitimately have some general concern about the quality of industrial management on which the economic prospects of the country may depend, it will also have a general concern about the quality of education. But this government (quite rightly) does not seek to monitor and direct the performance of industrial enterprises through a central plan as is common in Communist countries, or through management contracts with some public quango. It believes that such industrial planning is both infeasible and destructive of efficiency and liberty. So why does Mr Jackson believe that his government can monitor and improve the quality of higher education through central planning? At least in the industrial sector one natural measure of performance – profitability – does exist. No such unequivocal performance indicator is available for higher education, whose inputs and outputs are erratic and ephemeral.

Moreover, as the history of Soviet planning shows us, most attempts to use non-market indicators of performance lead to a system of incentives which systematically subvert the very objectives for which they were instituted. Thus measuring performance by the percentage of 'good' degrees which students obtain in relation to a measure of their A level grades on entry (a so-called value-added measure of teaching performance), merely produces 'grade inflation' – a process which can be seen at work in the pressures to 'perform' associated with the 1980s cuts in funding of higher education.

The ludicrous (were it not so deadly serious) proposal by the Universities Grants Commission to measure research performance by what they call 'bibliometric techniques', which in effect measure how many times a particular work has been cited, will lead to a further incentive 'to publish or be damned', to a marked increase in the citation of oneself and of one's friends, but not of one's opponents; while both those whose ideas become so well-known that no one bothers to cite them, and those who are 'sleepers' with ideas well ahead of their time, would fail miserably on their bibliometric indices. To cite just two examples of the latter from my own field, economics, Frank Ramsey – a brilliant mathematical economist – wrote two papers which were virtually forgotten by the profession for about three decades, but subsequently became the precursors of a fruitful and voluminous literature on the theories of optimal growth and optimal taxation. The second is the case of John Muth, whose 1961 paper on 'rational expectations' was rediscovered after nearly a decade, and has formed the basis of the so-called 'new classical' macroeconomics whose powerful intellectual artillery has fought the post-war Keynesian consensus.[62] Under Mr Jackson's new regime, on the basis of their bibliometric indices both

Ramsey and Muth would no doubt (having had their tenure abolished) have been asked to seek their fortunes outside the university. As politicians, perhaps?

The essential point about academic services is that it is not easy, perhaps not possible, to monitor them. The knowledge on which judgements of performance need to be based are necessarily local, personal and subjective. That is why most great universities have relied on internal moral codes, and on the pressure of a collegiate environment to ensure that quality is maintained and shirking eschewed. This collegiality, the only means of maintaining the 'intellectual dynamism' that Mr Jackson seeks to foster, is necessarily threatened by the bureaucratic apparatus that will be born, with colleagues here becoming the administrative arm of Mr Baker's quangos, there becoming fearful of non-conformity due to the abolition of tenure. His proposed means are likely to lead to the exact opposite of what they aim to achieve.

But perhaps most of these quasi-utilitarian arguments being advanced by Mr Jackson and Mr Baker are some kind of camouflage. One charitable interpretation is that they are trying to justify central planning, desired not for its own sake but as a means of reconciling the irreconcilable: that is, on the one hand honouring the commitments to reducing public expenditure, on the other adhering at least in appearance to the Robbins principle that all qualified school leavers are entitled to a publicly funded place at a university. We examine this dilemma more fully later. At the level of principles, however, no valid argument for the state direction of higher education exists. This leaves the question of the state financing of students in higher education, its justification and level.

QUESTIONS OF SUBSIDY

The major justification for a state subsidy to students in higher education concerns equity and equality of opportunity, together with some general cultural advantages of encouraging scholarly activities that would not attract private funds, but form an essential part of a civilised society.

As higher education is clearly one determinant of the lifetime income of an individual, limiting access to it to those with the ability to pay tuition fees would put the poor at a disadvantage – as well as perpetuate existing income inequalities. If all students, however, could borrow against their prospective future incomes, those who were unable to pay for their higher education out of their own or their families' current income could fund it. But as individual returns from this investment in higher education are highly risky, and students (particularly if they are poor) unlikely to be able to provide adequate collateral, private banks may well not wish to offer such loans. This so-called 'imperfection' of capital markets means that individuals cannot borrow to fund 'human capital formation', and underlies government proposals to provide loans or loan guarantees to help students finance their education.

Now under the current system of financing students, British students admitted to a university are in effect fully subsidised by the taxpayer. This public subsidy (which is over and above that implicit in removing the inefficiency in the market for 'human capital formation') is a pure transfer payment from general taxpayers to the students fortunate enough to gain a university place. As such it is a politically determined entitlement, and cannot properly be provided with an economic rationale. The nature and extent of this subsidy is concealed by the peculiar history of the subsidisation of British university students, and it is this non-transparency – whatever its political merits – which has led to much muddle about the proper role and extent of state financing of students in higher education.

In effect, the subsidy to students (and one must emphasise that this is what current arrangements amount to, even though ministers and journalists talk incorrectly of a subsidy to universities) is provided through the block grants made by the University Grants Committee to the universities, the nominal fees (of about £700 per annum) and the means-tested but mandatory maintenance grants paid for by the local authorities. The cost per university student of the first two components of this subsidy, which correspond to the full tuition costs (at constant 1986–7 prices), are given in Table 3.1 (which also shows what percentage of these come in the form of UGC direct block grants).

Two points need to be noted about these figures. First, compared with tuition fees in most universities in the United States, these 'full cost equivalent' tuition fees are highly competitive. Second, as nearly 22 per cent of university students come from fee-paying independent schools where parents have been paying similar sums for secondary education, this cost per student of a university education cannot be regarded as excessively high.

What is, unfortunately, extravagant is the Robbins principle, which in effect laid down that anyone qualified to go to a university has to be provided with a university education at public expense. In liberal terms this 'Robbins principle' is indefensible. For example, Hayek, considering state subsidisation of education (over and above that required to remove the imperfection in the capital market already discussed), noted that:

The situation is somewhat different, however, when the costs of a higher education are not likely to result in a corresponding increase in the price at which the services of the better-trained may be sold to other individuals ... but where the aim is the further dispersion and increase in knowledge throughout the community at large. The benefits that a community receives from its scientists and scholars cannot be measured by the price at which these men can sell particular services, since much of their contribution becomes freely available to all. There is, therefore, a strong case for assisting at least some of those who show promise and inclination for the pursuit of such studies. It is a different matter, however, to assume that all who are intellectually capable of acquiring a higher education have a claim to it. That it is in the general interest to enable all the specially intelligent to become learned is by no means evident or that all of them would materially profit by such an advanced education, or even that such an education should be restricted to those who have an unquestionable capacity for it and be made the normal or perhaps the exclusive path to higher positions.[63]

The open-ended commitment of public expenditure which the Robbins principle entails is equally indefensible. It is not surprising that at least since the early 1970s,[64] due to the unavoidable exigencies of public finance, the Robbins principle has in practice been repudiated by governments of both major political parties. Given the temper of the times no future government would attempt to implement it. Yet it is still invoked, at least rhetorically,[65] by part of the higher-education establishment. Perhaps this is not surprising since the maintenance of any semblance of consistency between Robbins and requirements of fiscal prudence dictates – does it not? – that creeping central planning of higher education under the aegis of the UGC and the officials of the DES, of which Mr Baker's full scale 'nationalisation' of universities is the latest sorry chapter. All those who revel in their current and prospective roles as the Platonic Guardians of Higher Education have sought to cover themselves with the mantle of Robbins whenever their ambitions have been questioned. Their statements should be seen for what they are – self-interested smoke-screens. Worse, though, by continuing to uphold Robbins even when in practice he has been repudiated, the evolution of a political consensus on alternative methods of financing students in higher education, which would in effect increase the access to higher education that Robbins sought, has been put back by some two decades.[66]

To conclude; while there is a case for state subsidisation of student finances, there is none for state direction, none for the effective nationalisation of universities.

FULL COST FEES – AND THEIR ENEMIES

How then can British universities be denationalised? The answer is simple. Every university should state that from next October it will charge full cost fees to all its students – just as they already charge their growing number of over-seas students (for whom the fees currently recommended by the Committee of Vice-Chancellors and Principals (CVCP) are £4,300 a year for arts, £5,700 for science and £10,500 for medical courses). This measure would remove anomalies such as the cheap education provided to students from the EEC (who only pay home-student fees) but not to those from the rest of the world. How these fees are financed by students (either home or overseas) should not be the universities' concern. If their current places are filled – and why should they not be, given the excess demand at the aggregate level for British university places? – their income would be no less (and possibly greater) than under the dispensation of funds through the UFC. As their income would thus arise directly from the services they provide, the UFC could then be abolished.

Since no legal obstacles prevent the universities determining their own fees (a principle which Mr Baker has recently endorsed), they could take this action unilaterally. But unfortunately (starting as one does from a situation wherein the government has a stranglehold over university finance through the deceptive means of granting home students a state subsidy through the UGC's block grants) the action would have to be taken collectively by a majority of the universities. Otherwise each university would face the well known prisoner's dilemma if it acted unilaterally and charged full-cost fees. If none of the other universities followed suit, the one which unilaterally raised fees and eschewed UFC funding could see its better home students melt away to other universities which offered *free* places.

Would universities agree to raise fees collectively? From the accounts of the recent meeting of the CVCP, which considered a watered-down version of such a scheme, they were split. It was difficult to discern the logic of those who opposed the move to full-cost fees.

Such a move, however, will clearly not be in the interest of the planners – the UGC, its successor body the UFC, the DES, the CVCP, all of which derive their existence and power from a dirigiste concept of higher education.

As regards the UGC (and now the UFC), it has never supported the raising of tuition fees to their real cost – despite the Robbins recommendation that there should be some increase in them to foster the autonomy of the universities. As Carswell noted,[67] the UGC disliked any substantial increase in fee income to the universities which would diminish the power of the UGC to control and dictate to them. Small wonder that Sir Peter Swinnerton Dyer, the last chairman of the UGC and new chief executive of the UFC, should feel such alarm at the heretical (from his mandarin viewpoint) market-oriented views of his new chairman, Lord Chilvers.[68] Similarly, despite their demurrals and flotation of fresh schemes for more market-based methods of financing universities (on which see the following) Mr Baker, Mr Jackson and their officials at the DES are not likely to relish the full implications of such a change.

This leaves one interest group: the academics. It is in the interest of the providers of the services – university teachers – that they charge, and in turn get paid, the market value of their services – unless of course under the current system they are obtaining more than the market would pay. But it is a sad fact that the hold of non-market ideas is so strong in academia that university teachers have failed to press for the obvious reform, which, according to the government's own professed principles, would patently be in their self-interest. The Association of University Teachers which should surely serve the real interest of its members, seems to be more interested in its anti-market ideology, arising from its dubious affiliation with the TUC and the Labour Party. Should it not, in that case, remind itself of those ringing words from one of the founders of its faith that, by embracing a system of higher education based on full-cost fees, it is arguing for a fair market price for the services of its members, and by advocating such a cause academics 'have nothing to lose but their chains. They have a world to win'?[69]

But, although the dirigisme of the UGC and DES may be discounted, it is worth considering further why many academics are suspicious of the privatisation of universities entailed by charging full-cost fees. Even though in the initial post-privatisation years, it might not be hard for universities to devise a collective agreement to charge nearly uniform full-cost fees, and implicitly to accept the current quotas for home students imposed by the UGC, over time we could expect that, depending upon the relative demand and supply, fees would differ by subject and university. If, as is desirable on economic grounds, academics are paid their market price, there would also be different remuneration of academics in different disciplines and universities. Also, as a result of market pressures and the decisions taken by this university and that, courses and departments would be restructured, with some disciplines expanding and others contracting in different universities. This differentiation is likely to be opposed by those who support the 'parity of esteem' supposed to exist between academics, all on a common national salary scale, and universities – all offering a similar breadth of subjects.

Of course, this 'parity of esteem' is a fiction. Esteem, especially amongst academics, has to be earned. It cannot be ascribed or legislated. The present system with its nationally uniform pricing of inputs and outputs, leads (as any economist would expect) to various non-price methods of adjusting demand to supply. In each subject and overall, depending in part upon their history, there is a pecking order of universities and departments in terms of earned esteem. With no financial differences in reward, academics and students want to belong to the 'better' universities. But without the ability to use differential financial rewards to attract academics (and, after a lag, students) from the more esteemed universities, the less esteemed are fixed in their position in the league table, in which their only satisfaction is the dog-in-the-manger one of seeing that their colleagues in the more esteemed establishments at least receive the same pay and perquisites as they do!

UNDERSTANDABLE FEARS AND MISGIVINGS

It is important to tackle the fear that a system based on market principles might entail the relative decline (and in some cases demise) of departments and universities for which there is a lack of demand at full-cost pricing.

First, it should be noted that cuts and closures are already taking place. The difference is that they depend on the judgements of the UGC made at the centre, with the inevitable politicisation that this entails. A market-based system of structural adjustment, on the other hand, would provide better signals of the different demands for different subjects; and, if the academics concerned wished to do so, they could take suitable countervailing action (on their salaries, student numbers etc.) rather than being subject to the *fiat* of a committee.

Second, nothing in the evolution of a market-based system would prevent a university from keeping this or that less popular subject, by cross-subsidising it from part of the revenues obtained for the more popular subjects.

Thus, the net effects of such a system of higher education

should in the long run be no worse, from the viewpoint of the self-interest of academics, than the current politicised system – especially since, once the universities charge full-cost fees and admit any one suitably qualified and able to pay them, they will no longer be limited to filling only the arbitrarily determined quotas laid down by the UGC: quotas based more on the exigencies of public finance than the true demand for higher education at its full-cost price.

But as inevitably the market solution will lead to short run distributional effects amongst universities and academics – with gainers and losers – it is unlikely that, however much privatisation is in their long-term interest, they will press for it. Even though in principle universities could, if they chose, readily escape, in practice public action might be required to 'force them to be free'!

Finally, there is an assortment of other misgivings that some may have about a fully privatised university system. Would the universities be able to fund their future capital needs and research activities out of the income they derive from full-cost fees? Or would there still be some need for direct grants from the government either through the UFC or the DES? It might be tempting for universities to base their fees to students on the costs of teaching alone, hoping that the research side of academic activity would continue to be financed by the government. But this would be a thin edge of a big wedge which might undermine their newly found independence.

If universities really believe their public rhetoric that academic research and teaching are inseparable activities, it does not make sense to cost these separately and charge students for only a part of their total costs. To quote Hayek again:

> On the highest level the dissemination of knowledge by instruction becomes inseparable from the advance of knowledge by research. The introduction to these problems which are on the boundaries of knowledge can be given only by men whose main occupation is research.[70]

The teaching that university students receive from scholars is assumed to be informed by research. The two functions must be inextricably entwined if universities are not to be mere 'vocational' machines.

Nevertheless it is impossible to argue that all British universities should aim to have a uniform balance between teaching and research. The planned system involves subjective judgements in the setting-up of fair standards for this balance, and imposes arbitrary standards in classifying some universities as primarily research-based and others as mainly teaching institutions. By contrast it is one of the strengths of a market-based system that it would allow diversity between universities, and hence in their relative costs and fees, to evolve in response to decentralised decisions by consumers and producers of their services.

Should universities under a new system be granted complete freedom to set their fees – if necessary differentiated by subject? The case for allowing them such autonomy may seem to be compromised by the following considerations. First, there are certain subjects where the costs per student include the costs of very expensive laboratories and equipment. If the fees for these subjects are based on their unit costs, they would be much higher than for many arts-based subjects. Would these high fees not discourage students from studying the very subjects that the government and the public believe – however erroneously – are essential for economic growth? Similarly, there may be some subjects of cultural importance which for whatever reason may not be able to attract many students, so that since a minimum infrastructure is required in terms of staff and services, their cost per student may also be above average. Universities might be tempted therefore to discriminate against such high-cost subjects.

Three points need to be made against these arguments for denying universities the autonomy to charge whatever fees they choose:

i) it would be open to universities to charge uniform fees for all subjects, and then cross-subsidise the high unit-cost subjects from the revenues obtained on low unit-cost ones in the general academic interest of maintaining the breadth of subjects vital to a good university;

ii) even if differential fees are charged it would be open to the public or charitable bodies who demand graduates in some subjects – e.g. physics school teachers and dons – to bear part of the costs of their education by for instance repaying the loans on behalf of the high fee payers. This would be preferable to a planning system whereby the government attempts to forecast the 'desired' number of these graduates, and finances a fixed quota in particular universities;

iii) to the extent that graduates – engineers, for example – are hired by industry, their relatively higher cost of production should in part be borne by the industry concerned, either through raising the salaries paid to these graduates or else by taking over the repayment of part of their loans.

The case therefore does not stand up for separating the 'normal' teaching and research costs of different universities, nor for prescribing any uniformity of fees charged by subject or university. Nevertheless, there would still be special, new emerging areas of expensive research in the sciences for which universities might not be able to pay out of their regular fee income. Public money in support of such ventures should be channelled through the research councils.

SETTING UP THE SCHEME

Government action is needed to underwrite its proper interest in financing students, once the current route via UGC block grants has been blocked, and universities become financially independent through charging full-cost fees. Observing the principles for state action in higher education sketched earlier, the ideal system is not far to seek. On grounds of economic efficiency, there should first be some system of public loans or publicly guaranteed loans which overcomes the inevitable imperfection of private capital markets, by enabling students to borrow against their increased earnings in prospect from their higher education.

Secondly, one must take account of the 'externalities' associated with higher education (of the sort adumbrated by Hayek in the passage quoted overleaf). As these essentially comprise some subsidy to the education of scientists, academics, doctors etc., whose services are demanded by public institutions including the government, the simplest solution would be to write off part of the higher education loans of those who joined the public services or the universities and stayed in these professions for some minimum period.

On grounds of equity the government might wish to encourage and subsidise clever poorer students. The principle of means testing already applies to existing maintenance grants, and could easily be applied in giving means-tested scholarships or vouchers to cover the full cost of a university education, to such students who gain university entrance.

These are the strictly economic subsidies, and their ideal form as described above is based on the sound principle put forward by welfare economists, that subsidies should aim directly at remedying specific distortions.

This leaves, however, the political entitlements to public subsidy of many students which are part of the present system of funding higher education. Being political, it is not, perhaps, for an economist to pronounce on their desirability. What can be said is that many of these entitlements accrue to the offspring of the government's supporters, who, as Sir Keith Joseph's unhappy attempts at introducing vouchers showed, will not balk at exerting political pressure to prevent their erosion.

For this reason a politically feasible privatisation of the universities might be effected in the following phases:

i) the government announces that from next year the universities are to charge full-cost fees to their home students at the same rate as to overseas students.

ii) the UGC/UFC block grant is abolished.

iii) the government gives bursaries, equivalent to the full-cost fees, to each and every home student who has been already allocated a place at university for the next few years by the UGC.

In effect the situation of the universities and their students, and the size of public expenditure, would be exactly as at present – but there are three important differences:

i) the quango UFC could be abolished.

ii) the principle, essential for their privatisation, that universities must derive their income from fees for the services they provide would be established.

iii) the way would be open to evolve a market-based system of higher education in any one of a number of possible ways that may be desired on political grounds.

This last point deserves some elaboration. The government could announce that after the first few years – the transition – when student numbers and the full-cost fees would correspond to the presently agreed plans for home student quotas and the implicit cost per home student (shown in Table 3.1), universities would thereafter be free to charge whatever fees they thought fit, to negotiate with their staff on its remuneration and terms of service in whatever way they thought fit, and could dispose of their capital assets – whose legal title should be passed on to the universities – as they saw fit. The state in turn would finance students, their number and the form of subsidy being along a number of possible lines, the choice of which could become part of the political debate (with the proviso that the state subsidy to students could not be open-ended, and would be subject to limits and political control, just as other forms of public expenditure). As universities could charge different fees for different courses, the government would of course still be able to exercise influence over the universities and the courses chosen by the students it was financing – because these would affect the total amount of public expenditure. Given that it fixed its commitment in advance, it would have a choice between financing fewer students on more expensive courses, or more students on less expensive courses.

The first step in freeing the universities could therefore be taken almost immediately, by a single change in the form of financing universities, and with no change in the current level of entitlements to students or in public expenditure. The raising of tuition fees to full-cost fees (equivalent to the average current public expenditure per student – excluding maintenance grants – in each university) and the substitution of student vouchers or bursaries to the home students (whose numbers and admission standards would be identical with current UFC plans) would replace the existing UGC block grants and nominal tuition fees paid by local authorities; and effectively denationalise universities at a stroke.

It might be argued that this change would be purely cosmetic as the universities, at least during the transition to alternative systems of financing university students, would still depend financially upon the number of home students they were allotted by the government. True, but the change in the environment in which university decision making takes place would be important. This can be illustrated by considering other goods which are mainly purchased by the government – for instance, many items of defence hardware. The current and prospective system of university management can be compared to a single nationalised organisation consisting of all the firms which provide, say, ordnance, ships, planes etc. for the government. In fact, however, the government recognises that even if it is the major consumer for the output of such defence industries, keeping them in private hands yields the usual efficiency gains. The same gains would accrue from privatising universities even if the government were the sole purchaser of *their* output.

But of course, it is only because of the conflict between the current practice of making mandatory awards to any student who gains a university place, and the legitimate desire to control public expenditure, that the government through the UGC has put quotas on the so-called full-time equivalent (FTE) number of home students any institution can admit. Thus, there are no restrictions on the number of high fee-paying overseas students that universities can admit; but home students, often of even higher academic calibre, and many of whom might be able and willing to finance their education, are turned away from British universities. This anomaly would disappear as soon as all students were charged the same full-cost fees (though, of course, all fees would not remain identical in a fully liberalised system). At the margin, those home students who failed to get one of the fixed number of vouchers (equivalent in number to the existing UGC/FTE quotas) would still have the option of obtaining a British higher education from their own means. In this way the discrimination against home students, which is a natural and scandalous concomitant of the present planned system, would be removed.

The question naturally arises, how in this first stage of reform will the fixed number of quotas and bursaries be distributed? If the necessary political support for denationalisation of universities is to be obtained from those who have come to expect free higher education as an entitlement, the full-cost vouchers or bursaries must go to those who would have obtained mandatory awards in the current system. As at this stage each university already has a quota of home students allocated by subject, vouchers for the full-cost fees to the students it would admit under its quota could be given to the universities to be handed to them. Any additional students admitted, whether home or from overseas would have to be financed from private means.

PRIVATISED UNIVERSITIES: THE FINAL FORM

The next stage of reform which must allow for the distribution of state-subsidised students between universities and subjects to be determined by consumer demand rather than by government planners – as is the case for overseas students – could take many different forms, ultimately depending on the manner and extent of state subsidisation of students.

While the simple act of charging full-cost fees for all students would lead to the immediate privatisation of universities, such a scheme is unlikely to be initiated by the government unless a credible and politically viable scheme of student financing of fees is also in place.

Assuming realistically that the overall public expenditure on higher education remains static in real terms, and given the average real full tuition cost per student in British universities (see Table 3.1), the government has to decide:

i) whether it will continue to provide a completely free university education to roughly the existing number of students in British universities, or whether it will provide an average subsidy less than the full-cost fees to a larger number of students;

ii) on what basis it will choose between different students who are to be subsidised; and

iii) what form the subsidy should take.

Several proposals have recently been aired dealing with these issues.[71] The fundamental choice must be based on an understanding of what the ultimate objectives of public subsidisation of higher education are. And this must surely be to create a system of funding higher education whereby:

i) on grounds of efficiency students who make rational, individual decisions on the expected costs and benefits of an investment in their higher education are able to implement them by being able to borrow against their expected increase in lifetime income.

ii) on grounds of equity and equality of opportunity, public subsidies may be granted to students who come from poor backgrounds who may be deterred from taking the risk involved in investing in their higher education by borrowing.[72]

iii) there must be a remedy for possible underinvestment in types of education which determine the supply of various professions – school teachers, academics, doctors – whose private rewards may be less than their social worth (at least in nationalised systems of education and health such as the British).

In addition there could be a case for at least some public grant to be paid to all university students. For example, the government has proposed top-up loans towards maintenance, though *not* tuition. The investment of the student will consist not only of the full-cost fees but also of alternative earnings foregone during the period of education.[73] His return is the incremental earnings made possible. But part of this increase is taxed by the government, or (putting it differently) part of the 'benefits' from higher education accrue to the public at large in terms of these tax revenues. It is as if the public at large had an equity stake in its graduates, its dividend being these 'extra' tax revenues. If students financed themselves solely from loans, the public at large would be receiving a 'dividend' without having paid anything for the equity it implicitly owned in its graduates. There would therefore be a case for some part of the costs of the student's education to be paid for out of public funds as a grant.[74]

Even amongst people with diverse ideological persuasions, a consensus is emerging that there needs to be some form of government guaranteed loan scheme at least partially to finance university students. There are problems. The government may worry about the incidence of default, and the borrower may worry that the income increase in the expectation of which the loan was taken out may not materialise.

In this context, the recent, much discussed proposal by Barnes and Barr is worth considering: state loans to students with income-related repayments made through a surcharge on the national income contributions of the graduates. This has two advantages. First, as most graduates will be earning, have a National Insurance Contributions (NIC) number, and be making normal NIC payments, a graduate NIC surcharge should be easy to collect, and hence avoid the problem of loan default that has plagued the US educational loan programme. Second, as the annual repayments are based on an NIC surcharge they are clearly linked to the incomes of the graduates, with relatively low earners paying less than high earners. It is important that the repayments should be finite, ending when the loan and accumulated interest are paid off; and not involving any redistributive element of post-graduation, income related subsidy or taxation. Earnings should not determine how much is repaid on a loan, as has been suggested for instance in the failed Democratic presidential candidate Michael Dukakis's proposal of a Student Tuition and Repayment System (STARS). The argument against any such redistributive system is based on the incentive it would create for loans to be used mainly by students who expected to earn relatively little – while those who expected to earn highly would have to pay back a lot, and might not wish to participate in the scheme.[75]

Whatever payments mechanism is used (and the use of the NIC system is the chief novelty of the Barnes–Barr[76] scheme), the essential point is that, on grounds of economic efficiency, some form of government guaranteed loans is justifiable as part of the financing of university students.

Might the servicing of such loans be considered too onerous by prospective students from poor backgrounds? It should be noted that in the current system only about 8 per cent of university students are from social classes 4 and 5. The way to subserve the second principle of equality of opportunity is to use part of the current public expenditure on higher education to give means-tested scholarships.

As regards the final reason for public action in higher education – the encouragement of this discipline and that for social reasons, or 'externalities' – the simplest solution would be for the government to 'pay back' the loans of students who enter the relevant 'professions'. As most of these – school teachers, doctors – are part of the public sector, the extent of this 'subsidy' will be directly related to the 'hires' in these professions by the public sector. So it should not lead to any open-ended commitment to public subsidisation.

A scheme which, while keeping annual public expenditure on higher education constant in real terms, provides a mixture of government grants and loans, with poorer students receiving completely free subsidised education could work as follows. With universities privatised and charging full-cost fees (assumed on average to be the same in real terms as at present), the government's fixed annual expenditure – currently given as block grant by the UGC, and tuition fees as part of mandatory grants by local authorities – is handed to a Universities Student Finance Committee (a suitable change in the role of the UFC, which would be redundant). This committee would give out full-cost scholarships to poor students, and to the remainder, 60 per cent of the full-cost fees as a grant and the rest as a real interest-free loan to be repaid over twenty years. Assuming that between 10–20 per cent of the loans are not repaid either because they are defaulted on or because they are forgiven (for graduates employed in the public sector, or whose incomes are too low), and that annual full cost fees are £5,000 per annum, the self-financing scheme would allow an expansion in students (over current numbers) financed by the agency of 4–5 per cent every five years, with 10–20 per cent of the students receiving full scholarships and the remainder paying back only £25 a month.

If the period of repayment were lowered to ten years, for the same monthly repayment of £25 by graduates who received loans the higher education system could be expanded at the same rate of 4–5 per cent, even if the grant-loan mix was changed to 80 per cent grant and 20 per cent loans.

Such a self-financing loan scheme which provided

increased access and completely free tuition to poor students, without any increase in public expenditure, and with only a modest monthly repayment burden on graduates, would seem to meet all the irreconcilable pressures on Mr Baker and Mr Jackson which we outlined at the start.

Although such a scheme might describe the ideal final system of financing students in higher education, it is unlikely that it could be legislated overnight, if for no other reason than the cry from those politically vocal groups who would protest against interference with their current entitlements. Why pay even £25 a month if you can manage to pay nothing? The transitional phase, therefore, could follow the lines adopted for other politically determined entitlements: namely, keeping their nominal value constant, but letting their real value erode as even low inflation takes its toll. This seems to be Mr Baker's – correct – policy in introducing student loans to 'top up' current maintenance grants, whose value is to be frozen. Similarly, while introducing a supplementary loan scheme for tuition costs, the government could also freeze the value and number of scholarships to cover full cost fees at the current numbers of students agreed by the UGC (except for poor students who gain admission to a university on some minimum grades in their A levels).

How should these scholarships be distributed? Given the political need to satisfy expectations based on existing entitlements, they will probably have to be rationed on the basis of A level performance (this seems to be similar to the scheme being floated by Mr Jackson.) Over time, the extra-nominal public funds available after deduction of the fixed-nominal charge on these politically determined scholarships should be used both to provide the full subsidies to poor students, and also to subsidise the loans of those who enter the professions with 'externalities'. Thus, gradually, we would move towards the 'ideal' system of financing students in higher education, with the rational balance between grants and loans in student financing discussed above.

As far as the universities are concerned, however, they would have been privatised at the first stage of these proposed reforms. As soon as they start charging full-cost fees, their financial independence would be established, together with the principle that they charge and earn a market price for the services they provide. Thus, irrespective of the means the government eventually adopts to finance university students, it can immediately free the universities by abolishing the UFC and its block grants, to be replaced by full-cost fees and by handing over the control of their existing capital assets to the universities. If Mr Baker fails to adopt one of these feasible methods of denationalisation, the suspicion must be that, for all his protestations, he wishes to remain the Commissar of Higher Education.

CONCLUSIONS

No good case for the recent 'nationalisation' of universities exists. The proposed direction of higher education will neither subserve the government's cherished principles in other fields, nor the vague and unjustified – generalised – concern which some of its agents express about the quality of British higher education. The paradox of a government which seeks to privatise, in effect nationalising, universities is explicable only in the light of the conflicting political pressures it faces. We have sought to show better methods than nationalisation, which the government rightly abhors, to reconcile these pressures.

Now, although there is no case for government *planning*
of universities, a case does exist on grounds of economic
efficiency and equity for some state *financing* of university
students, through a mixture of loans, grants and means-
tested scholarships. Whatever the appearances, the present
system of state financing does give public subsidy of the
full cost of students' higher education to themselves – not
to universities. Excluding maintenance grants, this average subsidy comes to about £5,000 a year: a sum which
represents the full-cost fees per student which would yield
universities an income equivalent to that which they now
receive through the block grants, politically determined,
from the UGC (or now the UFC).

The simplest way to privatise universities would be to
make them charge these full-cost fees to all their students,
thus removing the unjust discrimination against appli-
cants of British nationality, whose numbers are rationed
by the exigencies of public finance.

Once universities obtain their income from full-cost
fees the UFC can and should be abolished. Instead a
University Students' Funding Council would distribute
the loans, grants and means-tested scholarships which
are the proper concern of government – the number of
students supported and the mix of different forms of
financing being decided by the political process. We have
given some calculations which illustrate how (even with the
annual public expenditure in higher education remaining
constant in real terms, and with poor students receiving
completely free university education while the rest enjoy
a mixture of grants and loans) numbers of home students
could be expanded by 4–5 per cent a year. Thus, preservation of the Robbins principle, which has in practice been

rejected by both political parties, would be reconciled with the inevitable pressures to contain public expenditure. It must be noted that the cost to the students for receiving the loan would be no more than £25 a month, in real terms, spread over ten years.

The paper argues that one of the principal interest groups who would oppose such 'privatisation' from universities, the academics, can only stand to gain from universities charging the full market cost of their services to the students. Fears of structural readjustment, and of a market-based system of rewards are shown to be unfounded, especially when compared to the arbitrary and politically determined processes of today.

The opposition of the CVCP and the UFC to privatisation is perfectly comprehensible: it reflects a reluctance to lay down their tasks as the Platonic Guardians of Higher Education. This opposition can be eliminated by their abolition. More difficult to counter will be the antagonism of those students and their parents who have received, or can expect to receive, a large subsidy from other taxpayers. Here, tactics similar to those which the government has adopted to erode the real value of other politically sensitive but economically unjustifiable entitlements could be used.

Our recommendations could take place immediately, with no effects either on public expenditure or on the present, politically determined, entitlements of students. But, given today's system of financing it will require either collective action by the universities themselves, or else by the government. Nevertheless privatisation of Britain's universities remains essential not only for their future but also to resolve the most ironic paradox of the contemporary political scene.

TABLE 3.1

Govt. Expenditure
Per Student £(constant)
1986–7 prices

Year	UGC block grant plus home-student fees	UGC block grant	New under-graduate entrants 000s
1979–80	5,421	4,386.9	74.7
1980–1	5,773	4,671.6	76.4
1981–2	5,589	4,380.1	74.0
1982–3	5,796	5,095.3	71.6
1983–4	5,830	5,147.4	69.2
1984–5	5,790	5,096.2	70.5
1985–6	5,606	4,914.7	70.3
1986–7	5,552	4,855.1	70.7
1987–8	5,753	5,066.9	72.0
1988–9*	5,829	5,145.3	73.6
1989–90*	5,741	5,058.6	75.7
1990–1*	5,621	4,941.7	74.2

* Planned.

Source: Hansard vol. 135, Issues nos. 1453 and 1454, written answers 13.6.88 and 20.6.88 by Mr R. Jackson.

First published as 'Nationalised Universities', Policy Study No. 103, Centre for Policy Studies, London 1989.

CHAPTER FOUR

EMU: PUTTING THE CART BEFORE THE HORSE

INTRODUCTION

If Rip van Winkle had gone to sleep at the end of about 1870 and woken up in the last few years, he would find that little has changed in the world economy. He would note the various technological advances in transportation and communications (airlines, telephones and the computer), which have further reduced the costs of international trade and commerce and led to the progressive integration of the world economy, which was well under way – after the first Great Age of Reform – when he went to sleep.[77]

The terrible events of this century – two World Wars, a Great Depression and the battles against two illiberal creeds (Fascism and Communism), which led to the breakdown of the first liberal international economic order (LIEO) created under British leadership after the Repeal of the

Corn Laws – would form no part of his memory. Nor would the various and varying fads in economic policy – both national and international – during this century make any sense, e.g. exchange controls, the use of quotas rather than tariffs as instruments of protection, central-ised planning and associated controls on production and distribution, and restrictions on the free flow of capital.

Having read his De Tocqueville, he would also not be surprised that the US and Russia had become Great Powers in the latter part of this century – though the latter's greatness was to prove ephemeral. Nor that it took the US nearly a century to become the predominant power, just as it took Britain nearly a century from the mid-1700s, conflict with France till the end of the Napoleonic Wars to achieve its predominance. His reading of De Tocqueville would also allow him to see a natural progression from the rise of Great Britain – which was in a sense the victory of an aristocratic oligarchy over the divine right of kings – to that of the US, which is a victory of demos over aristocracy. Whether this is an unmixed blessing is open to question.[78]

He would be surprised by two features of the current world economy. For unlike the nineteenth century, when there was free movement of goods, money and people, today there are relatively free flows of goods and money but no free movement of labour. This is related to the second surprising feature he would observe: the welfare states to be found in most advanced countries, which, as he would soon recognise, have created property rights in citizenship. This necessarily leads to restrictions on immigration, for immigration creates new citizens with an automatic right of access to the purses of existing citizens through the transfer state.

Having gone to sleep in 1870 before the great scramble for empire by the nations of Europe, and the universal spread of the Romantic movement's ideal of nationalism, he would also not be surprised by two other features of the contemporary world. First, that the territorial imperative which had motivated competition between nation states since the end of the wars of religion was replaced by the commercial competition of trading states following the example of Great Britain in the first great Age of Reform. Second, that as more and more developing countries, particularly India and China with their vast pools of relatively cheap labour, are brought into an integrated world economy, a new international division of labour is emerging, with developed countries mainly providing services and developing ones manufactures. With this spatial division between 'the head' and 'the body' of economic activity, trade is becoming essential for the wellbeing of all countries, thus reducing the attractions of nationalism and war.[79] He would also not be surprised to see the world on a dollar standard as it is the currency of the dominant world power.

He would be surprised by the attempt to create an alternative world money in the euro, particularly as it is the single currency of what still remains a politically disunited union. He would recognise that the euro represents an unprecedented attempt to use economic means to achieve a political end – to recreate a new Holy Roman Empire. He would remember the failed attempt to create one under French arms during his lifetime, and would have read of the two failed attempts by the Germans to do the same while he was asleep. He would wonder if Germany had now found a cunning method – through

EMU – of achieving this end, and if it would be any more successful than past attempts. He would also wonder if, as during the period he was asleep, this new attempt at creating a united Europe under German hegemony might once again lead to the destruction of the newly emergent LIEO. It is these two questions arising from these latter of Rip's musings that I will explore here: firstly, what are likely to be the effects of a European Monetary Union (EMU) on globalisation and, secondly, whether EMU will promote or retard the process of globalisation within 'Euroland'.

EMU AND THE GLOBAL ECONOMY

The first question has two parts: the effects of EMU on the international monetary system and, secondly, on the world trading system. On the latter I can be brief. On trade matters, the EU has already been acting as a bloc with one voice – for good or ill – for a considerable period, including the various trade rounds that have markedly liberalised world trade under General Agreements on Tarifs and Trade (GATT) and now World Trade Organization (WTO) auspices. EMU does not alter this position. It might, however, for reasons I will come to in examining the effects of EMU on Europe, affect its stance in future trade negotiations. But the continuing mercantilist frictions – for instance in the recent banana and GM foods[80] disputes with the US – show that it retains its protectionist instincts.

What of EMU's effects on the international monetary system? As Rip noted, the world has in effect been on a dollar standard. A successful euro could challenge this dominance. The share of Euroland in global trade and production matches that of the US, and this could make it attractive as an international store of value and a vehicle currency for international transactions in goods and services, as well as for the dealings of the burgeoning international underground economy.[81]

But would this rivalry with the hitherto dominant dollar be in the global interest? A number of economic historians have maintained that part of the cause for the breakup of the nineteenth-century LIEO was that the decline of Pax Britannica was not smoothly followed by the rise of Pax Americana.[82] The economically and politically dominant power did not accept this new responsibility until the end of the Second World War. It is this US hegemony that Europe seeks to challenge. But, apart from the question of its likelihood of success, there is the danger that this attempt might create the type of frictions that led to the breakdown of the nineteenth-century LIEO.

However, if the euro can *successfully* challenge the dollar as an international store of value, a larger share of the world's money supply (including reserves) will be held in euros rather than in dollars. This will provide implicit revenue in the form of seigniorage to the European Central Bank.[83] But, there would also be two other global consequences. If there was a large enough shift out of existing US assets and of further flows from the world's savers into the euro, the current imbalance between savings and investment in the US would become untenable and its current account deficit unsustainable. A depreciating dollar, rising interest rates and a collapse of asset prices – not least in the bubble on Wall Street – would follow. But, nearly six months after the euro took its bow, this has not come to pass.

Nor has the other implication that, with the inflows of capital induced by a desire of world investors to diversify their portfolios, *ceteris paribus*, the euro would soar. This too has not happened so far. Why? The reason, I conjecture, is that the euro is not as yet perceived as being *credibly* as good as the dollar. This is because while there is no question in anyone's mind that the dollar, in which the US Treasury's long-term (thirty-year) bonds are denominated, will still be around when they are redeemed, no one can be as certain of the euro's survival when thirty-year euro bonds are issued by the European Central Bank (ECB) and come up for redemption.

This lack of credibility about its survival is intimately linked to the way the euro was set up: by putting the cart of monetary union before the horse of political union. The currency of a genuine political state is credible because the currency's demise would be coterminous with that of the state issuing it – which is unlikely. If not underpinned by a political union, a currency union is only credible if it fulfils the criterion of what economists call an 'optimum currency area' – within which exchange rates should be fixed. Europe does not fulfil these conditions. Hence, the bulk of respectable mainstream economists see the euro as a dangerous gamble with a high chance of failure.

EMU AND THE GLOBALISATION OF EUROLAND

Creating a monetary union without political union poses a number of political dangers which could undermine the process of globalisation within Euroland.

For a monetary union to work it is important either that there is wage and price flexibility to deal with the unemployment that asymmetric shocks to different regions in the currency area could cause, or else there should be easy migration possible – as in the US – between regions with deficient and excess demand for labour. Neither attribute exists in Europe.[84] Its labour markets are notoriously inflexible, and the major differences in customs and above all language make labour – except at the very top – largely immobile. When coupled with the 'stability' pact, countries in Euroland which suffer unemployment will be unable to deal with unemployment either via the exchange rate or expansionary fiscal policy. Nor, as in the genuine federal polity – the US – are federal fiscal transfers on a requisite scale likely to be forthcoming to offset regional unemployment. Here is the *first* serious source of political tensions, which have already emerged. An independent ECB, committed to an EU-wide inflation target, cannot loosen monetary policy to deal with the regional unemployment problems that will arise. Something has to give in this impasse, and it is becoming increasingly clear from the statements of the German and French governments – which have been legitimised by the fiddles so many aspirants to join Euroland made to meet the Maastricht criteria – that it is the 'stability' pact that will go.

This points to the *second* danger. If the ECB maintains a tight monetary policy, while various regional governments loosen fiscal policy – a policy combination last seen in Reagan's USA – the result will be a soaring euro. This will adversely affect the competitive position of Euroland industry in world markets – worsening its already serious unemployment problems. If, instead, the ECB heeds the interests of the regions suffering a deficiency of demand by loosening the common monetary policy, that would lead to inflation in the other regions, which is exactly the latent fear of so many Germans in their dislike of the euro having replaced their beloved deutschmark.

Euroland is, therefore, likely to be riven by inter-regional political tensions, because of the monetary union. These could inflame those very nationalist passions which the creation of Euroland was aimed to suppress. Some, like Martin Feldstein of Harvard, have even predicted a resurgence of the old European wars as a result of these tensions engendered by the advent of the euro.[85] Rather than leading to political union, monetary union could perpetuate the current political disunion and further lead to the breakup of the Common Market as economic nationalism is fed by these troubles.

The drive for European political unity is not helped by the fact that it is a political project that has tried to suppress normal politics in the member countries in getting through its various stages. It is a project borne out of the respective weaknesses of the participants and not their strengths. The French, despite their bravado and pride, are a defeated nation. They see the Anglo-Saxons, not least in their language and culture, triumphing worldwide. The French elite – most of whom seem to be associated in one way or another with the *École Nationale d'Administration* (ÉNA) (and can be properly called *énarques*) – has, therefore, seen the EU as its only hope of global influence in a Europe in which it would jointly exercise hegemony with the Germans – on its model of the Frenchman riding a German horse – in a new Holy Roman Empire.[86] Germany, because of its World War trauma, has gone along with this illusion, and used the clever ploy of promoting an economic union lead-ing to political union to tie down German nationalism as the best way to tame the passions which have led to two savage European wars. Italy has gone along because it wishes to unload the unending burden of subsidising the Mezzogiorno to a larger body of European taxpayers, while the rest of the Mediterranean countries and Ireland have looked upon the subsidies, through the CAP and other regional schemes they have obtained from Europe, as a drunk given free access to a liquor store.

And Britain? In search of a post-Imperial role and identity, a part of its elite, particularly in the Foreign Office, has come to the defeatist conclusion that the only role left for Britain is as a part of 'Europe' – where the inverted commas emphasise the artificiality of this project – where its worldly experience would allow it to join France and Germany in running Europe. To another part of the establishment and the general public the European project was sold as merely a common market which would provide the usual gains from trade in a larger unified economic space. The explicitly political aim of the European partners was said to be just window dressing. As this has been gradually exposed, Europe has become the great dividing line in British politics with – unsurprisingly – the euro at its centre.

Linking most of these elites there is also a not-too-hidden distaste for the United States and a desire to build a Europe which will be a bulwark against the crass and uncaring attitudes seen to be dominant across the Atlantic. Moreover, for the *énarques* – whose connections are Europe-wide – despite the lip service paid to 'subsidiarity' it will also be a Europe run by technocrats and not demos, or a free market. This is why we see the divide between big and small business in their support for 'Europe': with big business – which is more easily able to co-opt regulators to its benefit – being in favour of the regulatory state[87] favoured by the technocrats, and small business – more interested in the more level playing field a true free-market economy provides – being against.

There is a *third* and equally serious danger. With the setting up of the ECB, it has pooled the reserves of its constituent 'national' central banks. In a fractional reserve banking system, as we have known since Bagehot, one essential task for a central bank in the face of a financial panic is to act as a lender of last resort. The Maastricht Treaty is silent on who will provide this function in euro-land. Even if the 'national' central banks are willing to stem a regional financial panic, they may not be able as they have handed most of their reserves and the power to print national money to the ECB. By contrast, the ECB may be able but not willing to act in a regional panic because this could be taken as a bailout – at the wider EU taxpayers' expense – of regional bankrupts. In a nation state with both political and monetary union this would not matter because of the sharing of a common national identity. But Germans in the EU are unlikely to take kindly to the promised successor to the Bundesbank bailing out some feckless Italian financial institution. Another source of political conflict. Once again it seems the cart of monetary union has wrongly been placed before the horse of political union. What is worse, this paralysis in acting as a lender of last resort could in the face of financial shocks lead to a European slump on the scale of the US Great Depression.

There is *a fourth* danger. If the euro appreciates, there is likely to be a capital inflow whose obverse side is a trade deficit with the rest of the world. This will in the short run make it easier to finance budget deficits in Euroland, which are mainly caused by bloated and overgenerous welfare states. These have served the political purpose of keeping the lid on popular discontent arising from the unemployment caused by unreformed labour markets. The seemingly easy financing of these deficits by capital inflows would delay those badly needed reforms without which Euroland has no hope of competing in the global economy. By reducing the productivity of investment, this sclerotic labour market also damages growth. As has happened in so many Latin American countries, foreign investors are then likely to take fright, and the drastic measures which may then be required to deal with deficits that have become unsustainable could tear apart the social compact of the European 'social market economy'. The resulting wrath of the hitherto ignored and docile demos in Euroland could be terrifying.

The *final* danger is that, egged on by the rising trade deficits, the Eurocrats may try to create a Fortress Europe. This would also fit in with their 'nation-building' aims. As Hecksher emphasised in his magisterial work on mercantilism for the post-Renaissance creation of European nation states,[88] and Myint and I[89] found for the post-war Third World, this nationalist objective naturally leads to dirigisme. But, as worldwide experience has shown, this way lies the route to the poverty of the Second if not the Third World. It is also not viable in the long run.

Which of these various routes will undo the European project it is impossible to tell, but it is these political fears about the effects of the euro on Europe which I suspect will also make it difficult for it to replace the dollar as a world currency in the near future.

There is also a geo-political point to be made. The dollar's pre-eminence is based not merely on the US's economic strength but its geo-strategic hegemony. As the recent events in Yugoslavia show, a Europe which is unable to muster the requisite men and materiel to deal with a local tyrant within its domain, but must instead rely on those supplied by an increasingly reluctant America, can hardly be expected to challenge its supremacy as the world hegemon in the near future.

DINOSAURS VERSUS MODERNISERS

Euroland's embrace of globalisation is also being hindered by the contradictory expectations of the supporters of the euro. The first are the 'Dinosaurs',[90] the second the 'Modernisers'. The Dinosaurs look upon the euro and the whole European project as protecting that whole economic and cultural complex which is called by that oxymoron a 'social market economy' from – what are labelled – the neo-liberal effects of globalisation and the spread of Anglo-Saxon culture. The Modernisers by contrast look upon the euro and the stability pact accompanying it as the means to establish a flexible, dynamic and truly globalised economy as achieved in Thacherite Britain.

I think the Modernisers have logic on their side but the Dinosaurs can harness passions in domestic politics concerning what has been called 'the social question'[91] to stem the process of globalisation as their predecessors did at the end of the last century. The most important change in the global economy since the nineteenth century is an emerging new international division of labour. In the nineteenth century, the North mainly produced manufactures and the South, primary commodities. This led many to claim that without forced industrialisation the South would remain hewers of wood and drawers of water.[92] Now, as a result of globalisation, and after reversing their foolish import substituting industrialisation and protective trade policies, the countries of the South find that, under the impetus of the revolution in communications and differential labour costs, much of the North's manufacturing industry is shifting to them.

What of the North? It is coming to own what I call 'virtual factories'. This was the name given to this enterprise by a young and very rich entrepreneur I met in California, in the business of producing various consumer goods. His virtual factory consists of a few smart people with computers sitting in San Francisco, who have contacts with the major stores and designers in the US, as well as production facilities strung out all over the Asian Pacific Rim. Given the volatile and highly differentiated tastes of consumers for different products, the stores take orders for highly individualised products, which are then produced 'just in time' by the cheapest facilities the 'virtual factory' can find in Asia.[93] The virtual factory provides the 'head' for the parts of the 'body' scattered all over the South.

This new division of labour can be compared with that which underlay the nineteenth-century LIEO when the Industrial Revolution pioneered in Britain spread to other parts of Europe and North America. This is best seen by the nature of the first Industrial Revolution. The late Sir John Hicks used to emphasise that the major characteristic of the Industrial Revolution was that it led to the substitution of fixed capital for working capital in manufacturing. The simplest example is the substitution of the 'putting out' system of producing textiles with handlooms by the 'factory system' of textile mills. Later, as a result of Henry Ford's innovation of the production line, mass consumer goods could be produced by even semi-skilled workers. This factory system required both capital and technology – both by and large lacking in the south. But, now, enter the multinational or transnational corporation. It can provide both to the south. Relative labour costs then become the main determinant of where particular manufactured goods and increasingly their components are produced – and this is increasingly in the south.

So what is there left for northern workers to do? As my virtual factory example suggests, their future is increasingly in skill intensive activities, which are more in the nature of services than manufacturing. This new Industrial Revolution based on the microchip, therefore, involves substituting human for fixed physical capital in the north, whose traditional ways of making a living are moving to the South. In this way, as economists since Ricardo have known and preached, free trade leads to mutual benefits, with wages and incomes rising in both regions as they specialise in goods and services in which they have a comparative advantage.

But to obtain these gains, the processes of adjustment have to be allowed to work. In a market economy they are facilitated by wage signals, as can be seen in America – with the stagnation of the wages of the unskilled and a rising wage premium for each and every level of education. Though the income distribution has worsened, employment and per capita income have grown substantially. But this is not so in Euroland, where the views of the Dinosaurs still command widespread acceptance, and so the necessary wage signals have been muted and the unskilled are instead left unemployed but mollycoddled by generous welfare systems in these 'social market economies'.

It was precisely this so-called 'social question' which in part led to the unravelling of the nineteenth-century LIEO, as the redistributive and egalitarian politics arising from the rise of demos undermined that belief in classical liberalism, which underlay the intellectual underpinnings of the LIEO. With globalisation picking up where it left off, before this 'socialist' impulse – as we may call it – undermined the LIEO, the implicit philosophy underlying the so-called 'Washington consensus' on economic policy is underpinned by classical liberalism. In this sense, globalisation has put an end to what might be called the Age of Keynes.

One of the consequences of the breakdown of the nine-teenth-century LIEO was that convertibility of currencies and free mobility of capital were greatly attenuated and in many countries snuffed out by exchange controls. I need not remind you that in the UK these were only abolished when the first Thatcher government came to power. The bottling up of capital was essential for the Keynesian system to work. This was explicitly recognised in its inter-national expression (the so-called gold exchange standard established at Bretton Woods) which required controls on what were deemed to be short-term capital flows to allow the adjustable peg exchange rate system to work free from the speculative attacks which plague such systems.

The domestic consequence of this bottling up of mobile capital was that Keynesian remedies, requiring the taxation of capital to subsidise labour, would not work if capital was free to move and escape these arbitrary and exorbitant imposts. This is not the place to relate the story of how the world moved to free mobility of capital, but once it did, dirigiste states found it increasingly difficult to claim that they were able to promote national prosperity and welfare through fiscal policies to maintain 'full employment' and increases in redistributive taxation. Globalised capital markets, by allowing the prey to exit, have diminished the power of the predatory state to maintain, let alone increase, its take. Even those imbued by the 'socialist impulse' now recognise that their political prospects rely on the two Clintonian slogans: 'It's the economy, stupid!', and 'It's the bond market, stupid!' Moreover, as Mahathir Mohamad of Malaysia is soon about to discover, opting out of this emerging global market economy can only damage the prospects of that popular opulence which is now a worldwide demand and which this globalised economy can deliver to all its participants in an unprecedented manner.

There is also less danger today that the 'social question' posed by the current phase of globalisation will undermine the new LIEO as it did its nineteenth-century predecessor. This is because of the different nature of the 'losers' in the North in the two cases and the mitigating actions they can take to preserve their prosperity. The rise of the factory system in the nineteenth century and its spread to the North meant that the economic integration of the Atlantic economy by the LIEO led to relative declines or stagnation in the real incomes of the factors of production in each region which were relatively scarce, and a rise in the incomes of the more abundant factors.[94] This meant that in the US, which was labour-scarce and natural-resource-cum-land abundant, the distribution of income moved against labour. This led to the growth of populist politics and creeping protectionism on grounds first propounded by Alexander Hamilton. In Europe, which was labour-abundant and land-scarce, this nineteenth-century globalisation led to landowners relatively losing out. This then led to political coalitions such as the famous one between 'rye and steel' in Germany and growing protectionism justified by the 'infant industry' arguments of Friedrich List.

The UK alone stood by its free-trade creed, largely because having fought off the 'landed interest' at the time of the repeal of the Corn Laws and being the first industrial nation, the prosperity of both its industrial capitalists and workers was enhanced by the cheap grain flowing across the Atlantic as a result of the LIEO.[95]

While political action by threatened interest groups seemed inevitable to deal with the distributive consequences of globalisation at the end of the nineteenth century, the situation is much more benign in the current phase of globalisation. For whereas in the earlier phase the losers – the industrial workers in the US or the landowners in Germany for instance – could not acquire the means to prevent their relative decline, this is not so in the current situation in the North. The main losers are the unskilled, and unlike the industrial factory workers of the nineteenth century, who could not acquire the physical or financial capital to stem their relative decline in incomes, today's unskilled *can* acquire the necessary human capital to share in the immense gains from globalisation to their skilled compatriots in the North.

Secondly, and equally important, with most northern economies becoming primarily service economies, many more workers will be working in areas where the products produced are 'non-traded', i.e. sheltered from foreign competition. A hairdresser in Surbiton is not going to see his or her rates cut by competition from barbers in

Bangkok. But, many of these personal services require not just skills but also personal attributes like tidiness, punctuality, politeness and trustworthiness. Mothers are hardly likely to employ a member of the so-called 'underclass' as a baby sitter or housekeeper even if they are willing to accept the wages of a maid in India. The undermining of the Victorian personal virtues in the underclass created by Western welfare states provides yet another reason why their reform is so important for helping the potential 'losers' from the current processes of globalisation.

But within Euroland the Dinosaurs still cling to the dirigiste vision, with the preservation of their bloated welfare states being its major objective and look upon the euro as their saviour. The future prosperity of Europe therefore depends upon which of these two rival views wins in the near future. If the Modernisers win, Europe could challenge the US in efficiency and growth. But it should be emphasised the euro is certainly not necessary to further this process of globalisation within Europe. Unilateral removal of tariff barriers and eliminating capital controls are sufficient to integrate with the world economy.

Nor, as the successful city states of the Far East have shown, does size matter for prosperity in a globalised economy. Except for politicians, whose sense of self-importance may be fed by the size of country they claim to represent, the welfare of ordinary citizens is dependent less on where and what particular goods and services are produced domestically than on the highest return they can get for their labour, capital and enterprise and the cheapest price they can obtain for the goods they consume. The provision of local public goods and amenities is the only government-mediated action which would affect their welfare – apart from the usual provision of the classical public goods of law and order (including national defence).

CONCLUSIONS

For the euro successfully to challenge the dollar, not only would all these processes of globalisation need to be accepted in Euroland but in addition, as I have argued, there will be a need to create a genuine nation state with a true European identity. For only then will it be viable, as it is an economic area where the conditions for an optimum currency area are met. It is doubtful if, despite the spin doctors, there is any emerging European identity – witness the recent World Cup, where all the ancient tribal rivalries were often on bloody display.

As regards the conflict between the Dinosaurs and the Modernisers, which will determine whether Euroland globalises, perhaps the optimists will be proved right. The euro, although not in itself essential for globalisation, could act as a spur. EU politicians will bite the bullet and undertake the structural reforms necessary for Euroland to integrate fully with the global economy. I, however, remain a sceptic, partly because this is like asking whether pigs have wings. But, as I have argued, primarily because the euro is as much the problem as the solution for globalising Euroland.

First published as 'EMU and Globalization', Policy Series No. 17, Politea, London 1999.

CHAPTER FIVE

SMOKE GETS IN YOUR EYES

THE ECONOMIC WELFARE EFFECTS OF THE WORLD BANK—WORLD HEALTH ORGANIZATION GLOBAL CRUSADE AGAINST TOBACCO

INTRODUCTION

The publication of the World Bank's report in collaboration with the World Health Organization (WHO), entitled *Curbing the Epidemic – Governments and the Economics of Tobacco Control,* and the issuance of a provisional draft for a WHO framework convention on tobacco control (WHO, 2000) marks the unfortunate entry of these hitherto respected and technically proficient UN agencies into the West's current internal cultural wars. For complex reasons, which we cannot go into here,[96] many in the West have sought to demonise a perfectly legal but risky and addictive good which provides solace and comfort (summarised in the economist's notion of 'utility') to millions. It is illegitimate for international institutions which have been set up to provide technically sound advice to the international community to try and legislate the emerging tastes of many in the West to the rest of humankind. How well does this report stand up by technical standards, is the main question we shall investigate. As the report purports explicitly to be about the *economics* of tobacco control, it is with this aspect, and in particular with the wholly neglected effects on economic welfare, with which we will be primarily concerned.

It should be noted that as many reviewers of the report have noted it does not follow even minimal scientific or academic standards in deriving or documenting most of its conclusions.[97] Though the final report has removed some of the more extreme and indeed laughable assertions of the draft report (draft 4, February 1999)[98] the latter in many ways provides a clearer indication of the 'ideological' nature of the research and, even more disturbingly, of where these institutions want to take policy towards tobacco in the Third World – for instance, in the recommendation in the draft report that tobacco taxes be increased by 10 per cent per annum for ten years, which has now been moderated to be a once-and-for-all increase of the tax by 10 per cent. In our empirical estimates for the five countries and regions that we were able to get readily available and usable data – India, Korea, South Africa, Japan and the European Union – we therefore calculate the net welfare effects of both these policies as well as the welfare effects of the existing taxes in these countries or regions.

TOBACCO'S NET BENEFITS

The economic welfare effects of tobacco controls can be set out in terms of a simple supply–demand diagram (see Figure 5.1).

To simplify matters – and to avoid the problem of having to compute the effects on domestic production of various policies – assume that cigarettes can be bought at a given world price, Pw.

FIGURE 5.1

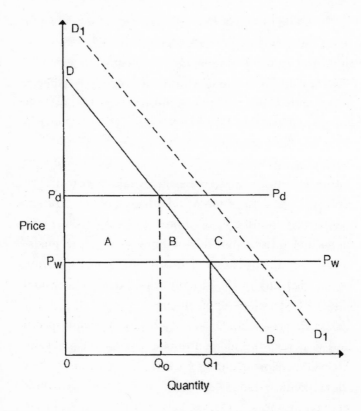

Quantity

These imports always supplement domestic supply, so that any change in domestic demand merely effects imports. With the existing taxes, the domestic price is Pd, and the loss in consumer surplus (CS) is the area A + B, where the former gives the tax revenue, and the latter the dead weight loss associated with the tax.

If taxes are handed back to consumers in lump-sum fashion, or the value of a rand of public funds is assumed to be at least equal to the value of a rand to the consumer, then the tax burden A can be neglected as a social cost, and the net welfare cost will be the deadweight loss B. But the social value of this tax burden depends crucially upon the character of the government to whose coffers it accrues. If the government consists of Platonic Guardians then it is plausible to say that a rand of public funds is worth more than a rand of lost consumption, and in some cases could be worth even more. But if most governments, particularly those in the Third and Second Worlds are predatory,[99] then the social value of this transfer of a rand to the government will be less than a rand and may even be worthless. Given the World Bank's ongoing crusade against corruption and for improved governance in many of its borrowers, implicitly it must ascribe the predatory rather than platonic end of this political spectrum to the character of the governments it advises. It would thus be best to look upon the tax burden as it is clearly to consumers – a burden – and which can only in special and specific cases and countries be set off as a social gain. We will therefore in our international comparisons eschew these political judgements and look upon the whole of the consumer surplus loss (CS = A+B) as a welfare loss to the consumer from taxation of cigarettes.

It should also be noted that the proposed taxation also violates the principles of horizontal and vertical equity recommended by traditional public finance principles. Horizontal equity requires equals should be treated uniformly. It is unfair to treat someone who is the same as everyone else, except for being a smoker, differently. Vertical equity requires that taxes should not be regressive. As the poor are predominantly smokers, tobacco taxes are inherently regressive. Against these principles of classical public finance which establish the case for uniform taxation, there is an argument based on modern public economics for non-uniform taxation which could be used in favour of tobacco taxation. This is the so-called Ramsey rule, which says that the excess burden of a tax (the dead weight consumer surplus loss (B) in Figure 5.1) is minimised by taxing goods in relatively inelastic demand – and the demand for tobacco is relatively inelastic. However, as Harberger has noted, 'to tax salt more heavily than sugar, simply and solely because it has a lower elasticity of demand is at least as capricious (from the standpoint of equity) as taxing people differently according to the colour of their eyes'.[100] Underlying these differences are different philosophies of government – the classical liberal view which favours neutrality defined as uniformity of taxation and the 'social engineering' view, which defines it on the Ramsey principle. We return to this important contrast in the next section.

What are the benefits of controlling tobacco? The most immediate is the reduction in cigarette consumption and the effects this may have on increased life expectancy. This is again a benefit which accrues to the consumer. What value can we impute to this possible extension of life?

There has been an interminable and inconclusive debate on the value to be placed on human life and hence on the value of years of life saved.[101] Two things need to be noted in forming a judgement on this issue. First, the diseases and hence deaths resulting from smoking occur late in life and hence the costs associated will only occur if life expectancy is already fairly high – which is in turn related to relative affluence. For many Third World countries where the traditional infectious diseases are still widespread and lower life expectancies, the smoker may well die off from other causes well before his smoking habit kills him. Here the World Bank report's egregious assumption that the normal life expectancy for everyone is that associated with the longest lived population – Japan's – allows it to define premature deaths from smoking in middle age to include deaths up to sixty-nine years. As I remarked of this: 'It is ripe to tell a landless labourer in rural India that he is dying prematurely at the age of sixty-nine because of his addiction to "bidis".'[102] Correspondingly its headline-grabbing figure of the ten million lives to be saved by its tobacco crusade are not credible.

Second, just as in national income accounting, despite the various complaints that have been made over the years that it does not provide a true measure of welfare (largely because of its neglect of distributional considerations[103]), GDP per capita remains a fairly robust and objective measure of the wealth of nations, the actual income and equivalent consumption lost as a result of reduced life expectancy is the simplest and most readily defensible value to be placed on the benefits of tobacco control. This is the measure we will use in deriving our estimates later on.

Are there any other costs and benefits? For developed countries with publicly funded health care and pension systems, various additional social costs and benefits have been identified. For the US it has been estimated[104] that in 1993 the social costs and benefits (including the dubious cost of second-hand smoke – on which more later) were as follows: Social costs – medical care $0.55, sick leave $0.01, group life insurance $0.14, fires $0.02, second-hand smoke $0.25, local taxes on earnings foregone $0.40. Total costs to society were therefore $1.37. Social Benefits – nursing home savings $0.23, pensions and social security payments saved $1.19, excise taxes paid $0.53. The total social benefits were $1.95, yielding a *net social benefit* of $0.58 per pack of cigarettes. If, as we see later, the wholly spurious social costs of second-hand smoke of $0.25 are disregarded, the net social benefit rises to $0.83 per pack!

For developing countries, as the World Bank report accepts, most of these purported social costs and benefits are irrelevant as they do not have extensive publicly or group funded health, insurance and pension systems. Apart from second-hand smoke, most of the other social costs and benefits adduced above are privately borne. Also this estimate takes no account of the consumer surplus charges associated with smoking and its taxation.

Moreover, even for developed countries most of the adduced social costs and benefits are pecuniary exter-nalities which are Pareto-irrelevant.[105] Thus, as in standard cost-benefit analysis all transfers including those relating to pensions, life insurance etc. should be netted out. This leaves only the true external costs namely the costs associ-ated with environmental smoke and probably from fires. As the latter are fairly small we will ignore them so that the only truly Pareto-relevant external effect – if it was proven – would be second-hand smoke which damaged the health of others. In fact the moral crusade against tobacco in the West has been fuelled by the claims made in a US Environmental Protection Agency report in 1992, which claimed there was scientific evidence of health damage from passive smoking. This was thoroughly discredited by a US federal court in 1998 for being inherently biased. As the only source of externalities remains damage from secondary smoke, it may be useful to summarise the available evidence on this.

The evidence, such as it is, is based on epidemiological studies. The scientific status of epidemiology is questionable, but be that as it may, Gori and Luik's survey[106] of all the available environmental tobacco smoke (ETS) studies shows (see their Tables 11, 12, 13) that the evidence from spousal studies, those of non-smokers exposed to smoke in the work place and of children exposed to ETS shows no increased risk to non-smokers and for work place and childhood exposure suggest reduced risk or *protection*.[107]

How can the World Bank report then claim that the health effects include 'disease in children and adults chronically exposed to second hand smoke'? While its claim that the other effects 'include low birth weight and increased risk of various diseases in the infants of smoking mothers', even if true, provides no basis for taxing tobacco. There are numerous risks that infants face, the most important arising from poverty – and particularly in developing countries from infectious diseases and unsafe water supplies. Should the poor then be taxed for having babies because of the differential health costs their children will have to bear?

Thus there is no credible Pareto-relevant externality[108] arising from smoking, and no need to go beyond the private costs and benefits we have already taken into account. The WB–WHO report's argument that there is a nuisance from tobacco smoke which is an externality is absurd.[109] There are many things which individuals do which others find annoying and irritating. For instance, I find the smell of cheap perfume very irritating. But that is no reason to ban or tax it. In fact much of civilisation has evolved as a system of manners which allow many personal habits to be self-controlled in public places.[110] Most civilisations thus teach children not to break wind in public and to feel a sense of shame when they do. With divergent tastes and habits, the purpose of these manners is to allow us all to move in the communal spaces we inhabit with consideration for others. Not taxation or prohibition is the answer to the annoyance of tobacco for non-smokers, but perhaps a course from Miss Manners in which smokers learn to ask in a public space: 'Do you mind if I smoke?'

Equally tendentious is the report's claim that consumers of tobacco in developing countries are ill-informed of the risks involved. The best empirical study found that in the US, smokers over-estimated the risks of smoking.[111] The report cites no evidence for its claim. But even if it were true this would merely justify a public information programme, not taxation or prohibition.

The argument that cigarettes are addictive and thus pose a special risk to the young is also without any merit. The addictive nature of tobacco can be taken into account in estimating the demand, as is done in our estimates below. That the young should be saved from risky behaviour which only hurts themselves, because they habitually underestimate the risks, would mean banning them from all risky activity such as bungee jumping, riding, boxing, skate boarding, rugby and much more. Moreover, as the report notes that much of teenage behaviour is based on rebellion, and as the evidence on the effects of bans and price increases in preventing teenage initiation into the tobacco habit is at best equivocal,[112] perhaps instead the rebellious urge could be put to use – by adults telling children how nice cigarettes are instead of how nasty!

It should be clear that as far as the economic welfare effects of tobacco policies are concerned, for the developing world we do not need to go beyond the simple net consumer surplus change measure we presented at the outset.

'PUBLIC HEALTH' AND PRIVATE HEALTH

It has been claimed in the draft of the World Bank report, and in Chaloupka and Warner[113] that there is a separate 'societal interest in the public's health' which it is the purpose of the public health community to foster. On the face of it this seems unexceptional, as clearly economists too recognise that there are externalities involved in many *infectious* diseases which require public health measures from improved sanitation to immunisation if a health epidemic is to be avoided. But this legitimate aim has now been stretched by the use of persuasive language to include people's lifestyle choices, which only affect their own health and not those of others. A typical example is provided in the very title of the World Bank report – *Curbing the Epidemic* (emphasis added).[114] Cigarette smoking may be widespread and growing, and it may lead to disease in later life, but it is not in itself a disease (any more than anal intercourse, which is implicated in transmission of the HIV virus leading to AIDS) and hence cannot in itself be an epidemic, which the Concise Oxford Dictionary defines as 'a widespread occurrence of a *disease* in a community at a particular time'. By using the persuasive term 'epidemic' the impression is created that smoking itself is a disease, like the flu, which can be transmitted to others.

But, the public health riposte will be that it is the responsibility of the public health authorities to prevent premature deaths, and hence it is justified in prohibiting or taxing personal behaviour which might lead to one's own premature death. But here the analogy with anal intercourse and AIDS is telling. Should the public health authorities ban anal intercourse which, even if consensual and in full knowledge of the consequences, could lead homosexuals to their premature deaths? Even more, the addiction and 'seduction of youth' argument used against smoking applies equally to homosexuality. In many countries (including the UK) the age of consent for homosexuality has been lowered to allow teenagers to be seduced by homosexuality. Just as with smoking there is a combination of tastes and heredity which make people homosexual and hence in danger of dying prematurely from AIDS. By converting teenagers to homosexuality there may be a similar 'addictive' effect as with smoking that might lead to their premature deaths. But does this mean that there is a public health interest in banning homosexuality as has been common in many parts of the world through most of history – or should people with their homosexual tastes and proclivities be free to choose – as liberal societies have rightly insisted – with the only public health function being to provide the necessary information about the risks involved?

This pinpoints the spuriousness and the 'ideological' nature of the arguments for prohibiting and taxing smoking by the public health profession. Just as liberal societies do not ban homosexuality on public health grounds even if it causes those who practise it possible health damage, similarly there is no separate public health case (apart from the standard economic arguments based on externalities) for banning or taxing tobacco. Smokers are now like homosexuals of yore, being punished for their tastes not shared by the majority of their fellows. There is thus a deep contradiction in the attitudes of supposedly liberal societies to these two different 'afflictions'.

The 'public health' case against tobacco, moreover, harks back to a paternalism which was the bedrock of those planned societies and economies we now know to have failed. The difference between it and the liberal view which has triumphed – and which at least in its other manifestations the World Bank promotes – is best expressed by the contrasting views of the liberal J. S. Mill and the socialist Douglas Jay.

As is well known, Mill, in his famous essay *On Liberty*, had stated one of the bedrock principles of liberalism, which is worth quoting in full. He wrote:

> The object of this essay is to assert one very simple principle, as entitled to govern absolutely the dealings of society with the individual in the way of compulsion and control, whether the means used be physical force in the form of legal penalties, or the moral coercion of public opinion. That principle is, that the sole end for which mankind are warranted, individually or collectively, in interfering with the liberty of action of any of

their number, is self-protection. That the only purpose for which power can be rightfully exercised over any member of a civilised community, against his will, is to prevent harm to others. His own good, either physical or moral, is not a sufficient warrant. He cannot rightfully be compelled to do or forbear because it will be better for him to do so, because it will make him happier, because, in the opinion of others, to do so would be wise, or even right. There are good reasons for remonstrating with him, or persuading him, or entreating him, but not for compelling him, or visiting him with any evil in case he do otherwise. To justify that, the conduct from which it is desired to deter him must be calculated to produce evil to someone else. The only part of the conduct of any one, for which he is amenable to society, is that which concerns others. In the part which merely concerns himself, his independence is, of right, absolute. Over himself, over his own body and mind, the individual is sovereign.[115]

By contrast Douglas Jay memorably summed up the paternalism underlying the 'public health' position when he wrote:

Housewives on the whole cannot be trusted to buy all the right things, where nutrition and health are concerned. This is really no more than an extension of the principle according to which the housewife herself would not trust a child of four to select the week's purchase. For in the case of nutrition and health, just as in the case of education, the gentleman in Whitehall really does know better what is good for people than the people themselves.[116]

This was the nub of the case for the planned society and economy. It is ironic that when the World Bank is advising these failed economies to move away from these dysfunctional beliefs it should have lent support to the 'public health' arguments which are based precisely on the same beliefs.

For a liberal society there is no separate public health justification for preventing people from slowly killing themselves by smoking. There is no evidence as we have noted that they damage others – even less so than homosexuals. In both cases banning, controlling or taxing the indulging of these private tastes is a sign of an illiberal society.

Furthermore, there are more serious reasons to doubt the 'public health' argument that is being used to affect people's personal lifestyle choices. As we have seen, public health is rightly concerned with infectious diseases, and at least in the developing world there remains much work to be done by conventional public health measures to eliminate these scourges. But in the developed world where this battle has at least been temporarily won, the public health professionals have invented a new set of scourges – lifestyles which purportedly kill us prematurely. The scientific basis for their identification is provided by the statistical techniques of epidemiology. But as is becoming increasingly apparent within the medical profession, the scientific standing of these findings is a sham. It is useful to explain why, because it was the respectable epidemiological study of smoking by Sir Richard Doll and his associates which gave credence to this technique, but which has since been grossly misused, not least in the EPA report on passive smoking already discussed.

In 1981, Sir Richard Doll – who in the 1950s with Sir

Austin Bradford Mill had used the statistical techniques of epidemiology to show the link between cigarette smoking and lung cancer – published *The Causes of Cancer,* claiming that apart from tobacco, food caused 70 per cent of cancers. His basic argument was that comparing the incidence of cancers recorded in the Connecticut Cancer registry with the lowest incidence of the same cancers in the world, different diets could be the only explanation for the differential incidence (e.g. he found there were 60.2 per million cases of pancreatic cancer in Connecticut, compared with twenty-one per million in India). He completely omitted to examine the relationship between ageing and cancer even though 'an eighty year old has a thousand times greater risk compared to when he was a teenager. This is *fifty* times greater than the twenty-fold increase Hill and Doll had found in the risk of lung cancer for smokers compared to non smokers.'[117] Though Doll subsequently conceded the weaknesses of his case, he never retracted it, and it has become the core of the claims still made by public-health lobbies to make us change our lifestyles. But what is the scientific validity of these claims?

The first thing to note is that epidemiology on which these claims are based is a purely statistical 'science'. But for economists who have been trained in modern econometrics the inferences drawn by epidemiologists will appear to be jejune at best. They often make the elementary mistake of identifying correlation with causation. The major problem all sciences of statistical inference face is what econometricians call the problem of 'identification'. Despite various purported advances by econometricians in solving the problem, it does ultimately depend upon accepting the form of induction recommended by the

Reverend Thomas Bayes in a posthumous paper in 1763. Bayes's famous theorem shows how given some prior belief about a *general* proposition (in terms of what would today be called subjective probabilities), current *particular* evidence will lead to revision of these prior beliefs, so that with this constant revision as evidence accumulates we will reach the true general proposition from particular experiences. Frank Ramsey, Keynes's young protégé in his famous *The Foundations of Mathematics and other logical essays,* showed this was the only coherent form of inference. Incidentally, Karl Popper, who misunderstood Bayes, was wrong to deny probabilistic induction. For economists, economic theory and their general knowledge of the world provide these prior beliefs, an aspect forgotten by the army of economic researchers currently throwing the cross-section data put together by Summers and Heston, for a large number of countries since the 1950s, into a computer and then trying to find *any* statistically significant relationship without any theoretical justification.

The same is true of epidemiologists, for whom the mantra is a 5 per cent significance level, using the multiple correlation methods recommended by the Cambridge mathematician and geneticist Ronald Fisher. He thought he had found a way around the inevitable subjectivity involved in prior beliefs associated with Bayesian methods. He claimed that, once the raw data was converted into a number giving the probability of getting the same correlations as the researcher found by mere fluke, then, if this probability level were below 1 in 20 yielding a significance level of 5 per cent, chance could be ruled out as the explanation. But as another mathematician, Harold Jeffreys, asked: why 5 per cent, and does this significance level imply that the chance that the effects are just a fluke is only 5 per cent? On the first, Fisher decided on 5 per cent because it was 'mathematically convenient'. On the second the definition of significance values is the convoluted one that it gives the probability of obtaining just as impressive results *assuming* pure chance is their cause. It does not tell the researcher whether the effect is *really just* a fluke. To do that there is no way to avoid Bayes's theorem, as the mathematician Richard Cox showed as early as 1946.[118]

To see the difference this makes, consider the chances of the correlations being nothing more than a fluke even if the significance level is 5 per cent, applying Bayes's theorem. Suppose that the prior belief is agnostic so that there is a 50–50 expected chance of the effects being real. Then the chance of the correlation being a fluke given a 5 per cent significance level is 22 per cent. So at least around a quarter of the results which are significant at a 5 per cent level are meaningless flukes! Much worse if the prior belief is that the presumed effects are extremely unlikely. Say this initial level of plausibility is 1 in 100, then the chance of the 5 per cent significant results being mere flukes rises to 96 per cent.[119]

Thus, consider the analysis of thirty-seven published studies of passive smoking by Hackshaw et al., which found an increased risk to those living with smokers of 26 per cent.[120] Once, however, studies of real-life measures of exposure to cigarette smoke are used to determine the risk, it falls to a negligible 2 per cent, largely because unlike the twenty-five cigarettes a day passive smokers were assumed to be exposed to by Hackshaw et al., Phillips et al. found that in real life the exposure was 1/50th of a cigarette a day![121]

These problems do not plague the epidemiology of *infectious diseases,* as the 'identification' is possible as these:

diseases occur only after exposure to specific bacteria, viruses and parasites. Indeed, it would be grossly unfair to lump all epidemiology together in view of the spectacular successes with infectious diseases – successes that have been possible precisely because absolutely undeniable causes could be identified and controlled. This is not the case for the study of most cancers and other conditions that are linked to a multitude of risk factors, none of which could be positively labelled as a cause.[122]

Sir Richard Doll himself was aware of the pitfalls of drawing causal inferences from epidemiology. He wrote:

> Epidemiological observations ... have serious disadvantages ... they can seldom be made according to the strict requirements of experimental science and therefore may be open to a variety of interpretations. A particular factor may be associated with some disease merely because of its association with some other factor that causes the disease, or the association may be an artefact due to some systematic bias in the information collection ... these disadvantages limit the value of observations in humans, but ... until we know exactly how cancer is caused and how some factors are able to modify the effects of others, the need to observe *imaginatively* what actually happens to various different categories of people will remain.[123] [emphasis added]

The emphasised word underlines the subjective nature of the resulting causal inferences drawn in epidemiological studies of non-infectious or 'lifestyle' diseases. This in turn has been justified by another epidemiologist, who says:

'...despite philosophic injunctions concerning inductive inference, criteria have commonly been used to make such inferences. The justification offered has been that the exigencies of public health problems demand action and that despite imperfect knowledge causal inferences must be made'[124]. But as Gori has rightly remarked about this view it is circular as it invokes exigencies of public health to justify these inferences which sustain the exigencies in the first place![125]

Not surprisingly, therefore, not only medical practitioners but also researchers are now beginning to question the scientific basis of epidemiology. Ultimately it can only be credible if the basics of biology are used, in the language of econometrics, to 'identify' the model. Most of the 5 per cent statistically significant results impugning nearly every aspect of our diets and lifestyles go against basic biology,[126] and hence the attempts to control or prevent disease by lecturing us on how we live is nothing short of statistical witchcraft.[127]

FROM FANTASY TO FACT

We have derived estimates of the net economic welfare effects of taxation of cigarettes in the technical appendix for five countries/regions for which we are able to get the relevant data. Three of these are developing countries – India, Korea and South Africa. The arguments we have given for ignoring the social costs and benefits associated with public pensions and health systems are readily applicable to these countries. In addition we have also provided estimates for two developed countries/regions: Japan and the European Union (the nine major countries in it viz. Belgium, Denmark, France, Germany, Ireland,

Italy, Netherlands, Spain and the United Kingdom). These estimates too are derived on the same basis as for the developing countries. They can be interpreted as the true social costs and benefits net of transfer payments, or if the current erroneous practice of taking account of pecuniary externalities is maintained as the effects which would occur if the public health and pension systems were privatised and individuals bore the relevant costs and benefits themselves.

In deriving these estimates we have to take account of the addictive nature of cigarettes in estimating their demand. Till recently most estimates of cigarette demand were based on assuming consumers were irrational or myopic. In the irrational case a sort of divided self was posited[128], with stable but inconsistent preferences with the 'short-run' self adoring tobacco while the 'long-run' self wanted clean lungs and a long life. In the myopic models, current consumption depends on the 'stock of habits' which is given by the depreciated sum of all past consumption.[129] So current consumption depends on past consumption but not future consumption. The rational addiction models repair this omission and show how, even with addictive goods, consumers maximise utility over their life cycle, taking account of the future consequences of their action.[130] These models capture many of the well-known features of addiction to tobacco. Due to reinforcement, consumption in adjacent time periods are complements.[131] So that current consumption of the good is related not only to the current price but also all past and future prices. The long-run effect of a permanent price change will exceed that in the short run, as will that of an anticipated price change from one which is

unanticipated. These models also lead to bi-modal distributions of consumption echoing the 'binge' and 'cold turkey'
type behaviour found amongst addicts. Also the model
implies that temporary events like a price cut, peer pressure, stress etc. can lead to permanent addiction. Finally,
the responsiveness to price changes will also depend upon
the individual's rate of time preference – the rate at which
he/she discounts the future. The rational addiction model
would thus seem to capture all the features that supposedly
make cigarettes 'different' from other consumption goods.

We have estimated our demand curves for the five
countries and regions for both the myopic and rational
addiction models, and invariably the latter performs
better. So our estimates of the welfare effects of tobacco
taxation is based on the estimated rational addiction
demand curves for each of our countries.

Next we estimated the consumer surplus (CS) lost per
smoker as a result of the current level of taxation, i.e. the
area A+B in Figure 5.1 (p. 98). With unchanging income,
this CS annual loss would accrue for each of the years
the consumer continues to smoke. Assuming that most
addicts get hooked on their habit at the age of twenty and
then never give up, this gives us CS losses in the years till
they die of their smoking-related diseases. This does not
take account of those smokers who quit, as we do not have
any data on this.

Manning et al. have used data from the Centre of Disease
Control and IJS life tables to estimate the relative risk of
smoking for two hypothetical cohorts of men and women
from age twenty to death: one cohort smokes, the other
does not.[132] From this they derive the figure that, for each
pack of cigarettes smoked, life expectancy at age twenty

declines by 137 minutes. We use this figure to estimate the duration of life saved by the reduction in tobacco consumption caused by the current tax rates. As explained earlier, we value these savings in terms of the yearly per capita income ($y(T)$) that the person would have had if they had lived their normal life expectancy (E). So for each pack not consumed, at the date $T = E-20$ (as we assume that all our smokers start at twenty years of age) there will be a benefit of $[137/(60\times24\times365)]\ y(T)$. This of course does not take account of the fact that with cigarettes there are threshold effects as, at a low daily consumption, numerous studies have found that, there may be no significant risk for smokers as compared with non-smokers.[133]

Without any income growth, therefore, the net welfare benefit of the tobacco taxes will be the CS losses from age twenty till the normal life expectancy in that country, against which have to be set the benefits of the extra years of life gained (valued at the per capita income) in the year T. But as a rand given up today is not equivalent to a rand gained tomorrow, we will have to discount these dated costs and benefits. The rational addiction model estimates provide the rates at which our average smoker discounts the future, but to take account of the 'misperception of risk' argument currently used against smoking we will be using much lower 'social' discount rates, namely 2.5 and 10 per cent to determine the net present values from the alternative levels of taxation of cigarettes.

Finally, we need to take account of the fact that per capita income will increase in the future. This will affect both the costs and benefit calculations. In terms of Figure 5.1, the demand curve will now shift in each year because of income growth. So in each year we will have the additional consumer surplus loss given by area C added on. This is readily derived from our demand curve estimates. Also the per capita income in year T when the benefits from increased life accrue will also be higher.

If n is the percentage of a year saved by not smoking a pack of cigarettes, and per capita income is growing at the rate of g per year, and d is the discount rate, then the present value of the benefits (PVB) from tobacco taxation is the reduction in cigarette packs per smoker (N) induced at our assumed starting age of twenty, so:

(1) $PVB = N. [n. y (1+g)^{T}] / (1+d)^{T}$

The present value of the consumer surplus (PVC) lost in each year C^{n} is:

(2) $PVC = N. [\sum_{n=0}^{T} C^{n} / (1+d)^{n}]$

The net present benefit NPB is then given by:

(3) NPB = (1) - (2)

In the Appendix these estimates have been made for (a) the current level of taxation in each of the five countries; (b) a 10 per cent increase in taxation as recommended by the World Bank report; (c) a 10 per cent increase p.a. for ten years as recommended in the draft World Bank report.

Table 5.1 summarises the estimates for each of these policies for each of the countries on the best guesses about the likely value of g, and assuming d=2. We give the figures for each smoker's change in welfare, and for the country in aggregate. The per capita income and GDP is also given for each country to allow a comparison of these net benefits to be appropriately scaled.

By any standard, the economic welfare losses from existing tobacco taxes are huge, and will further rise if the taxes are raised on either of the two policy recommendations. Thus for Korea the per smoker loss from current taxation is nearly 15 per cent of current per capita income, and the aggregate loss from current and future taxation (of a 10 per cent p.a. increase for ten years) would amount to 12 per cent of current GDP. For India, the per smoker loss from current taxation is nearly twice per capita GDP, and the aggregate loss from current and future taxation (of a 10 per cent increase for ten years) would be a massive 80 per cent of current GDP. For South Africa, the per smoker loss from current cigarette taxation is about 11 per cent of per capita income, and the aggregate loss from current and future taxation (of a 10 per cent increase for ten years) is 41 per cent of current GDP.

As the smokers who incur these losses are admitted by the World Bank report to be relatively poor, and if we were to apply the World Bank's project evaluation methodology,[134] we would have to apply distributional weights to them, so that an Rl loss to these poor would be socially more costly than an R1 loss to someone at the same per capita income. We have not made this adjustment as we do not have any income distributional data on smokers. But this does suggest that our estimates are likely to be underestimates of the true social losses from tobacco taxation in developing countries

CONCLUSIONS

Our conclusions can be brief. The World Bank report provides no cogent reasons for its crusade against tobacco in the developing world. With most of the costs and benefits being privately borne in these countries, the only case for intervention would be on the grounds of an externality. We have seen there are no such grounds. This crusade, as so much of past development policy, is based on an implicit contempt for the poor masses of the Third World. The conclusion of my survey of these dirigiste economic policies in 1983 is as applicable to this social dirigisme of the WB–WHO. In my *The Poverty of 'Development Economics'* I concluded:

> At its bluntest, behind at least part of the dirigiste case is a paternalistic attitude born of a distrust of, if not contempt for, the ordinary, uneducated masses of the Third World. This attitude is not confined entirely, nor primarily, to Western outsiders; it is shared by many in the ruling elites of the Third World. As a leading development economist [Paul Streeten] has observed about Gunnar Myrdal, one of the Western economists to have fuelled the *Dirigiste Dogma:*
>
>   'As a proud somewhat un-Swedish Swede ... he [Myrdal] finds it easier to identify with liberal Americans than with the English or French, and easier with Englishmen than with the Indian masses. It is partly for this reason that *An American Dilemma* is an optimistic book, and *Asian drama* a pessimistic one. He once said how kindred American aspirations and ideals, and the "American creed", were to his own beliefs, and how he could identify with these ideals when writing the book

on the black problem; and how, in contrast, when he visited an Indian textile factory, the thin, half-naked brown bodies struck him as utterly alien.' [135]

It is easy to suppose that these half-starved, wretched and ignorant masses could not possibly conform, either as producers or consumers to the behavioural assumptions of orthodox neo-classical economics ... it is the hallmark of much of development economics – together with the assertion that some ethereal and verbally sanitised entity (such as 'government', 'planners' or 'policy makers') which is both knowledgeable and compassionate can overcome the defects of these stupid or ignorant producers and consumers, and compel them to raise their living standards through various dirigiste means.[136]

And so it is with the WB–WHO report. The attempt to inflict the estimated large losses of economic welfare on poor people is wicked and shameful, when for so many of these poor the noxious weed is one of the only sources of pleasure in lives which remain 'nasty, brutish and short'.

APPENDIX: TABLE 5.1

Country/region	Current taxes	10% increase	10% a year incr. for 10 years
1. Korea *(2% pa. y incr, d=2%)* a) per smoker b) aggregate (billions) *per capita income:* *10,641; GDP (billions):* *489.38*	-1495 -23	-251 -4	-2463 -37

2. India *(3% pa. y incr, d=2%)* a) per smoker b) aggregate (billions) *per capita income: 209;* *GDP (billions): 196.23*	-455 -99.9	-20 -5.64	-280 -61.9
3. South Africa *(3% pa. y incr. d=2%)* a) per smoker b) aggregate (billions) *per capita income:* *29,404; GDP* *(billions): 316.90*	-822 -36.3	-153 -6.8	-2104 -92.8
4. Japan *(2% pa. y. incr. d=2%)* a) per smoker b) aggregate (billions) *per capita income:* *29,404; GDP* *(billions): 3717.00*	-3190 -106	-153 -6.8	-4309 -273
5. European Union (9 countries) *(0% pa. y incr. d=2%)* a) per smoker b) aggregate (billions) *per capita income:* *17,697; GDP (billions):* *5892.00*	-1998 -273	-354 -48	-6597 -900

Source: Lal, Kim, Lu and Prat (2000)

First published as 'Smoke Gets in Your Eyes', FMF Monograph
No. 26, Free Market Foundation, Sandton, South Africa 2000.

CHAPTER SIX

WILL TERRORISM DEFEAT GLOBALISATION?

Globalisation is the process of creating a common economic space. It leads to a growing integration of hitherto relatively closed economies through increasingly free movements of goods, capital and labour. It is not a new process. It has usually been associated with the creation and maintenance of empires. The latter have been created in part to provide 'order' in the larger economic space, by suppressing various threats to the productive and sedentary ways of life of civilisations from various roving bandits, who today are called terrorists. An elaboration of these points will allow us to answer the question posed in the title of this chapter.

One of the features of a closed economy is that goods and services do not enter international trade – they are non-traded. Their prices are set by domestic demand and supply. The efficiency gains which accrue from differences in the domestic and international prices of traded goods in an open economy cannot be obtained. These gains can be decomposed into the consumption gain, which allows consumers to obtain their consumption bundles at lower cost, and the production gain, which arises from the specialisation in domestic production on the basis of comparative advantage, allowing countries to use the more productive 'technology' provided by international trade to raise their output from given resource endowments.

Goods can be non-traded because natural barriers raise transport costs or because tariffs prohibit trade. In the millennial past when costs of communication and transport were very high, only high-valued, non-bulky goods entered into long-distance trade. This trade was always threatened by pirates and bandits of every kind. They imposed a further cost in addition to natural barriers to trade. If the costs of piracy were high enough, trade would cease as happened when the Great Powers's attempts to control the bandits failed.

Further, given the costs of doing international business, most traded goods were not locally produced. Domestically produced goods rarely faced foreign competition because they were not traded. The major gain from foreign trade was thus consumption. But the spice trade – which involved transfers between East Europe and the Tropics – did lead to production gains because meat from East Europe was stored for later shipment during long northern winters. This demanded new storage technology which was produced locally. Luxuries and the instruments of war were the major items involved in this long-distance trade. But the realisation of these gains required a modicum of order enforced by military power.

With the Industrial Revolution, and the creation of a British-led international economic order policed by the Royal Navy, there was an expansion in the goods traded around the world. This period of globalisation saw the growing integration of nearly the whole world into an international economy. The predators were kept at bay by the exercise of direct and indirect control over a vast economic space by British naval and military power. Nevertheless, there were still terrorists, mainly fuelled by nationalism as well as the romantic revolt against capitalism, who did disturb domestic order in the metropole and its dependencies.[137] This terrorism did not, however, raise the costs sufficiently to undermine the processes of globalisation. As long as the imperial peace was maintained, it was at worst a local irritant.

During this nineteenth-century liberal international economic order (LIEO) there were substantial consumption and production gains from the free mobility of goods, capital and labour. It was only during the first half of the twentieth century, with the decline of the British Empire and the ravages of the inter-war years, particularly the Great Depression, that domestic economic policy led to growing barriers to foreign trade in many countries, converting many previously traded goods into non-traded goods. These inward-looking policies had predecessors, most notably China in the Middle Ages and Japan under the Tokugawa Shogunate. Such regimes had completely banned foreign trade as they looked upon the accompanying foreign influences as sources of domestic disorder.

Order is required to maintain three elementary and universal goals that any society must pursue if any social life is to exist. These are, first, to secure life against violence which leads to death or bodily harm; second, that promises once made are kept; third, the stabilisation of possessions through rules of property. These are the minimal functions that any state in its domestic domain needs to perform. But, for international trade and commerce, there is also the need to protect the trading networks: to maintain international order. In an anarchical society of equally matched states, there is always the danger that internecine warfare will disrupt these trading channels. Given the high value of the objects traded in the past, taxing long-distance trade has always provided an important source of revenue for states. It has been in their interests to protect these channels.

But, as Jack Hirshleifer pointed out, in economics there is also the 'dark side of the force'.[138] For one can make a living by either making or taking. Disrupting or stealing a rival's long-distance trade can therefore form part of a country's strategy, of which war is the most extreme alternative. So state-sponsored terrorism, as we now call it, to both directly 'take' as well as damage the 'making' of a rival's income has also been a constant feature of human history.[139]

If an asymmetric advantage in military technology permits one state in an anarchical society of states to achieve hegemony, the resulting imperial state has usually been best able to provide the order over a larger geographical space, which is a necessary condition for the benign economic processes of 'globalisation' to operate. For these empires reduce the threats to these processes from roving bandits – either private or state sponsored. In fact, most of the ancient empires arose because of the threat posed by roving bandits to their sedentary ways of life. In long-term historical perspective, terrorists are best looked upon as roving bandits. They have threatened the sedentary civilisations of Eurasia for millennia. This is because these civilisations, which arose in the ancient river valleys of the Tigris and Euphrates in Mesopotamia, the Nile in Egypt, the Indus in India, and the Yellow River in China, were sandwiched between two areas of nomadic pastoralism: the Steppes to the north, and the Arabian Desert to the south. The nomadic pastoralists in these areas had not given up the hunter-gatherer instincts of their forefathers. They periodically mounted raids on the sedentary civilisations and sought to turn their inhabitants into chattel like their cattle.[140] All the sedentary civilisations had a common response to this terrorism. They sought to extend their frontiers to some natural barriers which would keep the barbarians at bay – thus creating their empires – and maintained specialists in warfare to protect them from the periodic barbarian invasions. They created man-made barriers and fortifications to protect their heartlands, of which China's Great Wall is the most notable example. They also invested in the latest military hardware to keep up with the nomadic Joneses.

Quite often the barbarian roving bandits turned themselves into stationary bandits by taking over the sedentary civilisations they had attacked and creating their own empire. The earliest example is the conquest by Sargon of Akkad in Mesopotamia in c. 2340 BC, who then created the first Sumerian empire. The one which reverberates to our day is the early Arab empire. These nomads from the southern fringes of antiquity fired by the messianic zeal of their prophet Mohammed, as well as their age-old desire for booty, smashed the world of antiquity. Unlike their

nomadic cousins from the north – who were absorbed
by the ancient civilisations – they created a civilisation of
their own. Osama bin Laden's daring raid on the heartland
of the current metropole on 11 September 2001 is resonant
of these earlier nomadic raiders who created a new empire.

The motives for creating these imperial states, apart
from this defensive one, have also included the desire for
glory (Alexander the Great, Genghis Khan), booty (the
Mesopotamian empires, the early Arab empire, the Iberian
empires), and the messianic desire to convert heathens (the
early Arab empire, the Iberian empires). But, once established, all these empires have, by providing an imperial
pax, reduced if not altogether eliminated roving bandits,
thereby facilitating the processes of globalisation. Thus,
the long period of the Pax Romana allowed commerce to
develop under the most favourable conditions. It eliminated the piracy and brigandage (terrorism) which had
continued to threaten commerce in the Hellenistic era, and
the Mediterranean became the major artery for trade and
commerce. Though the Romans did not place a high value
on commerce in their cosmological beliefs,[141] nevertheless
their Pax, and the associated development of Roman law
which spread with the expansion of the empire, created a
large economic space with a coherent legal framework for
economic activity.

Similarly, the Abbasid Empire of the Arabs linked the
world of the Mediterranean and the Indian Ocean, the
Mongol empire linked China with the Near East, the various Indian empires created a common economic space in
the subcontinent, while the expanding Chinese empire
linked the economic spaces of the Yellow River with those
of the Yangtze. Finally, after their victory at Waterloo, the

British created the first truly global empire, linking the whole world. In all these cases they provided protection against brigands and other predators. Together with the institution of an empire-wide legal system, the British promoted trade and commerce over a wide economic space, leading to those gains from trade and specialisation emphasised by Adam Smith and generating what I call Smithian intensive growth.[142] Thus, from the historical record, it would seem that suppressing international piracy and brigandage has been important for globalisation to occur throughout the ages. Second, the international order required for globalisation has usually been provided or at least assisted by a strong hegemonic power.

Since the Second World War, the United States has forged a degree of stability in world politics which has led to the current period of globalisation. This has come about both with the demise of the 'evil empire' of the Second World which challenged the global capitalism that is the hallmark of the new international economic order, and with the gradual acceptance by the Third World that its post-war 'inward-looking' policies were dysfunctional and needed to be reversed. Since the 1980s it too has joined the global bandwagon, with two major exceptions: Africa and much of the Middle East have remained aloof.

In this current period of globalisation, with the revolution in communications, there have been further falls in 'transport costs'. So that hitherto non-traded goods like various back-office services are now being traded. The call centres in India are part of the trend in outsourcing these services. At the same time the growing trade in components has led to the fragmentation of the production of goods: with parts being produced in the lowest-cost 'country' and being shipped for assembly for final consumption all around the world. This is leading to a finer and finer global division of labour.

But this global division of labour depends even more than in the past upon an intricate web of global communication networks, which are susceptible to damage by pirates and brigands as of yore. But do these terrorists pose more of a threat than did those when Pax Britannica held sway in the nineteenth century? One way of answering this is to see what the gains were from suppressing piracy and brigandage in the past, and then to see how current terrorist threats might affect the international order required for globalisation to proceed.

We do not have any quantitative estimates of what the gains from the imperial Pax in suppressing piracy and brigandage were for pre-modern times. But we do have some estimates made by Douglass North of the gains from suppressing piracy once the British Navy came to rule the waves in the late eighteenth and nineteenth centuries. North estimates that from the mid-seventeenth to the end of the eighteenth century there was a large increase in the productivity of shipping due to the suppression of piracy. Without any change in technology, freight rates on the Atlantic trade fell by a half, and from 1814 to 1850 before the technological revolution associated with steamships, productivity in shipping increased by 3–5 per cent per year. The decline in piracy, with the extension of the British international order, also reduced insurance costs by about two-thirds between 1635 and 1770.[143] Who are the current international pirates and brigands, and do they have the means to erode the current hegemonic system and thereby the processes of globalisation? Four major sources for these undesirables can be distinguished. The most important is provided by militant Islam. Its objectives are messianic and cannot be met with any compromise. If someone wishes to use the sword to establish their divine Kingdom on Earth, those reluctant to convert have only one option – to contain or kill the relevant purveyors of terror.

The second are sundry nationalists who in the name of a separate ethnicity or of religion wish to use terror to gain political ends – normally secession from an existing state and the creation of one of their own. They pose a difficult problem for the current imperial power. For since one of its high priests – Woodrow Wilson – pronounced the end of the Age of Empires and the dawn of that of Nations, its rhetoric has emphasised the principle of self-determination as the highest moral principle.[144] When does a freedom fighter become a brigand and a terrorist? This is a question which the proconsuls of the current hegemonic arrangement have great difficulty in answering. But the damage these terrorists do is more to their own people and those from whom they want to separate. The domestic disorder they breed rarely spills into international disorder which would damage the processes of globalisation.

But, as the failing state of Afghanistan shows, they can provide succour and shelter to terrorists of various other hues.

The third are closer to past pirates and brigands. These are the international Mafias linked to trade in illegal substances and humans. They are the result of particular policies adopted by states. The War on Drugs, for example, increases the price of banned substances and heightens the criminal return. Current policies also curtail the nineteenth century's liberal international economic order's free movement of people through immigration controls. The latter are in turn due to the creation of welfare states in developed countries which, through restrictions, makes citizenship itself an issue of great material and political importance. Changes in these drug and immigration policies would suck the lifeblood out of the brigands who feed on them. They do not however pose a direct threat to globalisation. For as they live by trade and commerce – albeit illegal – their interests do not lie in fouling the networks through which they operate.[145] Their threat is indirect. They can, however, promote domestic disorder leading to failed states, and by providing illegal and thereby secret sources of funds for the 'nationalist' and 'messianic' terrorists, help them in furthering their brigandage. The profits from drug smuggling by the Taliban in Afghanistan helped to support the state as well as to finance terrorism, for example.

Finally, there are the IT terrorists: the computer nerds whose motive is generally one of creating mischief for fun, but also increasingly theft – of money and identities – for personal gain. There is nothing new about theft, except in the mounting costs of the arms race between the law and thieves. IT technology provides a new avenue for cheating, which in turn requires further resources to countervail the thieving. This has further raised the dead weight costs associated with policing.

So the major threat, if any, to globalisation remains that of the messianic terrorists. These at present are mainly Islamists. How serious is the damage they can do? Considering their most spectacular terrorist act to date, the destruction of the World Trade Center, what were the effects on the US and global economy? It is difficult to separate out the effects of the global recession which coincided with the collapse of the Twin Towers in New York. But one crude indicator is that after 9/11 the consensus forecast for US real GDP growth was instantly downgraded by 0.5 percentage points for 2001 and 1.2 percentage points for 2002. The implied projected cumulative loss in national income through the end of 2003 amounted to five percentage points of annual GDP, or half a trillion dollars. The total loss for the three years was estimated at $630 billion. But, as Alice Rivlin has pointed out, these estimates certainly overstate the effects, largely because with the puncturing of the dotcom bubble and the sharp decline on Wall Street, New York was already going into a recession. Nevertheless, even if we take the expected loss for US GDP based on the changed forecasts after 9/11 as having been realised, this would still be only about 5 per cent of US GDP and a much smaller fraction of world GDP.

The specific damage from 9/11 has been estimated by Peter Navarro of the University of California, Irvine, as between $10 and $13 billion for property damage (the costs of the lost buildings, aircraft, public works and infrastructure, and corporate property like office equipment and software); the economic value of the lost lives in the range of $40 billion; the lost economic output in the immediate aftermath in the range of $47 billion (from lost airline and cargo shipping revenues, lost hotel industry revenues, lost advertising revenues in the first days during commercial free TV and radio, two-day work stoppage, lost consumer spending and retail sales). This gives a total of $100 billion which is less than 0.8 per cent of US GDP. Thus the economic damage from 9/11 to the US and the world economy was fairly small.[146]

Nor did New York's economy – the worst hit by the immediate aftermath of the collapse of the Twin Towers – suffer a long decline, as many had feared. Research by a team at the Russell Sage Foundation found that, comparing New York's performance before and after September 11 with its performance in past recessions, with the performance of the rest of the country before and after September 11, and with the experience of other large cities, it was not knocked off track in any fundamental way by 9/11.[147] Moreover, and most importantly, the communications networks on which globalisation depends did not collapse. Trading recommenced very speedily. The damage was to the US psyche.

What of future threats from biological and chemical weapons or a dirty bomb? Of these, for various reasons, the danger of a dirty bomb is the most pertinent. Biological and chemical weapons are not easy for private agents to use. They are more likely to be used by states and state-supported terrorists. But a dirty bomb is relatively easy to produce. It is difficult to estimate the damage, but most likely it would be to the real estate in the large area which was made radioactive.[148] I guess its effects would be similar to that of a massive earthquake in California. Being localised, its damage would again be more to the psyche than to the world economy.

A worse nightmare for globalisation would be if there were a series of explosions in the main shipping ports around the world in containers holding dirty bombs. It is difficult to estimate the damage this would do to shipping and commerce, but some estimate can be made from the costs of the insured losses from other recent disasters. Navarro provides estimates of these insured losses (adjusted for inflation). They are $5 billion for the 1989 Hurricane Hugo, $844 million from the 1992 Los Angeles riots, $16.9 billion from the 1992 Hurricane Andrew, $542 million from the 1993 World Trade Center bombing, $13 billion from the 1994 Northridge, California earthquake, and $127 million from the 1995 Oklahoma City bombing. Again, though tragic, these were not catastrophic losses.

The most serious costs associated with continuing terrorism are the general increase in the uncertainty associated with doing business that it might cause. But equally serious costs arise from preventive measures taken in a society seeking to be risk free from overreacting to the terrorist threat. Besides the direct costs of homeland security there are, for instance, the costs imposed on travellers in terms of the opportunity costs of the time lost in long security searches at airports. Navarro estimates these costs at between $16 and $32 billion annually. But while all these costs will reduce the gains from the ongoing developments in and spread of communication technology in the globalisation process, they are unlikely to hinder the globalisation process.

The most serious threat to globalisation arises from the Islamist terrorists, not because of the direct physical damage they can cause – as this is likely to be fairly localised – but because of their desire to sap the will of the metropole in maintaining its imperial sway. This could in theory succeed. To prevent this, it is important to realise that, despite protestations to the contrary, America presides over an informal empire. Since it overtook the British Empire in economic and military strength towards the first quarter of the last century, it has been the natural successor to the British in maintaining a global order. It can be argued that many of the bloody events of the last century were due to its failure to take over these responsibilities which Britain was too weak to carry out. Realising this error, the post-Second World War foreign policy elite has surreptitiously built an informal agglomeration of power.[149] But many, including President George W. Bush, remain frightened of the 'E' word. It goes against the American self-image.

It is claimed that the US is a hegemony but not an imperial power. Hegemons seek control over only the foreign policies of their dependencies. Empires seek control over both their domestic and foreign policies.[150] But in the current 'War on Terror' it is the domestic policies of states – providing money and succour to Wahhabi madrassas which breed terrorists, channelling money through Islamist charities to finance terrorist operations, building nuclear power plants which can be used to produce nuclear weapons as in Iran – that need to be controlled. Instead of the distinction between hegemony and empire, a much more meaningful distinction is between formal and informal empire. Of these an informal empire is always to be preferred, as it is less costly in maintaining an imperial order. The British knew this. A predatory choice – despite nationalist historiography denigrating British imperialism for being exploitative – was never the option. Direct imperialism was only reluctantly taken to control what would today be called 'failed states'. The informal route was always the preferred route. For instance, in areas of indirect British control, the imperial pax was maintained through gunboats and Gurkhas.

The same choice faces the US in maintaining its imperial order. But in making it and still retaining domestic political legitimacy, it is essential to be clearheaded in recognising that the American order involves imperial responsibilities. Perhaps the greatest inadvertent service Osama bin Laden's 9/11 raid has done is to make it easier for the foreign policy establishment to come clean about America's international role and responsibilities. The recent Bush doctrine, with its acceptance of pre-emptive strikes, is a departure along these lines, as is the war in Iraq. In maintaining the Pax which is essential for the processes of globalisation, the US will have to continue to bear the burden with probably changing 'coalitions of the willing.' The Wilsonian dream of securing the peace through collective security enforced by the United Nations was always a dream, and the Iraq war should have made this obvious. The UN only wishes to tie Gulliver down with a million strings. Relying on this ineffectual and increasingly redundant institution will only promote international disorder.

It is nonetheless true that maintaining an informal US hegemony is costly in terms of men and materiel. It also requires (as the British discovered and the US is currently learning in Iraq) the equivalent of a colonial service with the requisite political and administrative skills to run an empire. But today, the US's role is the necessary though perhaps not the sufficient condition for globalisation to operate. It is the hope of the messianic terrorists that the American people will not have the necessary will to bear the burden of empire. It is their attempt to sap American will through their acts of terror which constitutes the greatest threat to globalisation from terrorism. But an overreaction to the terrorist threat will also indirectly play into their hands. As the British discovered as an imperial power, the American homeland will continue to be subject to terrorism. The IRA has not yet given up its quest for reunion with Ireland, and has in the past bombed Britain to demonstrate this. But the British populace has learned to live with this threat for nearly a century without overreacting by restricting civil liberties – including the freedom to travel without restraint – and without giving in to terrorism. The citizens of the new US informal empire will have to learn to do the same.

First published as Chapter 3 of R. N. Rosecrance and A. A. Stein (eds), No More States?, *(Rowman and Littlefield, Lanham MD 2006).*

CHAPTER SEVEN

ENDANGERING THE WAR ON TERROR BY THE WAR ON DRUGS

INTRODUCTION

The United States is currently engaged in two wars, one of which is less than a decade old. The other has lasted over a century.

The first, the 'War on Terror' against Islamist fundamentalists began with Al-Qaeda's destruction of the World Trade Center's twin towers on September 11 2001. This led to the US invasion of Afghanistan, the defeat of the Taliban and the dislocation of Al-Qaeda's terrorist infrastructure, with Osama bin Laden and his deputy, Al-Zawahiri, having to flee to the lawless badlands between Pakistan and Afghanistan. With the creation of a democratically elected government under Hamid Karzai it might have been thought that the War on Terror in Afghanistan had been won. But as the Taliban-cum-Al-Qaeda scorpion had been squashed but not killed, it is now re-emerging with the resurgence of the Taliban and its continuing support for the refurbished Al-Qaeda terrorist network in the southern provinces (particularly in Helmand) of Afghanistan. This area also happens to be the major poppy-growing area in Afghanistan, for conversion into opium and heroin. In 2007 it provided 92 per cent of the world's opium supply, whose farm gate value was US$1 billion.[151] It is this opium economy which is now (as in the past) providing the Taliban with the money for arms, and growing control over the southern opium growing provinces, by offering farmers protection from the opium eradication programmes, spear-headed by the US as part of its 'War on Drugs'. The first part of this chapter shows why these drug-supply control measures are likely to fail, with dire consequences for the success of the War on Terror.

The second part, therefore, examines the century-old, US-led global War on Drugs which began with President Theodore Roosevelt. It examines whether in both theory and practice the supply control measures, which have formed a central part of this war, are justified, and if they have worked. It then presents the case for the US to cease its War on Drugs if it is not to jeopardise the much more serious War on Terror.

THE AFGHAN POPPY ECONOMY AND THE TALIBAN RESURGENCE
i)   History
The Afghan poppy economy is the result of the civil war which began with the Soviet invasion and occupation in 1979. With the rise of the Mujahideen resistance to Soviet occupation in 1979–80, most of the poppy-growing areas, concentrated in the southern provinces of Helmand and Kandahar and the eastern province of Nangarhar, ceased

to be under the central government's control. Opium production in 1932, (the first year for which quantitative estimates are available) was seventy-five tons of opium, produced on less than 4,000 hectares. By 1999 over 5,000 tons of opium was being produced from 92,000 hectares under poppy cultivation. This was the result of the civil war amongst the various factions in the 1990s after the Soviet occupation had ended. An opium economy developed, which combined opium production and trading for arms by the various factions. Opium production accelerated from 14 per cent between 1979 and 1989, to 19 per cent between 1989 and 1994.[152]

The rural areas with about 85 per cent of the population before the war, and with agriculture accounting for 68 per cent of employment (in 1998), saw a severe dislocation of the rural economy. Between 1979 and 1989 nearly half to two-thirds of all villages were bombed. There was a fall in livestock of 77 per cent, a destruction of a quarter to a third of the irrigation system, and one-third of all farms were abandoned. A third of the population fled the country and 11 per cent became internal refugees. Total food production by 1988 had fallen to about 45 cent of the level before the 1979 Soviet invasion.[153] The poppy economy offered various means of survival for those remaining in rural Afghanistan. First, it was highly profitable compared to other crops, though farmers reacted to the changing prices of opium in world markets by varying the area under poppy cultivation. Second, the poppy crop can be harvested earlier than wheat. Instead of growing wheat and merely obtaining additional fodder for livestock, growing poppies with their shorter period of cultivation allows farmers to also grow maize after harvesting the poppies.

They can thus achieve double cropping, raising profit-ability. Third, poppies are weather resistant and hence a more reliable crop than wheat. Fourth, the opium is easy to store, transport and sell. It therefore also provides poor farmers a simple means to smooth income, and thence inter-temporal consumption, in the absence of any formal credit markets.

The civil war amongst the various Mujahideen factions, after the Russian withdrawal with the implosion of the Soviet empire in 1991, led to the development of a large illicit economy providing the infrastructure for transport, communications, arms and protection. This was required by the various warring factions to retain their areas of control. The Afghan Transit Trade Agreement, which allowed landlocked Afghanistan to import duty-free goods in sealed containers from Pakistan, provided the major conduit for the development of this illicit economy. In the 1980s the illicit trade also extended to the Persian Gulf, transiting through Afghanistan to Pakistan. This illicit trade infrastructure came to be used for drugs and arms, and with the Taliban (one of the factions in the civil war) seizing control in 1996 of all the country's roads, cities, airports and custom posts, they became the major agents of the opium trade, supported by the powerful transport mafias in Afghanistan and Pakistan, and clandestinely by the Pakistan secret services – the ISI.

With the victory of the Taliban, and its control over most of the country, there was some economic recovery. But the poppy economy continued to flourish, with opium production doubling between 1996 and 1999.[154] The Taliban banned the production of cannabis, because 'it is consumed by Afghans and Muslims', but allowed production of opium, because 'it is consumed by kaffirs [unbelievers] in the West and not by Muslims or Afghans'.[155] The political reasons for letting farmers grow poppies were 'because farmers get good prices. We cannot push people to grow wheat as there would be an uprising against the Taliban if we forced them to stop poppy cultivation. So we grow opium and get our wheat from Pakistan,' the head of the Taliban's drug control force in Kandahar is reported to have said at the time.[156]

The Taliban also found the poppy economy profitable as they began charging a 20 per cent Islamic tax on all dealers moving opium. With the Taliban firmly in control, in 1996 opium production soared. The large number of Pashtun refugees returning to their lands in the Taliban-controlled southern provinces began cultivating the easiest and most lucrative cash crop available. It is estimated that by 2000 there were nearly one million Afghan farmers making over US$100 million from poppy cultivation. The Taliban's tax take was at least US$20 million.[157]

In July 2000, under intense international pressure over its human rights record, the growth of the poppy economy and its support of terrorism, and fearing stronger UN sanctions, the Taliban banned opium production. This decision might also have been influenced by the traders backing the Taliban regime who stood to gain enormous profits on their opium stocks with the rise in price resulting from the production ban.[158] The enforcement of the ban led to a fall in opium production in 2001 of 94 per cent, back to the level of the 1980s. But with no alternatives to making a living, along with a severe drought, farmers faced extreme hardships. Overall crop production more than halved and livestock were severely depleted, reversing the economic gains that had been made since the Taliban came to power in 1996.[159]

With the overthrow of the Taliban after 9/11, and the establishment of an interim government, a fresh ban on opium production was proclaimed in January 2002. But in that year the United Nations Office on Drugs and Crime (UNODC) found that opium production rose back to the level of 2000.

For the warlords, who still continue to rule much of Afghanistan, the opium economy provides a rich source of takings. In Helmand province the governor was removed when his central role in the opium trade was exposed, but his brother remained as deputy governor. As the UK MP Adam Holloway (who was a British Army officer in Afghanistan) noted after a trip to Helmand province in early 2006: 'I was told – actually by a police officer – that 99 per cent of the police in Helmand are either opium producers or traffickers or both, and that much of the opium is exported out of Afghanistan in police cars. The corruption engendered by the poppy has entwined the highest levels of government. Many small farmers despise the government and fear the Taliban, who promise to help fight the police while taking their cut of the opium crop, which provides them with income. So in practical terms, it is hard to draw a distinction between Taliban, warlord and drug trafficker – their interest is the same: instability.'[160]

The Taliban, with their bases in the lawless border area between Pakistan and Afghanistan, and with their associates in Al-Qaeda, have launched an insurgency against NATO forces in Helmand province, where the US with its continuing desire to wage its War on Drugs is at the forefront of the eradication programme, mainly through aerial spraying of the poppy crop. This has provided the Taliban a golden opportunity to recruit angry poppy farmers. Its 'hearts and minds program is to offer protection to farmers' opium crops from government eradicators, for a 10 per cent "tax", which is usually paid willingly'.[161]

ii)   The 'Alternative Livelihoods Programme'
The 'Alternative Livelihoods' Programme promoted by the UK Department for International Development has failed to persuade farmers to switch from poppies to other crops.[162]

This is unsurprising. An evaluation by UNODC of its Alternative Development Project between 1997 and 2000 in three districts of Kandahar province in southern Afghanistan found that, though the programme succeeded in raising the yields of legal crops (like wheat, cumin, beans, onions and fruits) by about 90 per cent, 'the data show that for Afghanistan as a whole the improvements reported from the three districts would not have been sufficient to make legal crops more profitable than opium poppy. The national average gross income from opium poppy was $1,071 in 2000, thus still above the gross income from legal crops in the three target districts of Kandahar province ($902).' These lower returns were due to the relatively low profitability of the main legal crops (wheat as a winter crop, maize as a summer crop) compared to opium poppy (combined with maize), and depended directly upon their price relative to that of opium. When the Taliban enforced the production ban in 2000 there was a massive rise in opium prices, with the average gross income per hectare from poppy cultivation (despite the fall in yields because of a drought and the prohibition on cultivation which affected the irrigated land in southern

and eastern provinces) rising seven-fold 'from about
$1,100 in 2000 to $7,400 in 2001'. By 2002, after the fall
of the Taliban, income per hectare from opium poppy rose
further to an average of $16,100. As the UNODC report
on *The Opium Economy in Afghanistan* ruefully concluded,
'at these gross income levels no other crop which could
be planted on a large scale would be competitive vis à vis
opium poppy in Afghanistan... Alternative development
efforts alone, though important for Afghanistan's medium-
and long-term future, cannot provide sufficiently strong
incentives to farmers to give up planting poppy.
Profitability of opium poppy is simply too high, at least
for the time being.'[163]

The UNODC's desired solution in this context seems
quixotic. It argues that given these high profits, poppy
production can only be achieved by '(a) a rigorous
implementation of the ban on opium poppy cultivation
across the country and (b) the creation of a security belt
around Afghanistan, in close cooperation with the Afghan
authorities, in order to reduce the outflows of opiates from
Afghanistan, thus lowering the demand for opiates within
the country'.[164] The first condition, as the experience from
the 2000 Taliban ban shows, will merely increase the price
of opium, further raising the profitability of the opium
poppy. The second requires an incorruptible effective
central government, whose creation is threatened by a
Taliban insurgency which would only be aided by a rigorous enforcement of the opium ban.

For, as the UK troops currently battling the Taliban
in southern Afghanistan have realised, protecting the
farmers' opium crop from government eradicators is the
Taliban's most potent recruiting instrument to their cause.

Besides providing them – through the 10 per cent tax they charge for this protection – the funding for their weapons, ammunitions and fighters, the drug lords controlling the drugs trade 'don't want the Afghan government authority that, in theory at least, comes in the Army's wake. For all the counter-narcotics efforts in Kabul and the stern words in Whitehall about tackling drugs, British soldiers understand the drugs problem very well. This spring [2008] as eradication teams made ready in Kandahar, the British were broadcasting radio adverts promising not to destroy opium around Musa Qala. Not this year, at least'.[165]

iii)   Alternative policies

If the War on Terror in its current epicentre in southern Afghanistan is to be won, this laissez-faire policy towards poppy cultivation needs to be made permanent. To deny the Taliban and the drugs lords the profits from the drugs trade which is financing the insurgency, a rational unsentimental response would be for NATO's development agencies to use the money they are currently spending on their failed economic development efforts in Afghanistan, as well as that on poppy eradication, to *purchase* the opium poppy crop directly from the farmers, in competition with the Taliban and drug lords. The farmers could be required to put the 10 per cent tax on income from poppy cultivation they currently pay the Taliban into development funds located and managed by locals to refurbish the destroyed agricultural infrastructure, which in time might be able to raise the productivity of alternative crops sufficiently to allow farmers to switch to non-poppy crops.

The opium purchased directly from the farmers could be used by the Western development agencies to provide morphine for easing the pain associated with various terminal illnesses, including AIDS, in many parts of the Third World, especially in sub-Saharan Africa.[166] Any surplus of opium remaining could be stored for future use for both medicinal purposes and to control the markets for opiates.

But such rational solutions to defeating the Taliban, by accepting the opium economy in Afghanistan and using it to win rather than endanger the War on Terror, can only be achieved if the US and UK give up their decades-old War on Drugs. Apart from having being unsuccessful in achieving its avowed aims (see the next section), it has, through its supply control measures, created a large global illegal economy where trafficking in illegal goods, from drugs to arms to humans, has also led to a vast shadow global money-laundering financial system, and to the creation of narcostates, as in the coca growing countries of the Andes.[167] The drug wars and the accompanying corruption to garner the massive illegal profits in this illicit trade are now reaching the very borders of the US as Mexico's democracy is being gradually undermined. We, therefore, turn to the War on Drugs and see if in theory and practice its benefits are likely to exceed its costs – which must include the cost of endangering the geo-politically more important War on Terror.

THE WAR ON DRUGS
i)   History
The international War on Drugs goes back to the Shanghai Opium Commission of 1909 and the first international drug treaty of the International Opium Convention of The Hague in 1912. The US has since been at the spearhead of

the international attempts to control drugs. It is instructive to see how this came about, and why it might be difficult for the US to call a halt on its War on Drugs despite its endangering its more important War on Terror.

The British empire, which preceded the current American imperium,[168] had not merely tolerated but promoted the opium trade with China from its Indian base, as a means to balance its large incipient trade imbalance with the Chinese. By the beginning of the nineteenth century, India was the largest opium producer in the world with the bulk being exported to South East Asia and China. The state monopoly of opium production and distribution, established by Akbar the Great in the sixteenth century, was resurrected by the British East India Company after it took control of the opium-producing regions of Bengal and Bihar with the victory at the battle of Plassey in 1757. The revenues from the opium trade financed the company's subsequent military expenditures in conquering the rest of the sub-continent.[169]

With the establishment of the British Raj after the 1857 Mutiny, the opium trade continued to provide substantial revenues for the continually fiscally constrained imperial power. In 1880 opium-related income provided 14 per cent of the annual income of the Raj.[170] It was to protect these interests that the British fought the Opium Wars in China in the nineteenth century, to keep their major opium-consuming market open, in the face of the successive attempts by Chinese emperors to crack down on opium imports to control the growing opium addiction in China. After the Second Opium War in 1856, the Chinese were forced to legalise the importation of opium with the Treaty of Tientsin in 1858. Subsequently the Chinese gradually removed restrictions on domestic production, and by 1906 China was producing more than 35,000mt of opium[171] (to be contrasted with the 9,000mt of opium produced in Afghanistan in 2007), to meet the demand from 23.3% of the male and 3.5% of the female adult population of China in 1906, who were consuming between 85%–95% of global opium supply at the beginning of the twentieth century.[172]

It was this Chinese opium crisis which led to the movement for international supply control measures fuelled by the perceived immorality of the opium trade. This consisted of the usual suspects. It included 'conservative religious groups, Chinese nationalists and left-wing critics of the impact of unfettered capitalism, the Victorian predecessors of today's anti-globalisation lobby'.[173] In response to their demands for abolition of the opium trade and its prohibition in British India, the British government set up a Royal Commission on Opium in 1893. Its Report of 1895 was based on rigorously collected information from a broad range of witnesses including doctors, the police, the military, local governments, lawyers, journalists, landowners, planters, merchants and missionaries. Its conclusions – apart from the obvious one that the loss of revenue and costs of enforcing prohibition could not be borne by India's precarious finances – were that the prohibition of opium, except for medical purposes, was neither necessary nor wanted by Indians, and so the government should maintain a laissez-faire policy to its production and consumption. But, most importantly, that opium consumption did not cause 'extensive moral or physical degradation', while it was impractical to disentangle the medical from non-medical consumption of opium.[174]

These reasoned conclusions were, of course, in accord with the classical liberal policies – whose most eloquent votary was John Stuart Mill – which informed public policy in Britain in the nineteenth century. Mill had explicitly attacked the temperance movement's demand to prohibit the consumption of alcohol as being in breach of his basic principle of liberty, which prohibited social control of individual's personal tastes and behaviour on moral grounds. As he stated: 'the sole end for which mankind are warranted, individually or collectively, in interfering with the liberty of action of any of their number, is self protection. That the only purpose for which power can be rightfully exercised over any member of a civilised community, against his will, is to prevent harm to others. His own good, either physical or moral, is not a sufficient warrant.'[175]

When, in its first imperial venture, the US occupied the Philippines in 1898, the large domestic demand from opium consumers was met by state-controlled monopolies, which provided a large part of the revenues of the preceding Spanish colonial state. The US initially sought to maintain a licensed opium trade and legal consumption. This plan was derailed by a powerful missionary prohibitionist lobby – the International Reform Lobby – at the instigation of its missionaries in the Philippines. Appalled at the US sanctioning the opium evil, it bombarded President Theodore Roosevelt with petitions from its supporters. Roosevelt caved in, and thus began the long and continuing US War on Drugs.

ii)   Social Ethics: J. S. Mill on Prohibition

Mill had foreseen the influence of the US's moralists in derailing his principle of liberty.

He discussed at length the temperance movement and its offshoots in Britain and its doctrine of 'social rights' which claimed a citizen's 'right to legislate whenever my social rights are invaded by the social acts of another. If anything invades my social rights, certainly the traffic in strong drink does. It destroys my primary right of security, by constantly creating and stimulating social disorder. It invades my right of equality, by deriving a profit from the creation of a misery I am taxed to support. It impedes my right to free moral and intellectual development, by surrounding my path with dangers, and by weakening and demoralising society, from which I have a right to claim mutual aid and intercourse.'[176] This 'monstrous principle', Mill goes on to say, 'is far more dangerous than any single interference with liberty; there is no violation of liberty which it would not justify'. This doctrine of 'social rights' seeking to justify prohibitions of actions in the private domain 'ascribes to all mankind a vested interest in each other's moral, intellectual and even physical perfection, to be defined by each claimant according to his own standard'.

Mill also deals with the other effects of alcohol and 'poison' which are claimed to harm others, what in modern parlance would be called negative externalities from the consumption of drugs. He deals with those still being paraded to justify prohibition: crime and social disorder. These purported 'externalities', Mill argues, merely require the usual punishment once the crime is committed, and though 'drunkenness ... is not a fit subject for legislative interference ... it [is] perfectly legitimate that a person, who had once been convicted of any act of violence under the influence of drink, should be placed under a special legal restriction, personal to himself; that if he were afterwards found drunk he should be liable to a penalty, and if in that state he committed another offence, the punishment to which he would be liable for that other offence should be increased in severity'.

Mill thus argued against any negative externalities flowing from the consumption of addictive substances which are claimed to require prohibition by the state. He provided cogent arguments which still have resonance against what he called the 'liberticide' of 'the projects of social reformers'.

But, there remains one other adduced externality arising from socialised medicine – which did not exist in Mill's day. It has been claimed that society has an interest in preventing addiction as it has to bear the costs of treating the medical consequences of addiction. But, Mill explicitly states that there can be no general argument against taxing addictive products for fiscal reasons (though not prohibitively as that would amount to illegitimate prohibition). Thus, the revenues derived from these legitimate 'sin taxes' can be used to cover the medical expenses of addiction. In fact a large part of the expenditures of the NHS are covered by the swingeing taxes on tobacco in the UK. If drugs were legalised and taxed like tobacco, the resulting revenues could be used to treat addicts. No 'medical' externality need arise.

iii)   The Divided Self and Rational Addiction
But, even where none of these externalities is adduced, it is nevertheless claimed that Mill's principle of liberty would

ensure prohibition. Because the drug addict or alcoholic would, in the rational 'long-run' part of a postulated divided self, demand the freedom of a non-addictive life which his 'short-run' myopic addicted self would prevent. Hence, basing themselves on Mill's correct argument against a person's freedom to sell himself into slavery,[177] it has been argued (e.g. by Amartya Sen about smoking tobacco – another addictive substance) that prohibition is justified on Mill's principles of liberty 'as habit-forming behaviour today restricts the freedom of the same person in the future'.[178] But as I and others pointed out subsequently, this is a complete misuse of Mill's argument against slavery.[179]

Mill's robust defence against bans on addictive substances like alcohol and opium does not mention his argument against slavery as being relevant in any way.

The argument for prohibiting addictive substances, based on assuming a divided self, postulates a negative inter-temporal consumption externality facing potential addicts. In the resulting myopic models[180] the current consumption of addictive substances depends on the 'stock of habits' which is given by the depreciated sum of all past consumption.[181] Hence, current consumption depends on past consumption but not future consumption. This omission is repaired in the rational addiction models of Becker and Murphy. They show how even with inter-temporally inconsistent preferences, consumers maximise utility over their lifecycle taking account of the future consequences of their actions in consuming addictive substances.[182]

These models capture many of the well-known features of addiction. Due to reinforcement, consumption in adjacent time periods are complements. So that current consumption of the good is related not only to the current price but to all past and (expected) future prices. The long-run effect of a permanent price change will exceed that in the short run, as will that of an anticipated price change from one which is unanticipated. These models also lead to bimodal distributions of consumption, echoing the 'binge' and 'cold turkey' type behaviour found amongst addicts. Also the models imply that temporary events like a price cut, peer pressure, stress etc. can lead to permanent addiction. Finally, the responsiveness to price changes also depends upon the individual's rate of time preference – the rate at which he/she discounts the future. The rational addiction model thus seems to capture all the features which supposedly make addictive substances like drugs and tobacco different from other consumption goods, and yet show that addiction could be perfectly rational. No divided self needs to be postulated.

Prohibition of these addictive substances, therefore, entails the same losses of economic welfare in terms of consumer surplus lost, as would occur if consumption of other goods were prohibited. My research students at UCLA and I studied the welfare losses entailed by raising the tax on tobacco by 10 per cent, within a rigorous cost-benefit framework, using estimates of the demand curves from the rational addiction model for India, Korea, South Africa, Japan and the European Union. It was found that these losses were large.[183]

The arguments against prohibition of addictive substances, therefore, remain cogent. The assumption that their consumption entails a consumption externality is insecure. But, even assuming that there *is* an externality, would it justify restricting supply, particularly through banning the international trade in drugs? For it is these

supply control measures which are at the heart of the
problems faced by the War on Terror in Afghanistan, and
it is to the relevant economic theory that I now turn.

iv)   Theory: Welfare Economics
The modern theory of trade and welfare offers a clear
argument against prohibiting free trade in drugs. The
presumed negative externality from consuming drugs is (in
this theory) a 'domestic distortion' in consumption, which
requires remedial domestic measures, but no interference
in international trade. The domestic remedial action could
range from a large tax to equalise the marginal social with
the marginal private value of consumption to prohibition.
For this consumption tax could be prohibitive. But, free
international trade to supply whatever demand remains
would be welfare maximising. The supply in a free trading world would be provided by the country which had a
comparative advantage in its production, and this would
(given appropriate measures to deal with the local domestic distortion in consumption) maximise world economic
welfare.[184] There would be no case for prohibiting the
Afghans from growing opium and exporting it, if they have
a comparative advantage in its production – as they seem
to have from our discussion in the previous section.

    What about the welfare maximising domestic policy
for dealing with the purported negative consumption
externality in the drug-consuming country? This question
has recently been definitively answered by Becker, Murphy
and Grossman within the standard cost-benefit framework,
considering both the positive and normative effects of
punishments seeking to make production and consumption of drugs illegal.[185] They assume that the social value is

negative, while the private value from consuming drugs is positive, given by private willingness to pay. They compare the effects of prohibition (optimally enforced) with those of legalising drugs and levying a tax on their consumption.

FIGURE 7.1: DRUGS — SUPPLY AND DEMAND

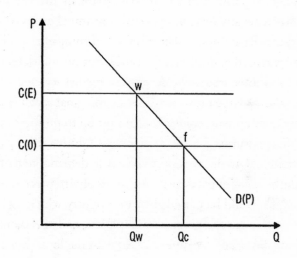

Assume drugs are supplied by a competitive drug industry with constant costs, in Figure 7.1. If the demand curve for drugs is given by D(P), the cost curve for drugs in a free market is C(0) and consumption is Qc, the free market equilibrium will be at 'f'. If the government launches a 'War on Drugs' and spends resources E on interdiction of drug suppliers and smugglers, the costs of supplying drugs will be C(E). Adding the costs to consumers of criminal punishments and other inconveniences in obtaining illegal drugs that the major thrust of the War on Drugs is to control supply so that T = 0, the War on Drugs equilibrium would be at 'w', with the resources devoted to drug production, smuggling and distribution being exactly equal to the revenues from drug sales in both the free and illegal equilibrium (the area under the demand curve at f and w). If the demand for drugs is price-inelastic, the more vigorously the War on Drugs is pursued, (>E, and hence higher C(E)), the greater will be the total resources devoted to supplying drugs, with only a small fall in consumption.

Being illegal, data on price and quantity consumed are scarce, so that there are few reliable estimates of the price-elasticity of demand for drugs. The few available estimates give an absolute value of less than one.[186]

As Becker, Murphy and Grossman conclude, 'Since considerable resources are spent fighting the war and reducing consumption, the drug war can only be considered socially optimal with a long run demand elasticity of about -1/2 if the negative social externality of drug use is more than twice the positive value to drug users'.[187]

A policy of prohibition and supply controls with optimal enforcement can be compared with legalising drugs and taxing them optimally at a rate which equals the difference between the marginal private and marginal social value of consuming drugs. Becker et al. show that this optimal excise tax would be higher than the implicit 'tax' that consumers face with prohibition and optimal enforcement. The resulting higher price with taxation of legalised drugs could thus reduce drug consumption by more than an efficient War on Drugs. But, as with all 'sin' taxes, high taxes would also foster the black market (as with prohibition), necessitating continued spending on enforcement. Becker et al. argue that the 'sin' tax on drugs needs to be accompanied with an optimal level of punishment for black market activities, which ideally would eliminate the black market. But, given the diminishing returns from increased punishment, there would be an optimal combination of tax and punishments, which would be less than the ideal, and hence a second-best outcome would be the best policy, where the divergence between the private and marginal social value of drug consumption would not be completely eliminated.

This then leads to a more radical alternative, in the spirit of J. S. Mill, to have a free market in drugs.[188] This would eliminate the costs associated with prohibition, including crime. But with lower prices and the elimination of legal threats to their use, drug consumption could increase. There are other more nebulous countervailing forces which might not lead to an increase. Many current abstainers would not become consumers as they consider drugs to be dangerous or repugnant (as with alcohol and tobacco). Those currently refraining because of legal threats would probably use the drugs responsibly for fear of other legal threats as with alcohol (driving under the influence, losing their job or reputation). Also, with legalisation, the consumption amongst the young, experimenting with illegal drugs because of their 'forbidden fruit' aspect, could fall. As we have no statistical estimates for these different factors, we cannot determine the increase in consumption of drugs with their legalisation. But as with other addictive substances (like alcohol and tobacco) it is not likely to be disastrous. For, the rules of the game which govern all markets, including those governing private property, tort and contracts, as well as the customs and traditions of society which control private behaviour, would make the market for drugs look very different from that with prohibition. 'With legalisation, market behaviour will look more like Budweiser, Marlboro and Coca-Cola, and less like Al Capone, *Miami Vice,* and *The Sopranos.*'[189] But, as Mill explicitly noted, even with legalisation there could be a case for taxing drugs which face an inelastic demand curve for fiscal reasons, as part of an optimal tax system to raise revenue.

Thus the theoretical welfare economics conclusions, even assuming that there is a negative social externality in consuming drugs are: *first*, this does not provide a justification for the restriction of their production in other countries, as the US is seeking to do about opium poppy cultivation in Afghanistan. The theory of trade and welfare establishes that where there are externalities in consumption (and not in production) production should occur in the countries with a comparative advantage in producing the good. Imports should be taxed at the same rate as that paid by domestic consumers. If domestic consumption is taxed to equate the marginal private with the marginal social value of the good, the same tax rate should be charged on imports. But domestic production like foreign production should not be taxed, so that the marginal rate of transformation between goods produced is the same wherever they are produced. This could imply that if the consumption tax is sufficiently high (prohibitive), there would be no domestic consumption of the good, even if the country had a comparative advantage in its production it should freely produce and export the good. This in effect was the policy the Taliban followed for most of the period it was in power in Afghanistan!

Second, even with a negative externality in the consumption of drugs, the optimal policy if the demand is price inelastic (as it seems to be) is not prohibition, but optimal taxation of consumption of legalised drugs. This optimal tax being higher than the implicit 'tax' with prohibition could also lead to lower consumption than with the War on Drugs.

Third, as this 'sin tax' would still create black markets, requiring punishments to be enforced for their control, the optimal 'sin' tax-cum-enforcement equilibrium would still leave a divergence between the marginal social and private value of consuming drugs. This leads to the most radical alternative, namely a free market, where any spillovers are regulated, as in other markets, by the law and custom. As with so many other purported 'domestic distortions' in the working of the price mechanism, the prescribed cures may be worse than the disease, so that laissez-faire is the best policy from the viewpoint of economic welfare.[190]

v)   Outcomes

Finally, we can briefly outline the outcomes of the continuing War on Drugs.

Its effects on endangering the War on Terror in Afghanistan have been outlined in the first section. This US-led war has led in the Andes to a succession of states which are or in danger of becoming narco-states. Colombia is the primary example, but with Bolivia and Ecuador not far behind. The Shining Path movement in Peru was supported by the Indian population incensed by the destruction of their coca crops. As I write, the head of the Mexican intelligence service is reported to have said: 'Drug traffickers have become the principal threat' to the country's democratic institutions 'because they are trying to take the power of the state'. The gangs which have become wealthy from the multibillion-dollar drug trade have 'co-opted many members of local police forces, judiciaries and government entities in their efforts to create local structures to protect their business... Congress is not exempt ... we do not rule out the possibility that

drug money is involved in the campaigns [of some legis-
lators].'[191] The US's foreign policy goals are continually
being undermined by its War on Drugs.

Equally sinister are the illicit markets in money laundering, illegal weapons and human trafficking that the
necessarily imperfect attempts to control foreign supply in
the face of stubborn domestic demand for drugs in the US
have spawned, generating huge profits for drug barons and
smugglers.[192] The extent of international money laundering,
which has been estimated to be between 2%–6% of world
GDP shows UNODC's estimate of the total value of the
global illicit drug market in 2003. In terms of retail value it
was $322 billion, just over 4 per cent of global licit exports.
Afghanistan is the major opium producing country today
and the cockpit of the current War on Terror. The gross
trafficking profits of Afghan traffickers are estimated to be
over $2.3 billion in 2006, which were nearly 33 per cent of
the country's GDP. In terms of the size of the global illicit
drugs market, the significant avenues for money laundering, and the massive profits that Afghan drug traffickers
(and through them the Taliban) can obtain as a result of the
War on Drugs, and the impossibility of weaning Afghan
farmers from opium cultivation in the short to medium
term, provides enough evidence that the US War on Terror
is now seriously threatened by its War on Drugs.[193]

Even given its avowed aims, the War on Drugs has been
ineffectual.[194] Its aim is to reduce drug use (particularly
amongst the young) and thereby its consequences – over-
doses, lost production and HIV infections. Sixteen million
Americans, 7 per cent of the population over age twelve,
use illegal drugs which is a $60 billion-per-year industry
in the US. This overall demand for drugs is made up of a

smaller proportion of the population who have an addiction problem. As Peter Reuter summarises the evidence, 'the
American drug problem is narrow and static. No more than
two and a half million Americans have substantial problems
with cocaine and/or heroin – less than one-fifth the number
for alcohol. Those with problems are heavily concentrated
in urban minority communities. Methamphetamine abuse
remains a much smaller problem, while marijuana dependence, a real phenomenon involving many more people, has
much less consequence for those who experience it.'[195] As
for preventing teenagers being initiated into drugs, official
figures show 'initiation of marijuana, cocaine, and halluci-
nogens went up in the 1990s and has stayed there'.[196]

The total expenditure by the US federal government on
drug control – has risen from about $12 billion in 2002
to $14 billion in 2008. In addition states and localities
spend at least as much.[197] So the total government spending
on controlling illicit drugs is about $30 billion annually.
The bulk of the increase in federal expenditure has been
on measures to reduce supply, spending on them having
doubled over the period, as compared with those to reduce
demand. This emphasis on controlling supply should have
been expected to raise the price of drugs,[198] and thus reduce
consumption. But 'the overall trend in cocaine and heroin
retail prices during the past two decades has been downward
(after adjusting for potency). That suggests *greater* availabil-
ity of drugs on the streets in the United States not less.'
Thus 'the price record suggests that supply control efforts
have failed to reduce the use of any established drug'.[199]

But, nevertheless, there has been no increase in cocaine or
heroin use. This reflects a pattern of drug use which is characterised by the time shape of a contagious epidemic. Drug use

is spread mainly through social contacts, but most users after becoming aware of the downside of drug addiction desist from use. The epidemic pattern is found for different drugs in many countries, each with its own drug-control policies, so other factors seem to be at work than government policies. 'The increases in drug use at the "outbreak" of an epidemic are also far faster than corresponding changes in underlying social variables (e.g. unemployment). The likely cause is that, while the epidemic is in outbreak mode, large numbers of light users are recruiting even larger numbers of lighter users. With the passage of time and the progression of consumers to heavy use, adverse effects become more apparent and the sheen begins to wear off the drug. Light use, with its risk of addiction and ill effects, no longer seems so attractive, and that dilutes the recruiting power of light users. Furthermore, as social circles amenable to drug use become exhausted of nonusers, the number of prospects left to recruit shrinks. Use of the drug begins to ebb, sometimes down to levels prior to the epidemic, sometimes stabilising at endemic levels. This cycle can take a long time, as heavy use careers can last many years. Hence, there remains a large number of people who continue to experience the problems of the affliction, even while there are few new cases.'[200] Thus the cocaine and heroin epidemics seem to have run their course, with few new heroin addicts since the early 1970s, and cocaine addicts since the 1980s. 'The addict population is getting older and sicker, though it is still criminally very active; the average age of heroin addicts is now about forty-five. With early deaths and increasing incarceration, the number of active cocaine and heroin addicts is very slowly declining.'[201]

The proportion of chronic drug users in the world population is small as is that of opiate users in the major consuming areas.[202] There is some evidence that there is a genetic element in creating a propensity to use drugs in a small proportion of the population, which can be activated by various environmental factors.[203] Peter Whybrow, the head of UCLA's Neuropsychiatric Institute reports that a novelty-seeking and risk-taking gene which is to be found in migrants is also found in those with a predisposition towards addictive behaviour, which often descends into manic depression (bi-polarity).[204] But this gene is rare, being at the tail of the normal distribution. Hence the small proportion of addicts in a population.

But, given this probable genetic basis for addiction, treatment not prohibition would seem to be the correct response to the drug problem. It has been estimated that 'drug treatment reduces drug use by 40 per cent to 60 per cent and significantly decreases criminal activity during and after treatment'.[205] But because of the high rates of post-treatment relapse and need to get addicts into treatment a number of times to take advantage of the in-treatment reduction in their drug use, it may be necessary to combine treatment with some form of coercion to keep them in treatment programmes. Treatment is more cost effective than enforcement of prohibitions.[206]

One other unintended consequence of the supply side emphasis in the War on Drugs is that with nearly three-quarters of the money to combat drug use being spent on apprehending and punishing drug dealers and abusers, 'the imprisonment rate in the US for drug offenses alone is much higher than the rates of most Western European nations for all crimes. For example, France imprisoned 95 per 100,000 in the population in 1995; that same year, the United States imprisoned 149 per 100,000 for drugs alone.'[207] Most of these are poor and Afro-American.[208]

Finally, even if supply side control measures are used to limit drug use, the estimates made by RAND researchers of the relative cost effectiveness of alternative enforcement strategies to avert cocaine consumption per million dollars spent (Figure 7.2) show that source-country control is the worst option. As the RAND survey of the research on US drug problems and policy concluded, not 'much can be expected of programs outside US borders, which have had little effect on US drug problems. Crop eradication and substitution, in particular, show minimal promise. Close to the drug source, costs are so low that enforcement induced increases are likely to have no observable effect on street prices. The same is true of increases in the cost of land and labour for producing coca or opium.'[209]

FIGURE 7.2: COST OF DECREASING COCAINE CONSUMPTION BY 1 PER CENT WITH ALTERNATIVE COCAINE-CONTROL PROGRAMS

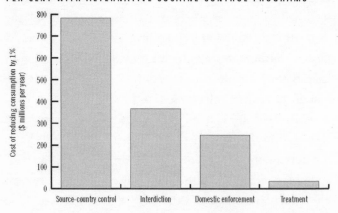

Source: Rydell and Everingham (1994), p. xiv

CONCLUSIONS

Our conclusions can be brief. The all-important War on Terror in Afghanistan is being undermined by the supply-control measures of the War on Drugs. These measures are ineffectual in dealing with the US drug problem, which is better dealt with through treatment based on 'coerced abstinence' of the small proportion of the population who are hardcore drug users rather than the enforcement of prohibition. As such J. S. Mill's views on addiction remain valid both in theory and in practice.

First published in World Economics, *vol. 9, no. 3, July–September 2008, pp. 1–29.*

CHAPTER EIGHT

BANISHING THE LORDS
OF POVERTY

oreign aid as a form of capital flow is novel in both its magnitude and its global coverage. Though historical examples of countries paying 'bribes' (see the following) or 'reparations' to others are numerous, the continuing large-scale transfer of capital from rich country governments to those of poor countries is a post-Second World War phenomenon. The origins of these transfers lie in the breakdown of the international capital market in the period between the two World Wars and in the rivalry for political allies during the Cold War.

The breakdown of the international capital market provided the impetus for the creation of the World Bank at Bretton Woods. Its purpose was to provide loans at market interest rates to poor countries that were shut out of Western capital markets – especially the largest, the United States – because of their widespread defaults in the

1930s and the imposition of the US government's 'blue sky' laws, which forbade US financial intermediaries to hold foreign government bonds. Meanwhile, European markets were closed through exchange controls; the United Kingdom, for example, had its exchange controls until 1979. Official loans to poor countries at commercial interest rates, as laid down in the charter of the World Bank's parent, the International Bank for Reconstruction and Development, would have been justified purely on efficiency grounds to intermediate the transfer of capital from where it was less scarce to where it was scarcer.

This purely economic case was buttressed by political and, later, humanitarian justifications for concessional official flows, that is, loans with softer – concessional – terms on interest and repayment. As to the political reasons for giving aid, little can be added to Lord Bauer's devastating critique that, instead of fostering Western political interests, foreign aid abetted the formation of anti-Western coalitions of Third World states seeking 'bribes' not to go communist.[210] A statistical study concluded that 'as an instrument of political leverage, economic aid has been unsuccessful'[211]. The end of the Cold War has removed this political motive. Currently, advocates of foreign aid emphasise the humanitarian and economic cases, though each rationale has seen many metamorphoses.

The humanitarian case for concessional flows was based on an analogy with the Western welfare state. The idea was that just as many people favour welfare to transfer wealth from the relatively rich to the relatively poor within a country, so they favour welfare to transfer wealth from relatively rich countries to relatively poor ones. But many commentators not necessarily hostile to foreign aid –

I. M. D. Little and J. Clifford, for example[212] – emphasised
that the humanitarian motives for giving aid may have
justified transferring Western taxpayers' money to poor
people, but not to poor governments: the latter may have
no effect on the former. With the likes of Marcos of the
Philippines, Bokassa of the Central African Republic,
Abacha of Nigeria, and a host of other kleptocratic
'tropical gangsters' in power, the money may simply be
stolen.[213] According to William Easterly, despite over $2
billion in foreign aid given to Tanzania's government for
roads, the roads did not improve. What increased was the
bureaucracy, with the Tanzanian government producing
twenty-four hundred reports a year for the one thousand
donor missions that visited each year.[214] Nor can the poor
of the world claim a moral *right* to welfare transfers from
the rich. While recipients of domestic welfare payments
depend on the existence of a national society with some
commonly accepted moral standard, there is no similar
international society within which a right to aid can
be established.[215]

The vast majority of foreign aid has failed to alleviate poverty. It has improved the lot of poor people in a
few cases. The people of Martinique, for example, are
probably better off because the French government
provides a very high percentage of their gross domestic
product. Also, foreign aid helped wipe out river blind-
ness in West Africa, keeping eighteen million children
safe from infection.[216] But a statistical study found that
foreign aid 'appears to redistribute from the reasonably
well-off in the West to most income groups in the Third
World *except* the very poorest'[217]. This is consistent with
the evidence from both poor and rich countries that the

middle classes tend to capture government transfers. By contrast, private transfers through either traditional inter-family channels or private charities (non-governmental organisations, or NGOs) are more efficient in targeting these transfers to the poor, as well as in delivering health care and education.[218] The centralised bureaucracies of the Western aid agencies are particularly inept in targeting these transfers to the truly needy because they lack local knowledge. Moreover, there is evidence that these inef-ficient public transfers tend to crowd out more efficient private transfers.[219] Not surprisingly, therefore, despite their claim that their mission is to alleviate Third World poverty, official aid agencies are increasingly subcon-tracting this role to the NGOs. Whether this official embrace of the NGOs is in the NGOs' long-term interest is arguable.[220]

The political and humanitarian justifications for foreign aid are in tatters. What of the purely economic case? One such case was the 'two-gap theory', the idea that foreign aid was required to fill one of two shortfalls – in foreign exchange or savings – that depressed the growth rates of developing countries below some acceptable limit.[221] The alleged 'foreign-exchange' gap was based on dubious assumptions. One such assumption was 'export pessimism', the idea that poor countries would not gener-ate many exports. Many development economists held this view despite a paucity of evidence for it.[222] Because both experience and theory have shown the irrelevance of this assumption, the 'foreign-exchange gap' justification for foreign aid has lost all force.

Nor has the 'savings gap' justification proved to be any more cogent. Contrary to the theory that foreign capital is necessary to supplement fixed and inadequate domestic savings, the savings performance of developing countries in the post-Second World War period shows that nearly all of them (including those in Africa until the early 1970s) have steadily raised domestic savings rates since the 1950s.[223] Moreover, a study of twenty-one developing countries between 1950 and 1985 confirms the common-sense expectation that differences in economic growth rates are related more to differences in the productivity of invest-ment than to differences in investment levels.[224] Finally, statistical studies of the effects of foreign aid on growth and poverty alleviation have not been favourable.[225] One found that, after correcting for the link between aid and income levels and growth, the effect of aid on growth is often negative (see Figure 8.1).[226] A survey of other such studies concludes that 'there is now widespread scepticism that concessional assistance does have positive effects on growth, poverty reduction or environmental quality'[227].

Except for sub-Saharan Africa, the World Bank finances less than 2 per cent of investment in developing countries.[228] Most of its lending continues to finance projects. The rates of return of more than 10 per cent earned by these projects are not a measure of the true effects of the aid provided, because money is fungible. A government can use aid to finance a high yielding project that it would have under-taken in any case, and then use its own resources to finance a project with a low rate of return (say, more armaments). This problem led to the growth of 'programme' lend-ing, which expanded in the 1980s along with the growth of 'structural adjustment' loans. Programme loans were based on a mutually agreed overall economic programme by the recipient government. Structural adjustment loans were given in return for specific commitments made to alter particular policies that damaged economic efficiency. Advocates of such loans hoped that by applying conditions to the programme loans they could give the governments an incentive to implement better policies, by, for example, avoiding price controls, moving toward free trade, and reducing high marginal tax rates. That way, these advocates believed, foreign aid would improve economic conditions. But numerous studies have found that policy conditionality is ineffective. Not only is aid not necessarily used for what it is directly intended, but also, on average, it has no effect on growth, either directly, or indirectly through improved government policies. What matters is the policy environment, but lending appears to have little direct impact on this.[229]

This is hardly surprising. As the adage has it, 'You can lead a horse to the water, but you can't make him drink.' Governments make all sorts of promises to get the loan, but then renege on them once they have taken the money, as President Moi of Kenya demonstrated repeatedly in the 1980s. Moreover, the aid agencies do not call their bluff, for they are part of a large international business in 'poverty alleviation' from which a large number of middle-class professionals derive a good living. These 'Lords of Poverty'[230] depend on lending as much as possible and persuading the public in rich countries that these loans will alleviate poverty. It is in the mutual interest of both the Lords of Poverty and the recalcitrant poor country governments to turn a blind eye to the non-fulfilment of the conditions on policy changes.

The latest justification for foreign aid is that, as the current ex-ante conditionality has failed, ex-post conditionality should be used instead. In other words, rather than seeking promises for better future actions, governments should be judged by their past actions, and only those whose past policy environment has been better than that of their peers should receive 'aid'. According to this rationale, not only will the laggards have a greater incentive to improve their policies, but aid will also be more effective. There are two problems with this justification. The whole economic argument in favour of aid was to improve the economic performance of countries unable to help themselves. If the basket cases are to be left behind because of their predator governments, what happens to the humanitarian arguments in support of aid? Second, and more important, with the opening of the world's capital markets to well-run developing countries, what incentive do these countries have to turn to the aid agencies – and their onerous procedures and conditions for loans – when they can borrow much more easily from a syndicate put together by the likes of Goldman Sachs? Any 'neighbourhood effects' whereby well-run countries are shunned by private capital markets because of their neighbours (as is claimed for Africa) can be readily countered by the aid agencies providing credit ratings for countries, just as Moody's does for the private sector. The large research capacity and information governments provide to the aid agencies would lend credibility to these ratings. No loans would be required.

The foreign aid programmes of the last half-century are a historical anomaly. They are part and parcel of the disastrous breakdown of the nineteenth-century liberal economic order during the inter-war period. But just as a new liberal economic order is gradually being reconstructed – with a milestone being the collapse of the Soviet Union and its allies and their growing integration into the world economic order – the various palliatives devised to deal with the dreadful woes bred by the past century's economic breakdown are becoming more and more redundant. Whether or not there was ever a time for foreign aid, it is an idea whose time has gone.

FIGURE 8.1 FOREIGN AID AND GROWTH ACROSS COUNTRIES, 1960–2002

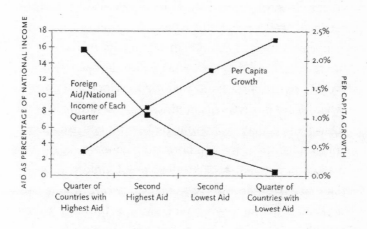

Source: William Easterly

First published in David R. Henderson (ed.), The Concise Encyclopaedia of Economics, *Liberty Fund, Indianapolis 2007.*

CHAPTER NINE

THE GLOBAL-WARMING SCAM

Since 1990 when I gave the Wincott lecture on *The Limits of International Co-operation* and unwittingly stumbled into the increasingly heated debate on global warming, I have been arguing that it is mankind's use of the mineral energy stored in nature's gift of fossil fuels which allowed the West and now increasingly, the Rest, to overcome the energy constraint imposed by the limited land-based sources of energy, which had formed the basis of pre-modern agrarian economies. This use of an unbounded energy source, accompanying the slowly rolling Industrial Revolution, allowed the ascent from structural poverty which had scarred humankind for millennia. To put a limit on the use of these fossil fuels is to condemn a Third World, in the process of converting its traditional land-based organic economies into modern mineral-energy-using economies, to perpetual structural poverty. Without going into the history of the debate since then, in this chapter I summarise where I see things standing at the moment (2011), concerning the science, economics, ethics and politics of global warming.

THE SCIENCE
Sun and Stars vs CO_2

The world is being spooked by climate change. The great and the good, aided and abetted by the International Panel on Climate Change (IPCC), and the Stern Report in the UK,[231] have convinced themselves and a large part of the electorates in the West that global warming is caused by human emissions of noxious greenhouse gases, particularly CO_2. India and China's rapid growth, with the two largest human conglomerations arising at long last from their pre-industrial slumber, will inevitably raise their noxious emissions. So that, even if existing concentrations of these pollutants were caused by the currently developed countries in their own escape from mass poverty, the future rise in emissions will come largely from the Asian giants. Hence the growing clamour by the developed countries to bring India and China into some global system of mandatory curbs on carbon emissions.

There is no dispute that global warming has been occurring. Though the stalling of the warming trend and the cooling observed over the last decade should give one cause to pause. The question is: what is the cause of the rise?

The current orthodoxy accepts the theory espoused by the IPCC that greenhouse gases, in particular the mushrooming CO_2 emissions since the Industrial Revolution, are responsible. A vivid popular depiction is provided by that redoubtable eco-warrior Al Gore's Academy award-winning documentary *An Inconvenient Truth*. It has successfully linked CO_2 emissions with catastrophic global climate change in the minds of the general public. Thus, one of the questions always asked by UCLA undergraduates in my sceptical lecture on climate change is: 'What about the ice-core evidence'? For Al Gore makes much of the apparent correlation between temperature and CO_2 concentrations as revealed in the Vostok ice-core data for millions of years. But, as I remind them, correlation does not imply causation. When a correct lagged regression is done of this and other ice-core data 'on long time scales variations in Vostok's CO_2 record lag behind those of its air-temperature record'.[232] So CO_2 cannot be the *cause* of temperature changes. It is changes in temperature which seem to cause changes in atmospheric CO_2.[233] But how?

The answer lies in the oceans, which are both the primary sink as well as emitters of CO_2. By comparison, the human contribution to global carbon emissions is negligible. When the oceans cool they absorb CO_2, when they warm, they emit CO_2. Given the vastness of oceans in the total surface area of the Earth, it takes a long time for the warming of the atmosphere to heat the oceans (and vice versa). Thence the lag between the rise in global temperature followed by a rise in CO_2, shown by the millennial ice-core evidence.

But what then causes global temperatures to wax and wane, as they have done for millennia? The alternative to the CO_2 theory is that changing levels in solar activity have caused changes in global climate over millennia. But it was argued that these changes in solar radiation were not large enough by themselves to explain the observed warming of the Earth by 0.6 degrees Celsius over the last century. Recent scientific work by Svensmark of Denmark,

Shaviv of Israel and Vezier of Canada, has now provided a fuller alternative theory of climate change which has been labelled 'Cosmoclimatology'.[234] They theorise that the climate is controlled by low cloud cover, which when widespread has a cooling effect by reflecting solar energy back into space and vice versa.

These low clouds, in turn, are formed when the sub-atomic particles called cosmic rays, emitted by exploding stars in our galaxy, combine with the water vapour rising from the oceans. The constant bombardment of the planet by cosmic rays, however, is modulated by a solar wind, which when it is blowing prevents the cosmic rays from reaching the Earth and thence creating the low clouds. The solar wind, in turn, is caused by the varying sunspot activity of the sun. When the sun is overactive with lots of sunspots, and the solar wind is blowing intensely, fewer cosmic rays get through to form the low clouds and the planet experiences global warming, as it is doing in the current transition from the Little Ice Age of the seventeenth to eighteenth centuries. Thus, on this alternative theory, global temperatures would be correlated with the intensity of the sun. When the sun is shining more brightly global temperatures will rise, and vice versa. This seems to be the case.

But there is still a missing piece in the cosmoclimatolgy theory. It depends on a hitherto untested physical hypothesis that cosmic rays influence the formation of low clouds. In 1998 Jasper Kirkby at the European Organization for Nuclear Research (CERN) particle physics lab proposed an experiment called CLOUD to test this theory. There were long delays in getting funding, and the experiment will begin in 2010. Meanwhile, Svensmark and his physicist son set up a mini-experiment in a basement of the Danish National Space Center in 2005, which found the physical causal mechanism by which cosmic rays facilitate the production of low clouds. When this is confirmed by the CERN CLOUD experiment, the final nail in the coffin of the CO_2 theory of climate change will be in place. The sun and the stars will have been shown to control our climate and not the puny, self-important inhabitants of planet Earth of current CO_2 orthodoxy.

The Continuing Scientific Wars

My wife and I recently went to see Bertolt Brecht's play *Galileo* at the National Theatre in London. This provides interesting parallels between the last large paradigm shift about man's relationship to the stars, and the current one in the new theory of cosmo-climatology.

The medieval scientific establishment was wedded to a theory which the celestial observations of the scientific sceptics, Copernicus and Galileo, contradicted. The Inquisition tried to suppress the heretics, by excommunication (Copernicus) or silencing them through showing them the instruments of torture (Galileo). Today, the peer-reviewed process of funding and validation of scientific research in climatology is equally controlled by the modern equivalent of the Collegium Romanum (the Vatican's Institute of Research), the IPCC.[235]

They, in turn, answer to the equivalent of the Inquisition, the Green ideologists, but who, mercifully, can only torment through derision or denying the heretics research funding, and not through the frightening instruments of torture – a visit to the museum in Carcassone will chill the bones of the most stout-hearted. But, even the Collegium Romanum was imbued by the rational scientific spirit, and confirmed Galileo's discoveries in his lifetime, though it took the Pope until 1993 to formally recognise the validity of Galileo's work. Finally, in both cases, the new theories were dismissed by the theologians as they seemed to downgrade the primacy of God's agents (human beings) in the universe.

FIGURE 9.1: A LONG, FAST DECLINE: 7 YEARS' GLOBAL COOLING AT 3.6°F (2°C)/CENTURY

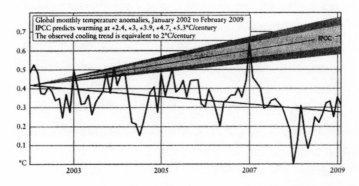

How the IPCC's projections of rising temperatures have increasingly diverged since 2001 from the trend in actual temperatures. Source: Science and Public Policy Institute.

Fortunately, it is much more difficult to suppress the scientific enterprise today. The International Panel on Climate Change (IPCC), the political body of scientists who have created the climate-change scare, still continues to claim that it is scientifically proven CO_2 emissions are the *cause* of global warming. But this is increasingly being questioned by climatologists. Particularly, as since 1997, both the terrestrial and more accurate satellite temperature readings (which are not contaminated by the 'heat island' urbanisation effect) show global cooling, even though there has been a large increase in CO_2 emissions (Figure 9.1). This is also the period in which the sunspot activity in the Sun has ceased.

In a remarkable March 2009 internal study on climate science suppressed by the US Environmental Protection Agency (EPA), but put into the public domain by the Competitive Enterprise Institute,[236] the whole scientific basis of the current CO_2 theory of climate change is put into question. It emphasises that 'global temperatures have declined, extending the current downward trend to eleven years with a particularly rapid decline in 2007–8. At the same time atmospheric CO_2 levels have continued to increase and CO_2 emissions have accelerated'. This means that 'the IPCC projections for large increases [in global temperature] are looking increasingly doubtful'. On the IPCC's rejection of the alternative explanation of solar variability as the *cause* of climate change it states: 'there appears to be a strong association between solar sunspots/ irradiance and global temperature fluctuations.' 'A new paper by Scafetta and Wilson (*Geophysical Research Letters*, 3 March 2009)[237] suggests the IPCC used faulty solar data in dismissing the direct effect of solar variability on global temperatures. Their research suggests that solar variability [rather than green house gases] could account for up to 68 per cent of the increase in Earth's global temperature.'

It then provides a table by Ken Gregory[238] which summa-rises the evidence for the alternative CO_2 and the Sun/ Cosmic Ray Warming hypotheses for climate change. This table (Table 9.1) shows that, on a number of predictions involving observable evidence on the two hypotheses, the sun/cosmic ray explanation for climate change wins hands down. Moreover, as on this hypothesis, it is the sunspot activity which controls the climate, as the sun seems to have gone to sleep over the last twelve years, there is a growing likelihood 'that sunspots may vanish by 2015. Given the strong association between sunspots and global temperatures, this suggests the possibility that we may be entering a period of global cooling.' Perhaps another Ice Age.

TABLE 9.1

Issue	Prediction – CO_2 Hypothesis	Prediction – Sun/ Cosmic Ray Hypothesis	Actual Data
Antarctic and Arctic temperatures	Temperatures in the Arctic and Antarctic will rise symmetrically	Temperatures will initially move in opposite directions	Temperatures move in opposite directions
Troposphere temperature	Fastest warming will be in the troposphere over the Tropics	The troposphere warming will be uniform	Surface warming similar or greater than tropospheric warming
Timing of CO_2 and temperature changes at end of Ice Age	CO_2 increases, then temperature increases	Temperature increases, then CO_2 increases	CO_2 concentrations increase about 800 years after temperatures increases

Temperature correlates with the driver over last 400 years	N/A	N/A	Cosmic ray flux and Sun activity correlates with temperature, CO_2 does not
Temperature during Ordovician Period	Very hot due to CO_2 levels>10x present	Very cold due to high cosmic ray flux	Very cold Ice Age
Other planets	No change	Other planets will warm	Warming has been detected on several other planets
Source: Gregory (2009)			

The first results from the CERN CLOUD experiment were published in 2011. It finds a 'significant' cosmic ray cloud effect.[239] The mystery of low cloud formation is what the CLOUD experiment is meant to uncover. As Professor Svensmark says, the CLOUD results 'basically confirm our own experimental results since 2006, and do so within a larger variation of parameters. It seems to say that ions [cosmic rays] are fundamental for the nucleation of new aerosols [tiny liquid or solid particles that provide a nucleus around which droplets can form from water vapour in the air]'.[240] The media, warmist scientists and the IPCC have denied or ignored the significance of this experiment.[241] But once, as I hope, Professor Svensmark and his associates who have developed the cosmo-climatology theory win the Nobel prize, the myth of anthropogenic global warming will be finally nailed. It will be recognised that humans cannot control the climate and must adapt as they have done for millennia to its continual changes.

THE ECONOMICS

It is ironic that many economists (and policy makers), base their climate-change policy recommendations on acceptance of the CO_2 theory upheld by the IPCC as the irrefutable scientific truth, the latest examples being the Stern Review put out by the UK government and the Garnaut Review[242] by the Australian government. But, there is nothing particularly novel about the cost-benefit methodology nor about the model, which is used to incorporate the IPCC-based scientific judgements, as William Nordhaus (the author of the most serious previous study of the economics of climate change), has noted in a recent review.[243] What is novel is its conclusion that, without drastic immediate action to curb greenhouse emissions, the world faces economic catastrophe 'on a scale similar to those associated with the great wars and the economic depression of the first half of the twentieth century'.

This is a dramatically different conclusion from earlier models of climate change which accepted the CO_2 theory of global warming,[244] and found that the 'optimal climate change' policies involve modest reductions in emissions in the near future. The reason for the contrary Stern results is the near-zero social rate of discount used to sum up future costs and benefits. This represents a contentious ethical judgement of the weight placed on the consumption of the future relative to present generations.

Any act of investment involves giving up current consumption to increase future income and consumption. If a one dollar cut in consumption today raises future consumption by a dollar and fifty cents, we need to decide whether this extra fifty cents (because of the productivity of investment) is worth giving up the dollar today. As for individuals who are mortal, 'a bird in hand is worth two in the bush', and the extra fifty cents tomorrow might not materialise, and moreover they may be dead and unable to consume it tomorrow. They would want to discount this future gain to make it commensurate with the dollar they are giving up today. The rate at which we discount this future income will then have two elements. One is a 'pure' time-preference component, reflecting our uncertainty about whether we will be alive to enjoy the extra income tomorrow. Another depends upon the fact that, with ongoing economic growth and increases in income, our future income and consumption will be higher in any case, so that by investing one dollar we are in effect transferring a dollar from our poorer self today to add an extra fifty cents to our richer self tomorrow. We now also have to make a distributional judgement on how much transferring one dollar of current consumption to make a richer future generation even richer is worth. These two components comprise the social discount rate. Even if we accept that for society as a whole the pure time-preference component should be set at zero, as society unlike individuals is in principle immortal, this still leaves the distributional weight to be placed on the intergenerational transfer of consumption from a poorer to a richer generation. If this is set close to zero it implies that any cut in the consumption of the current poor generation is justified to increase the consumption of the richer future generation by even an infinitesimally small amount. This is of course the policy which Stalin followed in his heavy industry-biased, forced industrialisation of the Soviet Union, justifying the building of seemingly redundant steel mills at the expense of industries supplying consumer goods with the quip: 'They cannot eat steel!'

The discount rate also crucially determines how far future costs and benefits need to be counted. If the discount rate is close to zero, the whole of the infinite future stream of costs and benefits becomes relevant. Hence, the highly speculative economic damage the Stern Review adduces from rising temperatures *two centuries from now* can be valued equally with any economic costs we have to currently incur to mitigate them. But, as Nordhaus rightly notes, this low discount rate can lead to absurd results. It would imply trading off a large fraction of today's income to increase the income stream of those living two centuries from now by a tiny fraction. For, with a near-zero discount rate, this tiny increase in the future generations, income stream is cumulated to near infinity.

By contrast, the estimates I made for the Planning Commission in the early 1970s[245] based on the same methodology as the Stern Review, but with more plausible parameters, yielded a social discount rate of 7 per cent for India. At this discount rate, the present value of Rs.1 (rupees) accruing seventy-five years from today would be worth nothing, making most of the speculative economic costs and benefits, and the apocalyptic predictions of the Stern Review, irrelevant for India.[246]

ETHICS

This mathematical politics, based on increasingly questionable officially sponsored climate science, to get the Third World (particularly China and India) to curb their CO_2 emissions, is also deeply immoral. The proposed new 'climate change' treaty in Copenhagen (which was fortunately scuttled in December – see below) seeks to put curbs on the carbon emissions of the Third World. If they do not comply they are being threatened by a draft bill going through the US Congress to levy carbon tariffs on their exports. This is a blatant attempt to prevent these countries from industrialising and achieving the standards of living of the West. For until technological advances can allow alternative 'green' energy sources to compete with the fossil fuels, whose use is gradually eliminating poverty in the Third World as in the West's own ascent from poverty, a call to put any curbs on carbon emissions is in fact to condemn their billions to continuing poverty.

While numerous Western economists and do-gooders shed crocodile tears about the Third World's poor, they are willing at the same time to prevent them from taking the only feasible current route out from this abject state. Nothing is more hypocritical and immoral than rich Westerners driving their gas-guzzling SUVs while emoting about the threat to Spaceship Earth from the millions of Indians who want to drive the new Tata Nanos. The salving of their consciences by buying carbon offsets (as Al Gore claims to do every time he jets around the world) is akin to the Papal indulgences sold by the medieval Catholic Church, which allowed its richer adherents to assuage their guilt and 'fornicate on clean sheets'. For Gore to have the lights in his mansion blazing throughout the night, and seek to restrict the emissions from Indian power stations, when most Indians don't even have an electric light bulb, is deeply wicked.

A study of the costs to the Indian poor of curbing carbon emissions has estimated that, over a thirty-year time horizon, with a 10 per cent annual emission restriction, the poor population *increases* by 21 per cent, even in the short run, and by nearly 50 per cent for a 30 per cent annual emission reduction.[247] Those development economists and sundry celebrities who, on the one hand, want to see the end of world poverty and on the other, to curb Third World carbon emissions, should be ashamed of themselves for advocating the latter path which will make the former goal impossible to achieve.

This is not to downgrade the serious current environmental problems caused by rapid growth in India and China. Anyone who has choked in the fetid air of Chungking, Xian, Beijing or Delhi, will know that no climate scares are needed to provide a case for dealing with their unhealthy air pollution. Similarly India and China face a growing water crisis irrespective of what is happening to global CO_2 emissions. Subsidies to energy and water use need to be removed for efficiency reasons. Given the political instability and growing political determination of supplies of fossil fuels from the countries where they are concentrated, it is sensible to diversify energy sources. Both nuclear power and coal reserves (abundant in India, China and the US) provide more secure alternatives. Biofuels, by contrast, have the disadvantage of competing for limited land with essentials like food. However, the Sun, which most probably controls the climate, also offers the backstop technology which will ultimately provide the unbounded energy for the Third World – living in tropical sunny climes – for continuing economic growth. In thinking about all these economic issues, the changing climate is a red herring.

POLITICS

On 29 October 2008, the country which had pioneered
the Industrial Revolution by learning how to convert the
mineral energy stored in its vast mineral resources of coal,
was experiencing its first October snow since 1934. Inside
the Palace of Westminster, the British House of Commons
was passing a 'Climate Change Bill' committing the country to an 80 per cent cut in CO_2 emissions in forty years,
by a near-unanimous vote, with only one MP, Peter Lilley,
questioning its potential costs.[248] If implemented it would
close Britain's industrial economy, make motorised transport impossible and turn off Britain's lights, transforming
the country into a North Korea.

This insanity had been preceded by the European
Union's 2007 pledge to reduce the EU's carbon emissions
by 20 per cent below 1990 levels. In June 2009, the US
House of Representatives narrowly passed the Clean Energy
and Security Bill which sought to cut US greenhouse emissions by 17 per cent of the 2005 levels in eleven years.
Both presidential candidates in the 2008 US elections had
endorsed measures to counter climate change. While, with
a change in government in Australia, when the government
of John Howard, a climate 'sceptic', was replaced by the
Labour government of Ken Rudd, an attempt to introduce
a climate change bill in a country 80 per cent dependent on
coal was only scuppered in August in its Senate, because of
the resilience of one senator – Stephen Fielding.[249]

The success of the global-warming hysteria is largely
based on the single mindedness and adroit manipulation
of bureaucratic structures by climate alarmists to generate
political pressures which elected politicians cannot resist.
Linked to this are various forms of corruption. The most

serious has been the corruption of the science by the IPCC. Nothing illustrates this better than the 'hockey stick' saga; what has come to be known as 'Climategate', and the latest revelation of scientific fraud labelled 'Glaciergate'. Here is a brief account.

THE 'HOCKEY STICK'[250]

In most climate histories, including that by Sir John Houghton, a former chairman of the IPCC and an environmental advisor to Tony Blair, there have been recognised to be distinct periods of warming and cooling over recorded history.[251] Thus, around 700–400BC there was the 'pre-Roman cold' period, followed between 200BC and sixth-century AD by the Roman warming, when vines were planted in Britain. This warming ended abruptly in the century, followed by three centuries of cooling during the Dark Ages. But from 900AD temperatures began to rise, giving way to the 400-year 'Medieval Warm Period' (MWP) when temperatures were higher than in the current twentieth century. From 1300 temperatures began to drop, leading to four centuries of the 'Little Ice Age', which lasted till the slow rise in temperature during the nineteenth century, leading to the 'modern warming' period. This climate history was in fact depicted graphically in Houghton (1994) and the first IPCC report in 1990 (see Figure 9.2). But it posed a serious problem for the proponents of man-made carbon emissions as the cause of global warming, like the IPCC. How could the Medieval and Roman warm periods be caused by human carbon emissions, as these were clearly part of the pre-industrial age where the technology to use fossil fuels to provide energy had not been invented.

FIGURE 9.2: CLIMATE CHANGE OVER THE PAST 1,000 YEARS AS SHOWN BY THE IPCC IN 1990

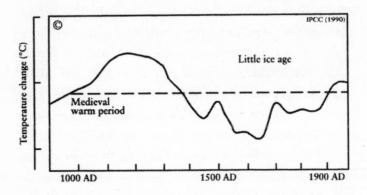

Climate change over the past 1,000 years: J. T. Houghton et al., IPCC First Assessment Report, 1990

In 1998 two papers by a recently qualified PHD physicist-turned-climatologist, Michael E. Mann, appeared, showing estimates from his computer models of global temperature extending back 1,000 years.[252] Lo and behold, the Medieval Warm Period and the Little Ice Age had vanished. The graph showed a gradually declining trend in average temperatures from 1000AD, and then a sudden shooting up in the twentieth century to an unprecedented level, The graph resembled a hockey stick, and became the iconic image 'proving' that man-made carbon emissions were responsible for the twentieth-century global warming.

Intrigued, Stephen McIntyre, a financial consultant and statistical analyst, and Ross McKitrick, an economics professor, asked Mann for the original data set. Examining this and the computer programme used by Mann, they found that 'there was an error in a routine calculation step (principal component analysis) that falsely identified a hockey stick shape as the dominant pattern in the data. The flawed computer program can even pull out spurious hockey stick shapes from lists of trendless random numbers.'[253] When they did the exercise properly, and after removing some dubious data on Californian pine cones used by Mann et al., the Medieval Warm Period appeared, confirming that the fifteenth-century warming exceeded anything in the twentieth century. So damning were these flaws that, despite their relative obscurity and that of the journal in which they published their findings, the issue became a cause célèbre because of the prominence the hockey stick had assumed in the public debate after it was made the centre piece of the 2001 IPCC report.

Two US congressional committees set up enquiries to investigate the claims and counter-claims about climate history. They upheld McIntyre and McKitrick, and one investigation chaired by Dr Edward Wegman, a leading statistician, excoriated the Mann papers, as well as his various highly place supporters who had tried to whitewash them. Wegman, however, also commissioned a 'social network analysis' of Mann's defenders to find out how independent they were. This found that they were 'closely connected and thus "independent studies" may not be as independent as they might appear on the surface'. Mann's supporters were 'a tightly knit group of individuals who passionately believe in their thesis. However, our perception is that this group has a self-reinforcing feedback mechanism, and, moreover, the work has been sufficiently politicised that they can hardly reassess their public positions without losing credibility.'[254]

This self-protecting clique of climate scientists controlling peer-reviewed journals were then found in a larger study of the purported 2,500 scientists who had put together the scientific chapter of the IPCC's 2007 report by an Australian IT expert, John McLean.[255] He found that the IPCC orthodoxy was based on the views of just fifty-three climate scientists who formed 'a disturbingly tight network of scientists with common research interests and opinions' with 'neither the papers nor opinions of the growing band of serious climatologists who doubt that humankind has an actually or potentially harmful influence on the earth's climate [being] adequately represented'. The IPCC authors relied heavily on the computer models of the Hadley Centre based at the University of East Anglia in the UK, These models had been programmed assuming anthropogenic global warming and, as it was, 'the *inputs* to the models that determined the extent of the imagined human influence on climate … analysing the *outputs* to determine the extent to which they demonstrate anthropogenic influences is meaningless and futile'. The clear biases observed in this chapter, McLean observed, showed it was 'not science but politics elaborately dressed up' to pretend to be science. He concluded, 'governments have naively and unwisely accepted the claims of a human influence on global temperatures made by a close knit clique of a few dozen scientists, many of them climate modellers, as if they were representative of the opinion of the wider scientific community'.

CLIMATEGATE

In November 2009, leaked e-mails from the Climate Research Unit (CRU) at the University of East Anglia, whose scientists have been at the heart of the IPCC scientific assessments, created a worldwide storm that was labelled Climategate by the British journalist James Delingpole.[256] Soon Google showed that the word appeared nine million times on the internet. What these e-mails revealed was that Professor Phillip Jones, the director of the CRU, which is the source of the most important of the four sets of terrestrial temperature data on which the IPCC relies, along with a tight network of colleagues, had for years discussed various tactics to avoid releasing their data to outsiders under freedom of information laws. They kept coming up with innumerable excuses to conceal the background data on which their findings and temperature records are based. Jones, astonishingly, even claimed in 2008 that this data from all over the world was 'lost'. But the e-mails show that scientists were told to delete large chunks of data. As this was done after a receipt of a freedom of information request, which is a criminal offence, the University of East Anglia had to agree to release the data in collaboration with the Met Office's Hadley Centre after obtaining the agreement of other met offices around the world.

The reason they did not want independent appraisal of the data was because they were desperate to rescue Mann's hockey stick. The e-mails reveal that they were trying to manipulate the data through computer programmes they did not fully understand, to flatten the historical record on temperature fluctuations and to 'adjust' the recent cooling temperatures upwards to show accelerating warming. Steve McIntyre had caught out James Hanson, the director of the US NASA's Goddard Institute of Space Science in 2008, which forced a revision of this other major source for global surface temperatures. While in Australia and New Zealand, when local scientists compared the official temperature record with the original data on which it was based, they found that a flat temperature chart had been manipulated to show temperatures steadily rising.

Finally, the e-mails revealed that the academics involved were willing to ruthlessly suppress any dissenting views by discrediting and freezing out any scientific journal which published their critics' work, and ensuring that this dissenting research was not include in IPCC reports.

GLACIERGATE

In its latest (2007) report, the IPCC claimed that the Himalayan glaciers could disappear by 2035. In January 2010 the IPCC's chairman, Dr Pachauri (a railway engineer), had to ignominiously admit that this claim had no scientific basis. This issue created a huge furore in India, as the huge Himalayan ice sheet feeds seven of the world's major river systems on which 40 per cent of the world's population depends. The EU had set up the 'High Noon' project on the impact of melting Himalayan glaciers, hoping that the resulting alarm would win Indian support for the climate change treaty to be negotiated in Copenhagen in December 2009.

It appears that a little-known Indian scientist, Dr Hosseni, had made this unsubstantiated claim in an interview with an Indian environmental magazine, *Down to Earth*, in April 1999, which was picked up by the *New Scientist*. This was the citation for its now-disowned claim in the 2007 IPCC report. Alarmed, the Indian government asked the country's most senior glaciologist, Dr Vijaya Raina, to examine the claim. He published his report in November 2009, showing that the Himalayan glaciers had not retreated in the last fifty years, that Dr Hosseni's claims were baseless and that the IPCC's claims were recklessly alarmist. Dr Pachauri reacted fiercely, saying Dr Raina's report was 'arrogant' and 'voodoo economics', A few weeks later he had to eat crow as he and the IPCC had to admit their predictions were without scientific foundation. He has been castigated by Jairam Ramesh, the Indian environment minister, and Dr Raina has asked him to apologise for his 'voodoo science' charge. Meanwhile (as I write at the end of January 2010) there is a growing clamour in India for him to resign from the IPCC.

But he is unlikely to do so for, as the *Daily Telegraph* journalists Christopher Booker and Richard North[257] have documented, his energy and resources institute (TERI) in Delhi has received substantial financial benefits from industry, foundations, governments and international agencies. This financial cornucopia has also covered the numerous scientists and economists who have led the global-warming hysteria. They, along with the numerous industries, see a whole trough of subsidies coming their way as governments, responding to the hysteria to curb carbon emissions, seek to promote alternative sources of energy. Thus the oil major BP now advertises itself as Beyond Petroleum! Meanwhile, if the targets for cutting carbon that the EU now has in place are met, the continent which ushered in the modern era will soon descend into the Stone Age.

THE COPENHAGEN DERAILMENT

The culmination of the Green takeover of the world was to be the Copenhagen conference in December to sign a new treaty agreeing to global curbs on emissions to save Spaceship Earth. The main purpose was to bring in the major deniers whose refusal to sign on to the Kyoto treaty had made the agreed curbs meaningless. With the new US President Barack Obama committed to tackling climate change, and with a carbon 'cap and trade' bill going through the US Congress, it seemed that the world's greatest polluter would now join the Green consensus. At the same time the coveted prize was bringing the major emerging economies of India and China into a new agreement to curb carbon emissions. The purported scientific 'consensus', the pressure of global public opinion and threats of carbon tariffs (which the WTO had surprisingly ruled would be legal) were all to be used as means to this end. But Copenhagen turned out to be a nightmare for the climate alarmists, particularly for the European Union which had preened itself as being the global leader in curbing carbon emissions, and was expected to take the lead in negotiating a new climate-change treaty.

Led by China, India, Brazil and South Africa the developing world made clear they were not willing to commit themselves to any mandatory curb on their emissions which would damage their growth prospects. Obama, unable to get his Congress to pass a climate change bill before Copenhagen, could do no more than express his commitment to get one in the near future with defined targets to limit emissions. All countries agreed to a meaningless voluntary accord to prevent global temperatures rising by more than two degrees Celsius. The developed countries were to set out their mandatory targets by the end of December. That was soon shelved by the UN agency running the conference as unattainable.

But the real story at Copenhagen was provided by a small vignette at its end. Wanting to use his charm to get the recalcitrant emerging markets of China and India to agree to mandatory cuts in their emissions, Obama asked to meet Manmohan Singh, the Indian PM, personally before a scheduled meeting with the Chinese President Hu Jintao. He was told Dr Singh was already on his way to the airport. Scheduled to see Hu Jintao, he was told he was in a room nearby. When Obama barged into the small room he found the Chinese President, the Indian PM and the Presidents of Brazil and South Africa in a huddle. There was not even a chair for Mr Obama, and one had to be brought in. During the next few hours they hammered out the meaningless Copenhagen Accord. The European Union, the self-proclaimed global leader on climate change, did not even get a look-in, leading to its Commissioner ruefully admitting after the conference that it was no longer a superpower.

The Copenhagen climate-change conference marked the shifting geo-political tectonic plates. The Third World was no longer going to be beholden to the First, and was no longer willing to listen to its diktats or cajoling. It was not going to commit economic hara-kiri like the West. It was determined to develop and alleviate its mass poverty as the West had done by converting from land-based energy-using to mineral-based energy-using economies. If the West realises that its global-warming hysteria will no longer lead to the global mitigation policies it has sought since the fall of the Berlin Wall, it will reverse the futile energy policies it has adopted, supported by 'junk' science and 'voodoo' economics. If it does so before the Great Chill, which some scientists are predicting as a result of the Sun going to sleep, it may even prevent itself from freezing. The derailment at Copenhagen by the Third

World of the Green agenda would have saved the world's
poor and the West from its self-created demons.

First featured in author's Indian Business Standard *column,
June and July 2007, August 2009, January 2011 and
September 2011.*

CHAPTER TEN

THE GREAT CRASH OF 2008

I t is now two years since the Great Crash of September/ October 2008. An immense amount has been written about its causes and the consequences are still being worked out, not least by policy makers divided by fears of future deflation or inflation. The crisis has brought all kinds of dirigiste panaceas to the fore, and there seems to have been a revival of crude Keynesianism amongst the commentariat and policy makers. Some have seen the crisis as the sign of the collapse of capitalism. In March 2009 soon after becoming President of the Mont Pelerin Society – of which Luigi Einaudi was one of my earlier distinguished predecessors – I organised a special meeting of the Society in New York on the theme 'The End of Globalizing Capitalism? Classical Liberal responses to the Global Financial Crisis'. I used the papers from the conference,[258] as well as my own op-eds from the Indian *Business Standard*, to give a lecture at the Adam Smith Institute in London in June 2009, with a title close to the one for this lecture. A revised version of this was published in the *Cato Journal* earlier this year.[259] As I stand by many of its arguments, in this lecture I will be largely basing myself on it with various addendums and additions.

I will begin by examining the major reason purported for this crisis based on so-called 'global imbalances', which I argue is mistaken, before going on to a major structural change in the US financial system (still disputed) and to list the commonly agreed policy errors which led to the crisis. I then discuss the alternative theoretical frameworks which provide a diagnosis of the crisis, and the errors of omission and commission of the monetary authorities which led to the crisis, as well as assessing their response in its aftermath. I then discuss the fiscal and regulatory responses to the crisis and their consequences. This leads on to the basic underlying cause of the crisis which is similar to that found in many developing countries – the creation of unsustainable entitlement economies. I end with what a classical liberal response would be to prevent or mitigate such crises in the future. I will not have time to discuss the equally important geopolitical consequences of the crisis. But for those interested, these can be found in my *Cato Journal* article.

GLOBAL IMBALANCES

The ongoing concern with 'global imbalances' (seen as a cause of the crisis, as well as of the 1980s Third World debt crisis and the likely source of another one in the near future) expressed by a host of commentators[260] and officials[261] gives me a tremendous sense of déjà vu. In my 1990 Wincott lecture[262] I had examined the case for international co-ordination to deal with the purported 'global imbalances' of the 1980s, and found it wanting. Though no doubt the purported problems leading to these 'imbalances' (the low consumption share in China and its undervalued exchange rate, the inflexible labour markets in Europe and dysfunctional welfare states, Japanese reluctance to allow immigration and foreign investment etc.) may be of concern to the citizens of the respective countries being lectured to, should they be of concern to the rest of the world? The discussion of 'global imbalances' implicitly assumes they are, because of the supposed spill-over effects of these various domestic policies on the global economy. But what are these spillover effects and should internationally co-ordinated public policy or international moral suasion be used to counter them?

To answer this question it is useful to look upon the global economy as an integrated economy, where governments, central banks, households and firms in each nation are all distinct economic agents acting in their own perceived 'self-interest', with their own objectives. The international markets for goods and assets will co-ordinate these myriad decisions into changing relative prices, which at the national level will be reflected in changing macro-economic variables like interest rates, real exchange rates, and savings rates. With both public and private agents maximising their own perceived interests, this decentral-ised international system is exactly like a market system.

The changes in prices and outputs that arise as a result of the different actions of these agents are exactly like the increase in demand, say, for shoes within a national econ-omy, which *ceteris paribus* raises the price of leather and hence affects the financial circumstances of the purchaser of handbags. The macroeconomic international spillovers are exactly like those affecting the handbag buyer, which (in the economist's jargon) are 'pecuniary' externalities mediated through the price mechanism and of no significance for the efficiency of the economy. They are synonymous with market interdependence and the price system, and irrelevant for public policy in contrast with 'technological' externalities like smoke from a factory which are not mediated through the price mechanism and could require public action. But, pecuniary externalities are not a sign of any 'market failure'. As at the national level, there is no need for any harmonisation or co-ordination at the international level further than that provided by the market.

What then are we to make of all the prognostications of various pundits on these 'global imbalances'? They are like the numerous stock broker reports trying to foretell market trends based on what each claims are 'fundamentals'. But we know that at best they are looking through a glass darkly. These local 'imbalances' may be of concern to particular economic agents. As a taxpayer in the US and UK I am naturally concerned about their respective fiscal deficits because of their implications for my future taxes. But for the rest of the world these are only of interest to agents in these countries if they choose to be holders of the relevant debt instruments financing them. They are not a global concern.[263]

CHANGING FINANCIAL STRUCTURES

In the early 1980s, I was working as the research administrator at the World Bank, while the Third World was engulfed by a debt crisis. The current global financial crisis has eerie similarities, but different outcomes. Why?

First, both the crises arose because there was a surplus of savings in a number of countries – the oil producers in the 1970s, the Asian economies and commodity exporters today – which was recycled through the international banking system. Second, highly liquid banks imprudently funneled cheap credit to uncreditworthy borrowers: the fiscally challenged and inflation-prone countries of Latin America and Africa in the 1970s, the *ninja* (those with no income, no jobs, no assets) subprime mortgagees of the current crisis. Third, there was a rise in commodity prices and a worsening of the terms of trade of the OECD, posing the stagflation dilemma for their central banks having aided and abetted the earlier asset boom. Fourth, the imprudent banks sought bailouts from taxpayers, claiming their demise would fatally damage the world's financial system.

But, the outcomes have been different. The 1980s crisis was finally solved after a prolonged cat-and-mouse game when the banks accepted substantial write-downs of their Third World debt, sacked their imprudent managers, and shareholders suffered large losses. But no systemic threat to the world's financial system (or the global economy) emerged. By contrast, today the Western financial system seems to be dissolving before our eyes, and with the US Federal Reserve's ever-expanding balance sheet, bailouts are no longer the exception but the norm. Many now foretell a deep and perhaps prolonged recession, with deflation, rising unemployment, and Keynes's famed liquidity trap about to engulf the world's major economies.

What then explains this difference in outcomes in the current global financial crisis from the Third World debt crises of the 1980s and 1990s? It cannot be purported 'global imbalances', even if they were, as is claimed, the origins of both crises. It is the differences in financial structures within which these temporally separated but largely similar crises occurred. In the 1970s the recycling of the global surpluses was undertaken by the offshore branches of Western money centre banks, which were neither supervised nor had access to the lender of last resort facilities of their parent country's central bank. Hence, when their Third World euro dollar loans went into 'default,' there was no direct threat to the Western banking system.

The present crisis emerged in a radically different financial structure: the rise of universal banks from the UK's 'Big Bang' financial liberalisation in the 1980s, and the Clinton-era abolition of the Glass–Steagall Act, which had kept a firewall between the commercial and investment banking parts of the financial system since the 1930s. The former had implicit deposit insurance and access to the central banks' lender of last-resort facilities. The latter did not. It is worth explaining why this matters.

This distinction between what were previously non-bank financial intermediaries and banks is important because it is only clearing banks which can add to (or reduce) the stock of money. A clearing bank holds deposits in cash (legal tender base money) from non-banks, repaying deposits in notes, and making payments for depositors by settlements in cash through an account in the central bank. When a clearing bank extends a loan it adds to its assets and simultaneously creates deposit liabilities against itself, increasing the broad money supply at 'the stroke of a pen'. This ability to create money out of thin air is limited by the bank's capital and cash. As cash can be borrowed from the central bank, the ultimate constraint on its ability to create money is its capital. But it is only because banks take in cash deposits – Keynes's 'widow's curse' – that they can create money.

By contrast, a non-bank financial intermediary, say a mortgage lender when it takes deposits or makes a mortgage loan, has to 'clear' these through deposits held at the clearing banks. Thus when someone deposits 'cash' at a Savings and Loan (S&L) this comes out of the depositor's bank account with a clearing bank. Similarly when the S&L makes a loan to a mortgagee this comes from the S&L's bank account with a clearing bank. Thus, the essential difference between non-bank financial institutions and clearing banks is that they cannot create the bank deposit component of broad money (M2 or M4).[264]

When the Federal Deposit Insurance Corporation (FDIC) was created as part of Roosevelt's New Deal to prevent the bank runs which the earlier universal banks' gambling had engendered, Marriner Eccles, who redesigned the Federal Reserve system for Roosevelt in the Great Depression, insisted that with deposit insurance the banking industry must be split in half: the public utility part of the financial system, which constitutes the payments system, *must* be kept separate from the gambling investment banking part, which is an essential part of a dynamic economy. For these gambles impart the dynamic efficiency through the cleansing processes of creative destruction. But if these gambles are protected against losses by taxpayers, as the payment system activities have to be because of deposit insurance, the gamblers will always win: keeping their gains when their gambles are correct and passing their losses onto taxpayers when their gambles turn sour. Hence the Glass–Steagall Act.

Given this 'moral hazard,' many classical liberals have favoured free banking. Banks combining the payment and investment functions and issuing their own notes should be monitored by their depositors, who would stand to lose if their banks undertook imprudent lending. But with the near universality of deposits as a means of payment, there is little likelihood of this monitoring function being effectively exercised, while the rise of demos precludes any government being able to resist pressures to bail out imprudent banks to protect their depositors. This makes deposit insurance inevitable, and to prevent investment banks from gambling with the taxpayer insured deposit base, something akin to Glass–Steagall remains essential.

The recent emergence of universal banking has, however, been lauded by many on the classical liberal side,[265] and the repeal of the Glass–Steagall Act is seen as a sensible measure of deregulating the financial system. Much of their argument is based on assessing whether the Glass–Steagall Act was necessary or an immoderate response to the Great Depression. As Meltzer states, 'As George Benston showed, proponents of the rule did not make a substantive case when they claimed that combined investment and commercial banking was a cause of the Great Depression'.[266] Similarly Calomiris, citing many studies which have examined the claim that there was a conflict of interest in mixing commercial and investment banking, whereby 'banks might coerce client firms or cheat purchasers of securities', demonstrates that this argument has now been discredited. But he also notes that another concern behind the Glass–Steagall Act 'was largely that of economists who correctly worried about the abuse of deposit insurance and the discount window – the possibility of government subsidisation of risk in new activities'. This is the worry which has not gone, particularly as he notes that deposit insurance is the only part of the 1933 Banking Act which now remains 'and it is difficult to imagine circumstances that will lead to its repeal'.[267] This is the nub, and it is difficult to see why he or Meltzer would therefore oppose keeping investment and commercial banks separate. It is deposit insurance alone that provides a reason for public regulation of any aspect of banking. If the Glass–Steagall firewall between commercial and investment banking is maintained, there is no reason why the investment banks should not be set completely free.[268]

POLICY ERRORS

The recent emergence of universal banking was followed by a number of public policy mistakes on the path to the current crisis. The first was the bailout of LTCM in 1998. Its failure posed no obvious systemic threat. Its public salvation changed expectations of market participants that non-bank financial institutions could also hope for bailouts. Next, the infamous Greenspan 'put', which put a floor to the unwinding of the dotcom stock market bubble, promoted excessive risk taking. Third, the promotion of 'affordable' housing for the poor by the Clinton administration, through the unreformed and failed Freddie mortgage twins, led to the development of subprime mortgages. Fourth, the Basle II capital adequacy requirements led banks to put their risky assets into off-balance-sheet vehicles – the SIVs – leading to the opacity currently being bemoaned. Fifth, when the housing bubble burst, and the credit crunch began with the gambles taken during it turning sour, the Fed chose to bail out Bear Sterns, sending the signal that the Fed's balance sheet was open to non-deposit taking 'banks' as signalled by the earlier LTCM bailout. Sixth, and most heinously given all that had gone before, the US authorities then chose *not* to bail out Lehman's – like a fallen woman suddenly finding virtue. This dashing of the bail-out expectations that the authorities had endorsed only in the spring, led to the intensification of the credit crunch. Seventh, as the authorities finally seemed to tackle the toxic subprime infected financial assets which caused the crisis through the Troubled Asset Relief Program (TARP), it calmed the markets. When TARP was changed to be used only to recapitalise banks, markets went into free fall. The essential step of forcing banks to come clean on their balance sheets, and then removing the toxic assets they reveal into a newly created institutional *cordon sanitaire*, has still not been taken. Worse, instead of recreating a firewall between the payment part and the gambling part of the banking system, even the pure investment banks, like Goldman Sachs, were pushed into becoming universal banks with access to the Fed's balance sheet and thence taxpayer's money.

Given these public shortcomings, the near-universal calls for greater regulation and state intervention is astounding. Public agents, not private ones – who reacted rationally to the implicit or explicit 'rules of the game' promoted – are to blame for the crisis. It would be foolish to blame the puppets for the failings of the puppeteer.

THEORETICAL REMEDIES

What of the remedies? In answering this it is essential to be clear of the nature of the crisis, and to view it from the

THE GREAT CRASH OF 2008

correct theoretical perspective. Because of the association of Keynes's name with the Great Depression, the crisis and its cures are being seen through 'crass Keynesian' lenses. Is this appropriate? To answer this question I briefly outline the alternative theoretical perspectives which seek to explain the current crisis as well as the remedies.

Here a personal note is in order. When I got my first academic job as a lecturer at Christ Church, Oxford, my senior colleague was Sir Roy Harrod – Keynes's first biographer and keeper of his flame. On having to provide a reading list for my tutorials on 'economic fluctuations and growth', I asked him what I should ask my pupils to read. I expected him to say Keynes, and his own work on trade cycles and growth. But after some reflection he said: Wicksell. So before I prescribed this to my pupils I immersed myself in *Interest and Prices* and *Lectures on Political Economy*. Since then I have been pleasantly surprised that most of the macroeconomic perspectives on offer really hark back to Wicksell.[269]

Wicksell asked how could the price level be anchored in a pure credit economy? Bagehot had observed in *Lombard Street* that the whole of the Bank of England's note issue depended on a slender and declining gold ratio. What if this ratio went to zero, asked Wicksell? His answer was that, if the Bank rate were set at the *natural* rate of interest, which balances productivity with thrift, the price level could be kept constant. This is, of course, the theory underlying inflation targeting, as embodied in the Taylor rule. As John Taylor has noted, it was the failure of the Greenspan Fed to follow this rule which led to the credit bubble after the dotcom bust.[270]

The reasons for this failure are provided by Hayek's refurbished Austrian theory of the trade cycle. Hayek saw divergences between the Wicksellian natural and market rates of interest as causing booms and slumps. If increased bank credit led to market interest rates below the natural rate, businesses will undertake relatively more capital intensive projects with relatively low rates of return. There will also be an unsustainable boom, with more projects undertaken than can be completed, leading to resource scarcities which end the boom. The financial crash which follows will lead to the liquidation of these 'maladjustments', followed by an economic recovery with resources being reallocated in line with inter-temporal consumer preferences and resource availabilities. While broadly accepting the quantity theory of money, Hayek argues that it assumed the absence of 'injection' effects, which even with an overall stable price level could lead to false signals in the pattern of inter-temporal relative prices, and thence to maladjusted investments. The recent US housing boom, with a stable general price level, provides an example of these 'maladjustments'.

But Hayek's prescription that the slump should be allowed to run its course came to be disowned even by his London School of Economics (LSE) circle led by Robbins in the 1930s. As Gottfried Haberler (1986: 422), a close friend and member of Hayek's Austrian circle, noted in his astute appraisal of Hayek's business cycle theory: 'Keynes, Robbins, and many others were correct: if a cyclical decline has been allowed to degenerate into a severe slump with mass unemployment, falling prices, and deflationary expectations, government deficit spending to inject money directly into the income stream is necessary. Moreover, Hayek himself has changed his mind on this point.'[271]

Though Keynes' General Theory, unlike Hayek's, provides no explanation for the boom preceding the slump, Keynes was right in emphasising 'effective demand' failures in the face of a financial crash, and the need for deficit spending. Though not, as advocated by many current Keynesians, through counter-cyclical public works. Thus, Keynes wrote:

> Organised public works at home and abroad, may be the right cure for a chronic tendency to a deficiency of effective demand. But they are not capable of sufficiently rapid organisation (and above all cannot be reversed or undone at a later date), to be the most serviceable instrument for the prevention of the trade cycle.[272]

A point reinforced by the Congressional Budget Office's assessment of the planned Obama infrastructure spending.

Friedman, unlike Hayek, was closer to Wicksell in concentrating on the effects of divergences between the natural and market rate of interest on the *general* price level, and not as Hayek's theory presupposes on *relative* prices. With the *real* (natural) rate being determined by productivity and thrift, monetary expansion will only raise *nominal* interest rates through inflationary expectations. Given the natural rate of interest there will also be a corresponding *natural rate of unemployment*. Monetary policy can only lead to transitory deviations from these natural rates, if capital and labour markets are efficient. There is little about credit markets in Friedman, or in his successors of the New Classical and Real Business cycle schools. As the current New Neoclassical synthesis is based on these models (with some twists of Keynesian 'imperfections'), but contains neither money nor finance, it is useless in explaining or providing cures for the current crisis.

Thus, though Hayek provides the best diagnosis of the cause of the current crisis, neither he nor Keynes provides an adequate explanation of the financial aspects of business cycles, assuming these are endogenous to the fluctuations in the real economy. It is Irving Fisher who provides the correct diagnosis of the nature and cures for the current crisis. Fisher saw a 'balance sheet recession' as an essential element in the Great Depression. He argued that, while there were many cyclical factors behind trade cycles, for Great Depressions the two dominant factors are '*over-indebtedness* to start with and *deflation* following soon after'. Like the Austrians he saw over-indebtedness was caused by 'easy money'. [273] This provides a succinct explanation of the current crisis and pointers to its cure. We have a Hayekian recession with Fisherian consequences. [274] I turn to examine the various means to deal with the crisis.

CENTRAL BANKS AND MONETARY POLICY

The first is monetary policy. The oldest central bank, the Bank of England, evolved over the centuries. With its notes becoming legal tender, it had two functions as the central banker: to maintain the purchasing power of its notes (monetary stability) and to ensure that the commercial deposit taking banks' deposit liabilities are always convertible into the legal tender at par (financial stability). [275] Inflation targeting by a central bank independent of political influence from the government (which has an incentive in democracies to use monetary policy to generate political business cycles) is now recognised as essential to maintain monetary stability. The Taylor rule provides a rough and ready guide to central banks to achieve this aim. As we have seen, it was the Greenspan put which neglected this rule, which led to the excessive growth in the US money supply, and was a proximate cause of the crisis.

The second part of the central bank's task to maintain financial stability is fulfilled in a crisis by following the rules Bagehot laid down in the nineteenth century in *Lombard Street* for dealing with a financial panic. The central bank should act as a lender of last resort to the commercial banks, by lending unlimited cash to a *solvent* but *illiquid* bank, at a penalty rate against good collateral. The Bank of England successfully followed these principles without any bank runs till the bank run on Northern Rock in September 2007. Its failure was in part due to the tripartite system which made the Bank of England independent with sole responsibility for maintaining monetary stability, while an independent Financial Services Authority and the Treasury were charged with maintaining financial stability. When the Northern Rock run started, the Central Bank with no knowledge of its balance sheet could not perform its traditional lender of last resort function. Instead, the bank was in effect nationalised with all the deposits protected, but with most of the shareholders wiped out. It turns out that the bank was illiquid and not insolvent.[276] The return of responsibility for financial stability to the Central Bank by the new Conservative–Lib Dem government is a move in the right direction, and should be able to avert similar panics in the future.

The US Federal Reserve, as Allan Meltzer's magisterial history shows, has by contrast:

in nearly a century of experience with financial failures
… never developed and announced a lender of last resort
policy. Sometimes it lets the institution fail: sometimes
it lends to keep it solvent. Failure to announce and
follow an explicit strategy increases uncertainty and
encourages troubled institutions to press for bailouts
at taxpayers' expense. The credit crisis after 2007 is the
latest example.[277]

This despite the fact that the Federal Reserve has recognised 'that it is the lender of last resort to the entire
financial system'[278].

The lender of last-resort role to provide liquidity to
solvent banks or to all financial institutions (as in the US)
would avoid financial panics. But what about the insolvent banks, and for the US (given the Federal Reserve's
extended lender of last-resort role) insolvent financial
institutions? They need to be closed down in an orderly
bankruptcy procedure. With the extension in 1991, by
the Federal Deposit Insurance Corporation Improvement
Act (FDICIA), of the FDIC's authority to cover even
solvent banks whose capital had been reduced – by
losses – below regulatory limits, and allowing them to be
merged or sold, a simple measure to maintain the financial
stability mandate would be to extend the FDICIA to *all*
financial institutions.

But, despite fulfilling the lender of last-resort function,
how can the central bank avoid the deflationary Fisherian
consequences of a financial crisis when – after the Hayekian
boom – deleveraging is required by most agents in the
economy? It has been claimed (most stridently by Paul
Krugman in his *New York Times* columns) that, once the

Central Bank has cut interest rates close to zero, it would face the fabled Keynesian liquidity trap,[279] and so the only recourse is to keep aggregate demand up through massive fiscal spending. Japan is cited as the prime example of a country which has been in such a trap with deflation and a stagnant economy since its asset price bubble burst in the early 1990s. But is this argument correct?

Central to answering this question is the transmission mechanism of monetary policy: whether monetary impulses work principally through changes in interest rates or through changes in broad money through the real balance effect which changes relative prices and net wealth. Meltzer shows clearly from charting the real interest rate against the growth of the real monetary base in the US from 1919 to 1951, that 'proposition one: when growth of real balances rises sharply, expansion follows whatever happens to the real interest rate... Proposition two: when real balances decline, or their growth is comparatively slow, the economy goes into recession even if the real interest rate is comparatively low or negative... Proposition three: if the real interest rate is comparatively high, the economy expands if real balances rise and does not expand if they fall.[280] So the transmission is from money to asset prices and inflation or deflation via the real balance effect and not through interest rates. If broad money expands, even with price deflation and hence rising real interest rates at the zero bound, the economy should expand.

Congdon, in examining the long Japanese deflationary episode, shows that it was due to concentrating inappropriately on the 'narrow' money definition of money, which the Central Bank controls through *money market* operations with the commercial banks.[281] If it had co-ordinated with the Ministry of Finance to expand broad money by *debt market* operations, it could have engineered an economic expansion even if there was deflation (of prices).

Ben Bernanke had clearly learned this lesson when he argued that the monetary authorities could always increase the broad money supply at a zero interest rate through 'unconventional' means, for which he was nicknamed Helicopter Ben. During the recent crisis he has fulfilled the pledge he made to Milton Friedman on his ninetieth birthday that he had learned the lesson of his great book with Anna Schwartz on the Great Depression, and through so-called 'quantitative easing' – which is a polite word for printing money – ensured the second leg of a Fisherian debt deflation did not take hold in the US. This has also been true of the Bank of England and the European Central Bank (ECB). The current worries are that these Central Banks will not be able to exit from 'quantitative easing' in time, before the inflationary consequences of their exploding balance sheets lead to inflation, and rising nominal interest rates on government debt, which would worsen the debt dynamics of the public sector. But by and large the 'liquidity trap' cited by the Keynesian fiscalists as leading to the impotence of monetary policy is a paper tiger.

FISCAL POLICY

For countries with a low or no structural deficit, raising aggregate demand in the face of a severe financial crisis by running a temporary budget deficit, above that resulting from automatic stabilisers, makes sense. This was the policy adopted by many of the emerging markets, notably India and China, and they have soon got back on to their high growth paths.

The US had an arguably unmanageable structural deficit. Moreover, the stimulus package it adopted in 2009 was a dog's breakfast and has failed to achieve its objectives. It failed to adopt the obvious means to restore household and firm balance sheets, by a massive across-the-board tax cut accompanied by an equivalent fiscal deficit. It is argued that most of this extra income will be saved, not spent. But this is to be bewitched by the wholly inappropriate Keynesian income–expenditure analysis, which fails to deal with balance sheets. If this Fisherian aftermath of a Hayekian recession is caused by attempts to reduce unsustainable debt, the 'savings' generated by the tax cut (i.e. reducing liabilities to the government[282]) will allow the necessary deleveraging, without a downward spiral in income and increased bankrupt-cies. By facilitating households to pay off their mortgage and credit card debts, it will prevent further impairment of bank assets. As the *Financial Times* reported, the parts of the Obama stimulus package that have worked were the 'fast acting tax breaks and transfer payments [which] largely explain why disposable income rose 2.9 per cent from January to May, even as earned income fell 0.7 per cent, allowing the savings rate to rise without a collapse in spending'.[283] If the whole of the $787 billion stimulus package had consisted of an across-the-board tax cut, there would have been a large deleveraging of the economy with an increase in private savings without an equivalent cut in private spending. The increased private savings being matched by public dis-savings would have been reflected in the increased budget deficit. Also the tax cut could be reversed once the economy recovered, providing an easy 'exit strategy' from the fiscal stimulus.[284]

This inept fiscal stimulus was then accompanied by the misguided health-care reforms which have added significantly to the US structural deficit. This has made any further fiscal stimulus politically impossible, while at the same time aggravating the problems with any further monetary actions through 'quantitative easing'. This makes a double-dip recession in the US more likely, if the extant monetary easing proves insufficient to give a nudge to the stalling economy.

In the UK, with a large structural deficit fuelled by increased welfare spending by the Labour government, there is little space for any further fiscal expansion. The new government is therefore right to create more fiscal space by a sharp cutback in public spending, by rolling back the unsustainable welfare state. But it has been wrong in keeping the 50 per cent tax on higher incomes instituted by the previous government, and also to raise VAT. If the spending cuts are made, they will give the Bank of England sufficient fiscal space to undertake further monetary easing through quantitative easing, if the need should arise.

Similarly in the eurozone, the ECB rightly undertook quantitative easing during the crisis while urging reduction of fiscal deficits. The success of Germany in following this advice, by reversing the stalling in its GDP, points to the success of this policy. The eurozone problems now concern financial stability related to the Greek debt crisis. As many of the banks in the non-Club Med members of the zone are exposed to Greek sovereign debt, a Greek debt default would lead to a serious eurozone banking crisis. To avoid this, an IMF-type stabilisation programme has been imposed on Greece by the ECB and IMF. But unlike similar stabilisation programmes in developing countries, two essential elements are missing: a large devaluation and a restructuring of the country's debt. The former is precluded by the fixed exchange rate of the euro, the latter by the external holdings of Greek sovereign debt by European banks. But the alternative imposed on Greece is a large *internal devaluation* to engineer a large fall in domestic wages and prices through a massive deflation. It is difficult to believe that Greek politics will allow the country to follow this path, particularly when even at its end Greece is likely to be left with a debt-GDP ratio of 150 per cent. A Greek default and exit from the euro seems the most likely outcome. The other Club Med countries should, however, be able to politically manage the fiscal retrenchment required in their less indebted economies.

FINANCIAL ENGINEERING

The story of financial engineering which created more and more complex debt instruments, in which tail risk was ignored, and was induced by the low interest rates during the Great Moderation, and exacerbated by the Greenspan put, is by now well known[285] and I will not labour it here. Two lessons, however, are important. First, it was the policy of the US government, ever since the Great Depression, to promote housing by giving implicit subsidies to homeowners through the financial system, which led to the sub-prime mortgage crisis. Second, it was the moral hazard begun with the LTCM bailout, and the subsequent bailouts of financial firms which were not commercial banks and whose bankruptcy did not threaten the deposit base – whose protection should be the sole public responsibility – which led to the mispricing of risk:

with financial intermediaries coming to believe that if their increasingly risky bets were successful they stood to make immense financial gains, and if they turned sour the authorities would get taxpayers to bail them out.

These distortions in the US financial system were then internationalised by the asset-backed securities which increasingly came to be held by banks around the world. By packaging a host of different securities including subprime mortgages into increasingly opaque securities, in the belief that this diversification of the assets in each security basket would lower the risk of holding the security, they made them even more insecure. It was like packaging different types of meat into pies and selling them around the world. When then it turned out that there was an infected piece of meat which had been baked into many of the pies, none of the holders of the pies around the world knew if their pies contained the infected meat. All interbank lending based on these opaque asset-backed securities ceased, and a global financial crisis was triggered.

The immediate official response to the crisis, in which the insurer AIG was bailed out, which then led it to fully repay its counterparties like Goldman Sachs, bailing them out in turn, only justified the beliefs of those who had undertaken the imprudent lending that any losses would be borne by taxpayers. Moral hazard increased even further. It was further accentuated with the classification of institutions as being 'too big to fail', and has given an incentive for the creation of even larger universal banks 'too big to fail'. With the authorities egging on the conversion of previous investment banks into bank holding companies, the US financial structure has become even more oligopolistic.

Much worse, the recently passed Dodd–Frank Wall

Street Reform and Consumer Protection Act now formalises the Federal Reserve's role in being the supervisor and lender of last resort of the whole US banking system, which is opposite to the classical liberal view that, once investment and commercial banking are kept separate (because it is politically impossible to end deposit insurance) the Central Bank should have nothing to do with the investment banking part. This should be allowed to follow whatever innovations and risk taking it chooses in competitive markets, but it must be made to bear the full costs of any mistakes it makes.

By contrast, as Peter Wallison of the American Enterprise Institute has argued, all 'financial firms will, under this new structure, inevitably be subordinated to the supervisory judgements about what the firms can safely be allowed to do... Where financial firms once focused on beating their competitors, they will now focus on currying favour with their regulator, which will have the power to control their every move. What may ultimately emerge is a partnership between the largest financial firms and the Federal Reserve – a partnership in which the Fed protects them from failure and excessive competition and they in turn curb their competitive instincts to carry out the government's policies and directions'.[286] In short, it is likely to substitute a sclerotic corporatist economic model, replacing the highly competitive and innovative model which, despite its flaws, has brought untold prosperity around the world.

THE ENTITLEMENT ECONOMIES

The financial crisis has ultimately been caused, like so many past crises,[287] by the particular country's past dirigisme.

Most government interventions in the economy are equivalent to taxes and subsidies. The implicit or explicit subsidies create politically determined income streams for various favoured groups which then have to be paid for by others through implicit or explicit taxes, with governments naturally favouring implicit taxes which cannot be easily monitored by the geese to be fleeced. But in time the expansion of these entitlements leads to tax resistance and a fiscal-cum-debt crisis.

In the case of the US subprime mortgages, which were the proximate cause of the crisis, there has been a commitment by the government since the Great Depression that home ownership should be increased. Apart from the explicit subsidy given by the tax deductibility of mortgage interest, the various government-sponsored enterprises (GSEs) like the Freddie mortgage twins, and various government mandates to the banking system to finance loans to the 'poor', were used to provide implicit subsidies to homeowners. The insolvent GSEs were then taken over by the government and their losses are to be borne by taxpayers. There has been no reform of these entitlements to housing. If they are to continue it would be best to make the subsidy given through the GSEs explicit through the budget.

But, ultimately these entitlements, which are explicit in the welfare states of Europe, are becoming unsustainable, as the current travail of Greece shows vividly. They inevitably lead to a fiscal crisis and a debt crisis whose resolution ultimately requires rescinding these politically determined entitlements. The UK has now bit this particular bullet. Greece and other Club Med countries are being made to do so by their actual or incipient fiscal crises.

The US, however, is still in denial. Instead of rescinding past politically determined entitlements particularly to health care, which the US comptroller general David Walker in August 2007 saw as the main cause of its unsustainable structural deficit of $500 billion at the time,[288] Obama has enlarged the entitlement with his misguided health-care bill. So the projected deficit is now in the trillions. As Walker emphasised, the incipient fiscal crisis (even with the smaller deficit in 2007) could not be cured by growing out of the problem, eliminating earmarks, wiping out fraud, ending the Iraq (and Afghan) wars or cutting defense expenditures, restraining discretionary expenditure spending, or letting the Bush tax cuts expire. The very policies Obama is hoping for will reverse exploding future deficits. Thus not only is the current US financial crisis not solved, the seeds are there for future – even more serious – crises.

CONCLUSIONS

My conclusions can be brief. First, to avoid future crises the entitlement economies which currently dominate advanced economies need to be tamed if not dismantled. Second, as long as deposit insurance remains, a separation between commercial banks which can create deposits, and investment banks which can gamble with these deposits in a 'universal' bank at taxpayers' expense, must be created.[289] Third, the investment banks should be free to take whatever risks they want without any possible bailout by the authorities. In the US, the orderly closure of failed and failing institutions should be done by the FDIC. Fourth, for the commercial banking part of the financial system the Bagehot rule for the lender of last-resort function of central banks should be formally established and publicised. Fifth, for the monetary stability part of their mandate central banks should monitor and control the broad money supply to mitigate booms and slumps. This in essence is the classical liberal perspective on dealing with financial crises, which will always recur.

The text of the XXIV Fulvio Guerrini lecture, held by Deepak Lal at the Centro Einaudi in Turin on 8 September 2010: an analysis of the causes, consequences and remedies to the crisis, from a classical liberal perspective.

NOTES

1   See Walters, A., *Britain's Economic Renaissance: Margaret Thatcher's Reforms 1979-1984*, Oxford University Press, USA, 1986.

2   Lal, D., *The Limits of International Cooperation, Twentieth Wincott Memorial Lecture, Occasional Paper 83* (1990), Institute of Economic Affairs. Reprinted in Lal, D., *Against Dirigisme*, ICS Press, San Francisco, 1994.

3   Lal, D. and Myint, H., *The Political Economy of Poverty, Equity and Growth: A Comparative Study*, Clarendon Press, Oxford, 1996.

4   Lal, D. *Fighting Fiscal Privilege*, Social Market Foundation Paper No. 7 (1990), reprinted in Lal, D., *Against Dirigisme*, ICS Press, San Francisco, 1994.

5   This was published as Lal, D., 'The Great Crash of 2008: Causes and Consequences', *Cato Journal*, vol. 30, no. 2, pp. 265–77.

6   Krantz, O., *Economic growth and Economic Policy in Sweden in the 20th Century: A Comparative Perspective*, Ratio Work Paper No. 32, London, 2004.

7   Bacon and Eltis have shown this to be the central cause of the UK's economic decline in the 1960s and 1970s, though stalled and partially reversed by the Thatcher reforms of the 1980s. See Bacon, R. and Eltis, W., *Britain's Economic Problem: Too Few Producers* London, 1976.

8   This is not an essential assumption; the platforms could be announced simultaneously. See Brennan, G. and Buchanan, J., *The Power To Tax*, Cambridge 1980, pp. 20–23 for a fuller discussion. They also derive the set of taxes based on classical liberal principles which would limit predation by the state.

9   In any given week there are advertisements for the myriad of local authority jobs advertised weekly in *The Guardian*, so that one group or other of welfare workers can deal with perceived social exclusion.

10 Burke, E. 'Speech to the Electors of Bristol' in Payne, J., (ed.), *Selected Workes of Edmund Burke*, vol. iv (Indianapolis) 1774 (1999).

11 Rauch, J., *Demosclerosis: The Silent Killer of American Government*, New York, 2004.

12 Zakaria, F., *The Future of Freedom*, New York, 2003.

13 The Thatcher reforms which curbed the power of trade unions and dismantled the vast panoply of nationalised industries illustrate the point.

14 This cycle of economic repression, crisis and reform was observed during the mercantilist period as documented in Eli Heckscher's magisterial book *Mercantilism*. See Lal, D., *The Political Economy of Economic Liberalization*, World Bank Economic Review, vol. 1, no. 2, 1987, pp. 273–99. Lal, D. and Myint, H., *The Political Economy of Poverty, Equity and Growth – a comparative study*, Oxford, 1996.

15 Caricatured by Carlisle's phrase 'anarchy plus the constable', or by Lasalles's simile of the night watchman.

16 Robbins, L., *The Theory of Economic Policy in English Classical Political Economy*, London, 1952.

17 Keynes J. M., *The End of Laissez-Faire*, London, 1926, pp 46–47.

18   Smith, A., *The Theory of Moral Sentiments*, Indianapolis, 1982/1759, pp. 184–5.

19   The 'Washington Consensus' was the term coined by Williamson to describe the policy package which had emerged as best able to promote efficient poverty alleviating growth as a result of the experience of developing countries in the 1970s and 1980s. It is close to that advocated by A. C. Harberger, as constituting the best technocratic advice based on experience. It is also the one emerging from the Lal–Myint study of twenty-five developing countries. Recently Williamson has sought to disown it partly as the anti-globalisation backlash has used it, particularly in Latin America, as the whipping horse in its denouncement of what it calls the 'neo-liberal' policies adopted in Latin America. But, as Mario Vargas Llosa has argued, there are hardly any countries in Latin America, apart from Chile, who have in fact adopted the full package, and hence to announce its failure on the half-baked liberalisation attempts in many countries is rather premature. T. N. Srinivasan rightly takes Williamson to task for his partial recantation. See Williamson, J., 'What Washington means by Policy Reform' in Williamson, J., (ed.), *Latin America Adjustment: How Much Has Happened?*, Peterson Institute for International Economics, 1990; Harberger, A.C., *World Economic Growth*, San Francisco, 1984; Llosa, M. V., 'Liberalism in the new millennium', in Vasquez, I. (ed.), *Global Fortune*, Washington D. C., 2000; Srinivasan, T. N., 'The Washington Consensus a decade later: ideology and the art and science of policy advice', *World Bank Research Observer*, vol. 15, no. 2, 2000, pp. 265–70.

20   Hayek, F. A., *The Constitution of Liberty*, Routledge and Paul, London, 1960, p. 402.

21   See the discussion in Lal, D. and Myint, H., *The Political Economy of Poverty, Equity and Growth*, Oxford University Press, USA, 1996.

22   In Lal, D., *Nationalised Universities – paradox of the privatisation age*, London, 1989, I have outlined how this can be done

for higher education in the UK, and in Lal, D., *A Premium on Health: A National Health Insurance Scheme*, London, 2001, how the NHS can be reformed in line with these principles.

23   Keynes, J. M., *The End of Laissez-Faire*, London, 1926.

24   Eichengreen, B., *Globalizing Capital*, Princeton, N.J., 1996.

25   As discussed by Berlin, I., *Two concepts of Liberty*, in *Four Essays on Liberty*, Oxford Paperbacks, Oxford, 1969.

26   See Sen, A. K., *Development as Freedom*, Oxford Paperbacks, Oxford, 1999 and Sugden, R., 'A review of 'Inequality reexamined' by Amartya Sen', *Journal of Economic Literature*, vol. 31, no. 4, 1993.

27   De Jasay, A., *Before Resorting to Politics*, Edward Elgar Publishing, Aldershot, 1996, p. 23.

28   If, as is usually the case, there is no clear boundary to the possible harms a particular action could cause, it will be impossible to prove that a feasible action is harmless. Similarly with obligations (which confer corresponding rights), it will be impossible to prove that some right has not been violated. In the common law tradition the *prosecutor* has to prove that, in pursuing a particular action, the defendant has violated obligations or caused harm to others. In the continental law tradition it is for the *defendant* to prove that he has not violated *any* right or caused *any* possible harm.

29   See Nozick, R., *Anarchy, State and Utopia*, Oxford, 1974, p. 92. De Jasay's position on rights is different from R. Nozick. One of the senses in which Nozick uses rights: 'rights that is permissions to do something and obligations on others not to interfere'. De Jasay rightly notes: 'rights are not permissions but claims for performance by another. Yet liberties are not permissions either; if they were they would be most confusingly misnamed. Who would be competent to grant permissions and on what authority?' He also contests Nozick's position on property rights.

30   De Jasay, *Before Resorting to Politics*, Aldershot, 1996, p.30.

31   Minogue, K., 'The history of the idea of Human Rights', in Laqueur, W. and Rubin, B., (eds) *The Human Rights Reader*,

New York, 1979, pp. 14–15.

32 Hart, H., 'Are there any Natural Rights?' in Quinton, A., (ed.) *Political Philosophy*, Oxford, 1967.

33 Isaiah Berlin refers to human rights as 'a frontier of freedom' which no one is allowed to cross (p. 165). But as Little rightly notes: 'an infinite list of rights is not as convincing as a frontier. The frontier is properly constituted by the quite limited list of things that one may not do to human beings.'

34 But as there are an infinite number of such 'rights', it will be impossible to delineate them all, which would give rise to endless legalistic disputes.

35 De Jasay, *Before Resorting to Politics*, Aldershot, 1996, p.51.

36 Coase, R. H., 'The Nature of the Firm', *Economica*, n.s.4, 1937. The existence of corporations depends upon there being various contracts which cannot be specified at arm's length. Because workers acquire various skills which are specific to the firm through on-the-job training, this form of firm-specific capital is of value to the firm but not the worker, who cannot cash them my moving to another firm. These firm-specific skills are to be distinguished from the general skills acquired from on-the-job training, which can be marketed outside the firm. Because of the importance of firm-level skills there will have to be a more permanent relationship between employer and employee than the arm's length transactions of a spot market for labour. This means that the employer will now have to incur the policing type of transactions costs in monitoring workers to see that they are not shirking. This would require the hierarchical organisation of firms. As part of this task the employer may choose various forms of contracts with the workers which could include 'co-determination', like having workers on boards of companies. But given the diversity of conditions faced by different firms, in a free market, the types of contracts will be varied, including the types advocated by promoters of 'stakeholder capitalism'. What would go against the functioning of the free market was if a particular type of contract, viz. the

stakeholder type, was forced on all employers by legislative *fiat*.

37 This can be seen as part of the set of feasible actions they can take, based on the offer made by the strong, which does not infringe the rules of justice that the owner is free to dispose of his endowment as long as he does not violate the constraints of harm and obligation.

38 Lal, D. and Myint, H., *The Political Economy of Poverty, Equity and Growth*, Oxford University Press, USA, 1996.

39 These set of optimum taxes were derived by Frank Ramsey, a Cambridge mathematician, as the formal answer to a puzzle set for him in the 1920s by A. C. Pigou. What set of taxes would minimise loss of welfare to raise a *given* revenue? Ramsey's answer was that the optimum pattern of taxation was to impose higher taxes on goods for which (in economists' jargon) the price elasticity of demand was low – like cigarettes and alcohol. Imposing such taxes would reduce the excess burden (in terms of loss of consumers' surplus) associated with raising a given revenue. The explanation: suppose that there are two goods: cigarettes, for which price elasticity is low, so that when their price rises, consumption does not drop substantially; and restaurant meals, for which the price elasticity is high, so that an equivalent percentage increase in their price reduces their consumption substantially. As a welfare measure of the loss of satisfaction to consumers depends on the reduction in the quantity of goods consumed induced by the price rise, the tax on cigarettes will involve a lower loss of consumer satisfaction than a tax yielding equivalent revenue on restaurant meals.

40 It is Ramsey's optimal tax, because the tax yield from any given ad valorem tax on cigarettes in inelastic demand will be greater than an equivalent tax on restaurant meals with an elastic demand. Because of their addiction smokers will find the tax on cigarettes inescapable, while consumers of restaurant meals, being more easily able to reduce their consumption, can escape the tax.

41   See http://www.hm-treasury.gov.uk./media/CFA/92/foi_flat-tax010805.pdf

42   Mill, J. S., *On Liberty*, Everyman's Library, London, 1859/1910.

43   Marx, K., 'Critique of The Gotha Programme', in Marx, K. and Engels, F., *Selected Works*, Moscow, vol. 3, 1970, pp. 9–30, p. 19.

44   With an exchange rate of $1.5 = £1.0, the sum is £950 per family member.

45   'Uncertain benefits of health contracting', *Financial Times*, Letters, 7 August, 2000.

46   'A private remedy for public ills', *Financial Times*, A Personal View, 21 July, 2000.

47   '"Command and control" will not deliver better health care', *Financial Times*, Letters, 14 August, 2000.

48   I have dealt with these theoretical economic issues in my 'The role of the public sectors in health financing in developing countries', HRO Working Paper no. 33, The World Bank, June 1994, reprinted in Lal, D., *Unfinished Business*, Oxford University Press, Oxford, 1999.

49   The reasons for the uninsured in the US health system is due to the tax subsidy to employers' health plans, which was granted during the period of wartime wage and price controls. Employers sought to get around the wage freeze by offering health insurance benefits to employees. The Internal Revenue Service went along – granting business a tax deduction and excluding the fringe benefits from employee incomes. Subsequently, given these tax advantages, most health insurance in the US is provided by employers, which leaves those without large and generous employers having to depend on self-insurance, or much more costly private insurance. See Green, D., *Challenge to the NHS – A Study of Competition in American Health Care and the Lessons for Britain*, Hobart Paperback 23, London, Institute of Economic Affairs, 1986; Goodman, J. C., and Musgrave, G. L., *Patient Power: Solving America's Health Care Crisis*, Washington DC, Cato Institute, 1992.

50   Feachem, R. G. A., Sekhri, N. K. and White, K. L., 'Getting More For Their Dollar: A Comparison of the UK's NHS with California's Kaiser Permanente', *British Medical Journal*, 19 January 2002, pp. 135–41.

51   See Hayek, F. A., *The Constitution of Liberty*, Routledge and Paul, London, 1960, for some of the arguments.

52   It was reported in the Press that when Mr Baker visited the USSR his opposite number quipped that while Mr Baker was centralising power, *he* was looking for methods of decentralisation.

53   See Carswell, J., *Government and the Universities in Britain*, Cambridge University Press, 1985, for an excellent discussion of the power of this motive which fuelled the desire for the expansion of higher education in the 1960s and 1970s, a movement that was largely led by the 'red brick' universities.

54   *The Times*, 6 January 1989.

55   Mill, J. S., *On Liberty*, Everyman's Library, London, p. 161.

56   *Higher Education – Meeting the Challenge*, Cm. 114, HMSO, April 1987, p. 1–2.

57   Maddison, A., *Phases of Capitalist Development*, Oxford University Press, Oxford, 1982, p. 110–111.

58   See Lal, D., *The Poverty of Development Economics*, Hobart Paperback No. 16, Institute of Economic Affairs, London, 1983.

59   From recently leaked papers, it appears that it was the Treasury and not the DES which has sought to use manpower planning to determine the demand for higher education. See the report in *The Times* by Sam Kiley, 'Rift over the Allocation of Funds', Tuesday 1 November 1988 p.2. It is unclear whether the Treasury believes in manpower planning or is using its professed faith merely as a tactical device to contain public spending on higher education.

60   From a transcript of an unscripted talk by Robert Jackson: 'Policy Funding for Higher Education', 17–18 March, Churchill College, Cambridge, distributed as Appendix 2 to Marris, R., 'How to Measure Performance Genuinely',

paper for LSE Suntory-Toyota Conference on 'Funding
and Management of British Higher Education', 20
September 1988.

61   Centre for Policy Studies, London, 1988.

62   According to the Social Science Citation Index which begins
in 1966, Muth's paper, published in 1961, had the following
number of citations: 1966–5; 1967–3; 1968–2; 1969–2; 1970–
4; 1971–2; 1972–9; 1973–10; 1974–10; 1975–20; 1976–33;
1977–41; 1978–47; 1979–44; 1980–71; 1981–56; 1982–74.
As Donald McKloskey, from whose book *The Rhetoric of
Economics*, University of Wisconsin Press, 1985 (p.87), these
figures are taken, notes on this 'sleeper': 'There was a tiny flash
and long afterwards a boom'.

63   Hayek, *The Constitution of Liberty*, p.383.

64   See Carswell, op. cit, p. 132 and following.

65   Most recently by Sir Peter Swynnerton Dyer, the last chairman of the UGC and the chief executive of the new UFC.

66   Thus, writing in 1964, Lord Robbins said, 'I have little doubt
that, as time goes on and the advantages of higher education
are more generally perceived and the burdens of financing
its expansion are more severely felt, there may easily come a
change in public attitudes such that the equitable arguments
for a considerable replacement of grants by loans will become
practically relevant', in his *The University in the Modern World*,
Macmillan, London, 1966, p.30.

67   Carswell, op. cit. p. 113.

68   See the report in *The Times* Higher Educational Supplement,
28 October 1988, p. 11.

69   Marx, K., *Communist Manifesto*, London, 1848.

70   *Constitution of Liberty*, op. cit. p. 388.

71   See for instance: Barnes, J. and Barr, N., 'Strategies for
Higher Education', paper at LSE Suntory-Toyota conference, op. cit. 10.

72   In economist's jargon they may be highly risk-averse. This may
not matter in itself, as different degrees of risk-aversion are like
differences in tastes. But if, because of this, highly risk-averse

children from poorer backgrounds do not enter higher education the 'cycle' of deprivation which may be a social concern
could be perpetuated.

73 We assume that the student would have to maintain him or
herself in any case even if they did not go to university, so this
element in the 'costs' of the two alternatives nets out.

74 It may be objected that on a similar line of argument, given
the existence of a capital gains tax, there is a case for the
public subsidisation of shares and stocks, as the general public
benefits through the tax on the capital gains on these equities.
This argument, of course, shows why the capital gains tax is
a bad tax, and is an argument against it, and not against the
proposal in the text. For even on grounds of ideal taxation,
there would be a place for an income tax – with some progressivity – to fund essential public goods such as defence and the
legal system. With such an income tax, the above argument
for some grant element in student financing would hold.

75 See Becker, G. S., 'Why the Candidates are Missing the Point
on College Costs', *Business Week,* 14 November 1988.

76 The Barnes-Barr proposal is also more open-ended, as given
their redistributive predilections they at times suggest using
their repayments scheme as a redistributive device. Also, as
has been pointed out most recently by the Institute of Fiscal
Studies, NICs are a bad tax. It would be preferable to eliminate
them. The income tax system, despite the Inland Revenue's
resistance, could be used as the repayment mechanism.

77 This pamphlet in part is based on Lal, D., 'The World
Economy at the end of the millennium' in Mueller, J. (ed.),
Prosperity, Politics and Peace, Westview Press, New York, 1999
and Lal, D., 'The Euro', *Intercom* 21 (ISOP, UCLA), 1999.

78 See Lal, D., 'Participation, Markets and Democracy' in
Lundahl, M. and Nudulu, B. J. (eds), *New Directions in
Development Economics*, Routledge, London, 1996 and Lal,
D., 'Unintended Consequences: the impact of factor endow-
ments, culture and politics on long run economic perform-
ance', *The Ohlin lectures*, MIT Press, 1998.

79 See Rosecrance, R., *The Rise of the Trading State*, Basic Books, New York, 1986, for the first and Rosecrance, R., 'The Virtual State', *Foreign Affairs*, 1996, for the second of these points.

80 This dispute is particularly ridiculous. We are now told some butterflies are at threat from the pollen of GM maize which attacks their caterpillars. Part of the reason for genetic modifications of food crops is to make them resistant to pests. Caterpillars which feed on shoots clearly damage the crop. To say that they have greater rights to survive than the people who will benefit from the GM maize is yet another example of the politically correct eco-fundamentalism so prevalent today in the West. See Lal, D., 'Eco-Fundamentalism', *International Affairs*, vol. 71, 1995, pp. 515–28 for a critique of this latest fad. It should also be noted that the Green Revolution which has changed the prospects of the South feeding its burgeoning population is based on genetically modified crops. If these are to be banned because of Green sensitivities it will condemn a large part of human kind to starvation and poverty. This underlines the immorality and frivolity of the latest EU position.

81 Bergsten notes: 'The EU accounts for about 31 per cent of world output and 20 per cent of world trade. The US provides about 27 per cent of global production and 18 per cent of world trade. The dollar's 40–60 per cent of world finance far exceeds the economic weight of the US. The total also exceeds the share of 10–40 per cent for the European national currencies combined' ('The Dollar and the Euro', *Foreign Affairs*, no. 76, pp. 83–95, 1996). Fortes and Rey (1998) state that: 'the dollar is used in 83 per cent of two way transactions in foreign exchange markets... In 1992 48 per cent of world exports were invoiced in dollars, 15 per cent in DM, 18 per cent in other European currencies, and only 5 per cent in yen' (pp. 311–12). Rogoff concludes that based on various estimates about '40–50 per cent of US currency is held abroad' in the underground economy, a large part of which is related to

drugs – see Rogoff, K., 'Blessing or curse? Foreign and underground demand for Euro notes', *Economic Policy*, vol. 13, no. 26, 1998, pp. 261–303.

82   For instance, Kindleberger, C. P., *The World in Depression, 1929–1939*, University of California Press, Berkeley, 1973.

83   Portes and Rey estimate that the seigniorage derived by the US from the use of the dollar as an international currency is about 0.2 per cent of its GDR. By contrast the purported savings in transactions costs of converting one European money into another are likely to be trivially small. The oft-repeated experiment of a traveller taking a fixed sum in one currency and then converting into other European currencies in local foreign exchange bureaux ignores the fact that only a moron would now do this. As any well-travelled teenager will tell you, they should carry a piece of plastic which gives them local currency and bills them in their home currency at the market rate without incurring any of these costs of 'dealing'. See Portes, R., and Rey, H., 'The emergence of the Euro as an international currency', *Economic Policy*, vol. 13, no. 26, 1998, pp. 307–43.

84   See Charles Wyplosz (esp. pp 8-10) for a summary of the studies which have tried to see if empirically the EU meets the optimum currency criteria. Of the three criteria, openness to mutual trade, the diversification of individual economies and mobility of inputs particularly labour over the area, the evidence on the first two is ambiguous, but it clearly shows that on the third criterion of labour mobility, Europe is not an optimal currency area compared with the US, (Wyplosz, C., 'EMU: Why and how it might happen', *Journal of Economic Perspectives*, vol. 11, no. 4, 1997, pp. 3–22).

85   See Feldstein, M., 'The political economy of the European Economic and Monetary Union: Political sources of an economic liability', *Journal of Economic Perspectives*, vol. 11, no. 4, 1997, pp. 23–42 and 'EMU and international conflict', *Foreign Affairs* 76: 60–73, 1997.

86   That it is the Holy Roman Empire which is being

reconstructed is shown by the reluctance of many EU member states to grant Muslim Turkey and the Orthodox Slav states full membership of the EU.

87 For a critical discussion of regulation and how it has replaced planning as the chief method of current dirigisme, as well as ways to escape it, see Lal, D., 'From Planning to Regulation: towards a new Dirigisme?' *Cato Journal* 17, 1998, pp. 211–27.

88 See Wolf, M., *The resistible rise of Fortress Europe.* London: Centre for Policy Studies, Trade Policy Unit, Rochester Paper No. 1, 1994, for such an interpretation of EU trade policy.

89 Lal, D. and Myint, H., *The Political Economy of Poverty, Equity and Growth: A Comparative Study*, Clarendon Press, Oxford, 1996.

90 In case you think 'dinosaur' is a pejorative word, those of you with young children in the last ten years will know they will not agree as they look upon dinosaurs with as much affection as their kittens and dogs.

91 See Judt, T., 'The social question redivivus', *Foreign Affairs* 76, 1997, pp. 95–117.

92 See Lal, D., *The Poverty of Development Economics*, London: IEA, 1987, 2nd edn 1997, for these old debates on trade and development.

93 See Lal, D., 'Taxation and regulation as barriers to international investment flows', *Journal des Economistes et des Etudes Humaines* 9, 1999, pp.3–29, for evidence on the size of this 'virtual' production.

94 This is called the Stolper–Samuelson theorem in international economics. There is an ongoing and unsettled debate amongst economists whether the current wage trends in the US and other developed countries are due to the growing economic integration promoted by the current LIEO, in particular of the low-wage and abundant-labour countries of Asia, or due to technological changes. See Feenstra, R., 'Integration of trade and disintegration of production in the global economy', *Journal of Economic Perspectives* 12, 1998, pp. 31–50.

In my judgement it is likely to be a bit of both, with it

being very difficult empirically to assign the relative shares to these two increasingly complementary forces. The empirical evidence on the effects of the income distribution effects of the ninetenth century LIEO is in Williamson, J. G., 'Globalization, Labour Markets and Policy Backlash in the Past', *Journal of Economic Perspectives* 14, 1998, pp. 51–72.

95 See Rogowski, R., *Commerce and Coalitions*, Princeton University Press, Princeton, NJ, 1989 for this 'factor-price' explanation of changing trade policies in the nineteenth century.

96 See Harris, R., *Murder a Cigarette*, Duckworth, London, 1998.

97 See Tren, R. and High, I. I, 'Smoked out', *IEA Working Papers*, Institute of Economic Affairs, London, 2000.

98 See Lal, D., 'Up in smoke', *Business Standard*, 2 September 1999.

99 See Lal, D., *The Hindu Equilibrium*, Clarendon Press, Oxford, 1998 and Lal, D. and Myint, H., *The Political Economy of Poverty, Equity and Growth*.

100 Harberger, A. C., 'Neutral Taxation', *The New Palgrave* 3, 1987, pp. 645–7.

101 Chaloupka and Warner provide a comprehensive survey though with an irritating politically correct 'spin' of the economics of smoking, which provides references to this literature. The reason for the spin becomes clear when it is noted that Chaloupka is credited as the co-leader of the team which produced the World Bank report! See Chaloupka, F., J., and Warner, K., E., 'The economics of smoking', NBER Working Paper No. 7047, NBER, Cambridge, Mass, 1999. For the illogicalities in the attempts made to provide some quantifiable measure of the closely related QALYs (quality of life years) and DALYs (disability adjusted life years) saved by various medical interventions see Broome, J., 'QALYS', *Journal of Public Economics* 50, 1993, pp. 149–67.

102 See Lal, D., 'Up in smoke', *Business Standard*, 2 September 1999.

103 See Lal, D. and Myint, H., *The Political Economy of Poverty, Equity and Growth.*

104 Viscusi, K., *Smoking,* Oxford University Press, New York, 1992.

105 Buchanan, J. and Stubblebine, W. C., 'Externality', *Economica* no. 29, 1962, pp. 371–84.

106 The judgement is given in full in Gori and Luik and provides a devastating critique of this report. Gori, G. B., and Luik, J. C., *Passive smoke,* Fraser Institute, Vancouver, 1999.

107 The biological reason for this is that many toxins are beneficial in small doses, e.g. toning up the immune system through immunisation, sec Neese, R. M. and Williams, G. C., *Why We Get Sick,* Times Books, New York, 1995.

108 Pareto-relevant externalities are sometimes called 'technological' externalities which are not mediated through (the price mechanism, in contrast with Pareto-irrelevant externalities also called 'pecuniary' which are so mediated; see Buchanan and Stubblebine, 'Externality'.

109 It writes: 'Other direct costs' to non-smokers 'include irritation and nuisance from smoke'.

110 See Elias, N., *The Civilising Process,* Pantheon, New York, 1978.

111 Viscusi, W. K., *Smoking,* Oxford University Press, USA, 1993.

112 See the references to these studies in Chaloupka and Warner, though for the reason given earlier their assessment of these studies is dubious.

113 Chaloupka, F. J. and Warner, K. E., 'The economics of smoking'.

114 World Bank, *Curbing the Epidemic,* World Bank, Washington DC, 1999.

115 Mill, J. S., *On Liberty,* pp.72–73.

116 Douglas Jay in 1937 cited in T. E.B. Howarth: *Prospect and Reality: Great Britain 1945-1955,* Collins, London, 1985, p. 30.

117 Le Fanu, J., *The Rise and Fall of Modern Medicine,* HarperCollins, London, 1998.

118   Cox, R. *Am J Physics*, vol. 14, no. 1, 1946.

119   See Matthews, R. A. I., 'Statistical snake-oil'. *Prospect*, November 1998.

120   *British Medical Journal*, vol. 315, no. 629, 1997.

121   *Int Arch Occup Environmental Health*, vol. 7, 1998, pp. 379–90.

122   Gori, G. B. and Luik, J. C., *Passive Smoke*, The Fraser Institute, Vancouver, 1999.

123   Doll, R. and Peto, R., 'The causes of cancer: quantitative estimates of avoidable risks of cancer in the United States today', *Journal of the National Cancer Institute*, vol. 66, 1981, pp. 1191–308.

124   Rothman, K. J., *Modern Epidemiology*, Little Brown, Boston, 1986, p. 17.

125   Gori, G. B., 'Epidemiology and public health: Is a new paradigm needed or a new ethic?', *Clin Epidemiol* 51, 1998, pp. 637–41.

126   See Le Fanu, *The Rise and Fall of Modern Medicine* and Lal, D., 'Hearts and minds', *Business Standard*, 7 October and 'Statistical witchcraft', *Business Standard*, 4 November, 1999.

127   In this context it should be noted that there is now conclusive evidence that peptic ulcers which were supposed to be caused by stress in certain personality types are now known to be caused by the Helicobacter bacillus, while there is growing evidence that heart disease is due to a new strain of the bacterium Chlamydia, (see Le Fanu, 1998) While the two massive trials of heart disease in the US (the MRFIT study) and Europe in which an 'intervention' group was made to change its lifestyle, unlike a control group, which continued to live its rotten lifestyle, have finally exploded this lifestyle view of heart disease. The results showed that for every 1,000 subjects in the intervention group 41 died of a heart attack while for every 1,000 in the control group 40 died! (Ebrahim, S., *British Medical Journal*, vol. 314, 1997). As Le Fanu (1998) explains, the social and dietary theory of disease is doomed to failure as the body's mechanisms are like a thermostat, so that changing the *exterieur* (e.g. the amount and type of food consumed)

will not change the *milieu interieur*, the physiological functions, such as the level of cholesterol.

128   See Schelling, T. C., 'Egonomies, or the art of self-management', *American Economic Review* 68, 1978, pp. 290–94.

129   See, for example, Houthakker, H. and Taylor, L., *Consumer
demand in the United States 1929-1970*, Harvard University
Press, Cambridge, Mass, 1966.

130   See Becker, G. and Murphy, K., 'A Theory of Rational
Addiction', *Journal of Political Economy*, 96, 1988, pp.
675–700, and Becker, G., Grossman, M., Murphy, K.,
'An Empirical Analysis of Cigarette Addiction', *American
Economic Review* 84, 1994, pp. 396–418.

131   A good which is a 'complement' with another is one for which
the demand increases/decreases for both goods together, when
the price of one falls/rises. This contrasts with goods which are
'substitutes' where the demand for a good rises as that for the
other good falls with a rise in its price.

132   Manning, W. G. et al., 'The taxes of sin', *JAMA* 261, 1989,
pp. 1604–9.

133   See Gori, G. B. and Mantel, N., 'Mainstream and environmental tobacco smoke', *Regul Toxicol Pharmacol* 14, 1991,
pp. 88–105.

134   Squire, L. and van der Tak, I. I., *Economic analysis of projects*,
Johns Hopkins, Baltimore, 1975.

135   Lal, D., *The Poverty of 'Development Economics'*, Institute of
Economic Affairs, London, 2nd ed. 1997, referencing Streeten,
P., *Development Perspectives*, 1981, Macmillan, London.

136   Lal, D., *The Poverty of 'Development Economics'*, Institute of
Economic Affairs, London, 2nd ed. 1997, p. 104

137   See Dangerfield, G., *The Strange Death of Liberal England*,
Stanford University Press, Stanford CA, 1935.

138   Hirshleifer, J., *The Dark Side of the Force: Economic Foundations
of Conflict Theory*, Cambridge University Press, Cambridge,
2001.

139   The Royal Navy, which created and maintained the British
Empire, was itself the result of the state-sponsored pirates who

had previously raided the Spanish Main. See Herman, A., *To Rule the Waves*, HarperCollins, New York, 2004.

140 See McNeill, W. H., *The Human Condition*, Princeton University Press, Princeton, NJ, 1980.

141 The distinction between the material and cosmological beliefs of a culture is outlined and discussed in Lal, D., *Unintended Consequences*, MIT Press, Cambridge, MA, 1998. The former are concerned with ways of making a living, the latter with, in Plato's words, 'how one should live'.

142 This implied a rise in per capita income based on the Smithian gains from trade. But it was bounded because the ancient agrarian economies depended upon a fixed factor of production – land. The Industrial Revolution converted these agrarian economies into mineral energy economies which were no longer bounded by land but could use the near-unlimited stock of fossil fuels for energy. This unleashed modern economic growth which allows a sustainable and continuous rise in per capita income. These two forms of *intensive* (with rising per capita incomes) are to be distinguished from *extensive* growth (where output grows pari passu with population, leaving per capita income unchanged), which has been ubiquitous through human history. See Lal, D., 'Unintended Consequences: the impact of factor endowments, culture and politics on long run economic performance', the Ohlin lectures, MIT Press, 1998.

143 Douglass North, 'Sources of Productivity Change in Ocean Shipping, 1600-1850,' *Journal of Political Economy*, no. 5 (1968).

144 The fatuity of this principle was noted by Dean Acheson in a speech at Amherst College on 9 December 1964. He said this high sounding moral principle of self-determination 'has a doubtful moral history. He [Woodrow Wilson] used it against our enemies in the First World War to dismember the Austro–Hungarian and Ottoman Empires, with results which hardly inspire enthusiasm today. After the Second World War the doctrine was invoked against our

friends in the dissolution of their colonial connections. On the one occasion when the right of self-determination – then called secession – was invoked against our own government by the Confederate States of America, it was rejected with a good deal of bloodshed and moral fervour. Perhaps you will agree it was rightly rejected' (Acheson, 'Ethics in International Relations Today,' in Larson, D. L., ed., *The Puritan Ethic in U.S. Foreign Policy*, Van Nostrand, Princeton, NJ, 1966, pp. 134–35.

145 The illegal drug trade was estimated to be about $400 billion in 1997, compared with a value of legal world exports of $5 trillion that is about 8 per cent of the value of legal world trade. The profits from the trade are enormous. Thus, a kilogramme of cocaine base sells for between $650 and $1,000 in Bolivia or Peru. It can be processed into cocaine hydrochloride for export for between $900 arid $1200, which sells for between $13,000 and $40,000 wholesale in the US before reaching consumers at a retail price of between $17,000 and $172,000. Heroin from Burma begins its progress at $70 per kg to the Burmese producer, to $3,000 after processing in Thailand, whence it is exported from Bangkok at $6,000–$10,000. It sells wholesale in the US for between $90,000 and $200,000, and at retail for nearly $1 million (Krueger, A. and Aturupane, C. E., 'International Trade in "Bads"', in Giersch, H. (ed.), *Merits and Limits of Markets*, Springer, Berlin, 1998). The direct budgetary costs of enforcing the prohibition of drugs in the US have been estimated to be over $20 billion per annum. Yet the war shows no sign of succeeding. There is a strong case for legalisation, while Krueger and Aturupane rightly contend that following the theory of trade and welfare, the correct policy is not to prevent production by the most efficient worldwide producer, but only to seek to tax or prohibit domestic consumption.

146 Navarro, P. and Spencer, A., 'September 11, 2001: Assessing the Costs of Terrorism,' *The Milken Institute Review*, Fourth Quarter 2001, pp. 19–20.

147 See Krueger, A. 'New York's Economic Resilience,' *New York Times*, 16 September 2004.

148 Allison, G., 'Globalization, Terrorism, and the U.S. relationship with Russia', in Rosecrance, R. N. and Stein, A. A. (eds), *No More States?*, Rowman and Littlefield, Lanham MD, 2006.

149 See Lal, D., *In Praise of Empires*, Palgrave Macmillan, New York, 2004.

150 See Doyle, M., *Empires*, Cornell University Press, Ithaca, NY, 1986.

151 United Nations Office on Drugs and Crime (UNODC), *World Drug Report 2008*, UN, New York, 2008, p. 40.

152 UNODC, *The Opium Economy in Afghanistan*, UN, New York, 2003, p. 90.

153 Ibid.

154 UNODC, *The Opium Economy in Afghanistan*, p. 92.

155 Rashid, A., *Taliban*, Yale University Press, New Haven, 2000, p. 118, quoting the remarks of the head of the Taliban's anti-drugs control force in Kandahar.

156 Ibid.

157 Rashid, A., *Taliban*, p. 119.

158 A US Congressional Research Service by Perl of 5 October, 2001, just before the US invasion of Afghanistan, noted that after the Taliban ban on poppy cultivation in July 2000, the price of opium in Afghanistan jumped from $44/kg to $350–$400/kg. It was estimated by UNDCP officials that before the ban up to 60 per cent of opium stock had been stored for future sales. The UK government estimated that in 2001, 3,000 tons of opium were stockpiled in Afghanistan with a substantial portion held by bin Laden and his followers. There were also indications that bin Laden serves as a middleman for Afghan opium producers, using this income to finance terrorist training camps in Afghanistan. See Perl, R. F., *Taliban and the Drug Trade*, CRS Report for Congress, RS 21041, Library of Congress, Washington DC, 5 October 2001.

159 UNODC, *The Opium Economy in Afghanistan*, p. 93.

160 Holloway, A., 'Opium, corruption and the Taliban: the deadly alliance that our troops have to meet', *Daily Telegraph*, 23 April 2006 (available at www.telegraph.co.uk).

161 Meo, N., 'The obstacles facing NATO in Afghanistan', *Daily Telegraph*, 22 June 2008 (available at www.telegraph.co.uk).

162 Phelps and Castillo have suggested channelling reconstruction aid through the central government to provide price support for legal crops (e.g. cotton), and once the output of lawful crops increases to provide the necessary technical knowhow and credit for the local industrialisation of these crops. But as I noted in my letter in response, 'War on terror cannot be won through the war on drugs', *Financial Times*, 8 January 2008, this would only work if there was a viable Afghan polity, which could only be established if the Taliban insurgency could be defeated. The simplest means being the measures suggested later in this article. See Phelps, E. S. and Castillo, G del., 'A strategy to help Afghanistan kick its habit', *Financial Times*, 4 January 2008.

163 UNODC, *The Opium Economy in Afghanistan*, p. 105.

164 Ibid.

165 Meo, N., 'The obstacles facing NATO in Afghanistan', *Daily Telegraph*, 21 June 2008 (available at www.telegraph.co.uk).

166 McNeill Jr notes that 'the World Health Organization reports that 4.8 million people a year with moderate to severe cancer pain receive no appropriate treatment. Nor do another 1.4 million with late stage AIDS. For other causes of lingering pain it issues no estimates but believes that millions go untreated'. The vast majority of these are in developing countries. Thus McNeill cites a report from the UN's International Narcotics Control Board, that 'Six countries – the US, Canada, France, Germany, the UK and Australia – consumed 79 per cent of the world's morphine according to a 2005 estimate. The poor- and middle-income countries where 80 per cent of the world's people live consumed only about 6 per cent'. Morphine is inexpensive: 'One hospice in Uganda, for example, mixes its own liquid morphine so cheaply that a three-week supply

costs less than a loaf of bread. It is not used because of the fear of addiction. As David Joranson of the University of Wisconsin medical school [has said], 'Pain relief hasn't been given as much attention as the war on drugs.' See McNeil Jr., D. G., 'Fear of morphine dooms third world poor to die painfully', *International Herald Tribune*, 9 September 2007.

167 See Naim, M., *Illicit*, Arrow Books, London, 2005.

168 See Lal, D., *In Praise of Empires,* Palgrave Macmillan, New York, 2004.

169 Kapoor, L. D., *Opium Poppy: Botany, Chemistry and Pharmacology*, New York, 1997, p. 11; Trocki, C. A., *Opium, Empire and the Global Political Economy*, London, 1999, p. 37.

170 UNODC, *World Drug Report 2008*, p. 176.

171 Zhou (1999), p. 13.

172 UNODC, *World Drug Report 2008*, p. 177.

173 Ibid.

174 Richards, J., *Opium and the British Indian Empire: The Royal Commission of 1895*, Cambridge, 2001.

175 Mill, J. S., *On Liberty*, pp. 72–3.

176 Mill, J. S., *On Liberty*, pp. 145–6.

177 Namely that 'the principle of freedom cannot require that the person be free not to be free. It is not freedom to be allowed to alienate his freedom', Mill, J. S., *On Liberty*, p. 158. legislation.

178 Sen, A. K., 'Unrestrained smoking is a libertarian half-way house', *Financial Times,* 11 February 2007.

179 See Lal, D., 'Mill would have been appalled at tax on risky, pleasurable activities', Letters, *Financial Times*, 15 February 2007. The best response to Sen's article was from Stuart Simpson, who as a heavy smoker since his teens wrote that 'So strong is Prof. Sen's commitment to liberty that he feels we must now go beyond the traditional assumption of individual free will and seek to liberate the individual from himself or herself. I have myself been in a state of bondage for over 15 years and I was entirely unaware of this state until two weeks ago. This has left me feeling uneasy. Perhaps Prof. Sen can be given a regular column to enlighten us to other states of

bondage we may find ourselves in. Each week he may identify for us a personal behaviour from which we require to be
liberated with the aid of state sanctions. In time the government may be persuaded to set up a new ministry to deal with
the required legislation. I suggest we call this ministry the
Ministry of Liberty.' ('Liberate us from all our states of bondage', Letters, *Financial Times*, 2 March 2007.)

180 See Schelling, T. C., 'Egonomies, or the art of self-management'.

181 See Houthakker and Taylor, *Consumer Demand in the United States*.

182 See Becker and Murphy, 'A Theory of Rational Addiction';
Becker et al., 'An Empirical Analysis of Cigarette Addiction'.

183 See Lal, D., Kim. H., Lu, G., and Prat, J., 'The welfare
effects of tobacco taxation: Estimates for 5 countries/regions',
UCLA Dept. of Economics working paper, 2000, and Lal,
D., 'Smoke Gets In Your Eyes', FMF Monograph no. 26, Free
Market Foundation, Sanditon, Johannesburg, 2000.

184 See Krueger and Aturupane , 'International Trade in "Bads"'.

185 Becker, G., Murphy, K, and Grossman, M., 'The Market for
Illegal Goods: The Case of Drugs', NBER Working Paper,
No. 10976, NBER, Cambridge, Mass, 2004.

186 Caulkins, J. P., *Estimating the Elasticities of Demand for
Cocaine and Heroin with Data from 21 Cities from the Drug
Use Forecasting Program, 1987–1991*, ICPSR version, Rand
Corp., Santa Monica, 1995; van Ours, J. C., 'The price
elasticity of hard drugs: the case of opium in the Dutch East
Indies, 1923-38', *Journal of Political Economy*, 103, 1995, pp.
261–79. Only a few studies have attempted to use the rational
addiction model to estimate the demand for cocaine by young
adults, surveyed in Grossman and Chaloupka. These models
imply that the long-run price elasticity of demand exceeds
the short-run one. Grossman and Chaloupka emphasise an
'estimate of the long run price elasticity of total consumption
(participation multiplied by frequency given participation) of
-1.35. When, however, they include individual fixed effects
to control for unmeasured area-specific effects that may be

correlated with price and consumption, the elasticity becomes -0.67. One problem with the latter estimate is that biases due to random measurement error in the price of cocaine are exacerbated in the fixed-effects specification' – Becker, Murphy and Grossman, 'The Market for Illegal Goods: The Case of Drugs', n. 2, p. 15.

187 Becker, Murphy and Grossman, 'The Market for Illegal Goods: The Case of Drugs', p. 15.

188 See Thornton, M. and Bowmaker, S. W., 'Recreational drugs', in Meadowcroft, J. (ed.), *Prohibitions,* Institute of Economic Affairs, Profile Books, London, 2008 for a lucid and succinct discussion of the case for a free market for drugs against that for other forms of legalisation – government monopoly, government regulation, sin taxes – and prohibition.

189 Thornton and Bowmaker, 'Recreational drugs', p. 72.

190 For a theoretical justification of this position in the context of the theory of trade and welfare, see Lal, D., 'Free trade and laissez-faire – has the wheel come full circle?', *The World Economy* 26 (4), 2003, pp. 471–82, Lal, D., *Reviving the Invisible Hand,* Princeton University Press, Princeton, NJ, 2006 and Thompson, A., 'Democracy in Mexico under "threat" from drug cartels', *Financial Times,* 14 July 2008.

191 Thompson, A., 'Democracy in Mexico under "threat" from drug cartels'.

192 See Naim, *Illicit,* for a chilling account of these often linked illegal and increasingly globalised markets, which are becoming a serious threat to global order.

193 Sources: United Nations Office on Drugs and Crime (UNODC), http://www.unodc.org/unodc/en/money-laundering/globalization.html; United States Department of State, Bureau for International Narcotics and Law Enforcement Affairs, International Narcotics Control Strategy Report, Volume 2, March 2008 (p. 5); International Monetary Fund, World Economic Outlook Database, April 2008; United Nations Office on Drugs and Crime (UNODC), World Drug Report 2005 (p. 127); United Nations Office on Drugs

and Crime (UNODC), World Drug Report 2007 (pp. 195, 209, 212, 223–227).

194 See MacCoun, R. and Reuter, P., *Drug War Heresies,* Cambridge, 2001; Miron, J. A. and Zwiebel, J., 'The economic case against drug prohibition', *Journal of Economic Perspectives,* 9(4) pp. 175–192; Miron, J. A., *Drug War Crimes,* Independent Institute, Oakland, California, 2004.

195 Reuter, P., 'Supply-side drug control', *The Milken Institute Review,* First Quarter 2001, p. 16.

196 Caulkins, J. P., Reuter, P., Iguchi, M., Y., and Chiesa, J., 'How Goes the "War on Drugs?": An Assessment of US Drug Problems and Policy', Occasional Paper, RAND Corp., Santa Monica, 2005, p. 5. This report by RAND presents a succinct summary of the research on the US War on Drugs.

197 Reuter, 'Supply-side drug control', p. 16.

198 Caulkins et al., 'How Goes the "War on Drugs?": An Assessment of US Drug Problems and Policy', p. 7.

199 See The White House, National Drug Control Strategy FY2009 Budget Summary (p. 13).

200 Caulkins et al., 'How Goes the "War on Drugs?": An Assessment of US Drug Problems and Policy', pp. 11–12.

201 Reuter, 'Supply-side drug control', p. 16.

202 See United Nations Office on Drugs and Crime (UNODC), World Drug Report, 2007.

203 Vanyukov, M. M. and Tarter, R. E., 'Genetic studies of substance abuse', *Drug and Alcohol Dependence,* 59, 2000, pp. 101–23.

204 Whybrow, P. C., *American Mania,* Norton, New York, 2005 and Lal, D., *Reviving the Invisible Hand,* pp. 3–4. The novelty seeking, risk taking 'migrant' gene of our ancestors who walked from our homeland in Africa to the four corners of the Earth has been confirmed by the work of Cavalli-Sforza, L. L., *Genes, Peoples and Languages,* Farrar, Strauss and Giroux, New York, 2000; Chen et al., 'Population migrations and the variations of dopamine D4 receptor allele frequencies around the globe', *Evolution and Human Behavior,* 20, 1999,

pp. 309–24 and Chang et al., 'The world wide distribution of allele frequencies in the human dopamine D4 receptor locus', *Human Genetics,* 98, 1996, pp. 91–101.

205 Leshner, A., 'Science-based views ofdrug addiction and its treatment', *JAMA,* 282 (14), 1991, pp. 1314–16, and Duhamel, L. M., 'Drug use outcomes in four substance abuse treatment studies', NEDS Fact Sheet 29, Center for Substance Abuse Treatment (Washington DC.), 2000.

206 Caulkins et al., 'How Goes the "War on Drugs?": An Assessment of US Drug Problems and Policy', p. 38.

207 Reuter, 'Supply-side drug control', pp. 16–17.

208 Nearly half of those imprisoned on drug charges in the US are African-American (see Maguire, K. and Pastore, A. L., *Sourcebook of Criminal Justice Statistics 2000,* Bureau of Justice Statistics, Govt. Printing Office, Washington DC, 2001; Harrison, P. M. and Beck, A.J., *Prisoners in 2001,* Bureau of Justice Statistics, Washington DC, 2002.) They tend to be part of the vast numbers (about 200,000) involved in retailing drugs, and earn little above the minimum wage. The reason they are willing to take the risk of imprisonment and violence at the hands of competitors and collaborators for such meagre rewards is due to the low earnings in alternative occupations for the underclass. See Reuter, 'Supply-side drug control'.

209 Caulkins et al., 'How Goes the "War on Drugs?": An Assessment of US Drug Problems and Policy', p. 38.

210 Bauer. P., *Dissent on Development,* Harvard University Press, Cambridge, 1976.

211 Mosley, P., *Overseas Aid,* Wheatsheaf, Brighton, 1987, p. 232.

212 Little, I. M. D. and Clifford, J., *International Aid,* Allen and Unwin, London, 1965.

213 Klitgard. R., *Tropical Gangsters,* Basic Books, New York, 1990.

214 See Easterly, W., 'Does Foreign Aid Reach the Poor?' SAIS Lecture, December 2004, online at: http://www.sais-jhu.edu/programs/i-dev/Easterly%20 Presentation.pdf.

215 See Lal, D., *Poverty, Power and Prejudice,* Fabian Society, London, 1978, and Lal, D., *The Poverty of 'Development*

Economics'. 3rd ed. London: Institute of Economic Affairs. Cambridge: Harvard University Press; Cambridge: MIT Press, 2002.

216 Easterly, op. cit.

217 Mosley, P., *Overseas Aid*, Wheatsheaf, Brighton, 1987.

218 Lal, D. and H. Myint, *The Political Economy of Poverty, Equity and Growth: A Comparative Study*, Clarendon Press, Oxford, 1996.

219 Ibid.

220 Lal, D., 'Participation, Markets, and Democracy.' in M. Lundahl and B. J. Nudulu (eds), *New Directions in Development Economics*, Routledge, London, 1996.

221 Lal, D., 'The Foreign Exchange Bottleneck Revisited: A Geometric Note.' *Economic Development and Cultural Change* 20, no. 4, 1972, pp. 720–750.

222 Lal, D., *The Poverty of 'Development Economics'*, 3rd ed., Institute of Economic Affairs, London, Cambridge: Harvard University Press; Cambridge: MIT Press, 2002.

223 Lluch, C., 'ICOR's, Savings Rates and the Determinants of Public Expenditure in Developing Countries.' in Lal, D. and Wolf, M. (eds), *Stagflation and the State*, Oxford University Press, New York, 1986.

224 Lal, D., and Myint, H., *The Political Economy of Poverty, Equity and Growth: A Comparative Study*, Clarendon Press, Oxford, 1996.

225 Easterly, W., *The Elusive Quest for Growth*, MIT Press, Cambridge, 2001, and Gilbert, C., Powell, A. and Vines, D., 'Positioning the World Bank', *Economic Journal* 109, no. 459, 1999, F598–F653.

226 Boone, P. 'The Impact of Foreign Aid on Savings and Growth', *Mimeo*, London School of Economics, London, 1994.

227 Gilbert, C. et al., 'Positioning the World Bank'.

228 Krueger, A. O., 'Whither the World Bank and the IMF', *Journal of Economic Literature* 36, no. 4, 1998, pp. 1985–2020.

229 Gilbert, C. et al., 'Positioning the World Bank'.

230 Hancock, G., *Lords of Poverty: The Power, Prestige, and*

Corruption of the International Aid Business, Macmillan, London, 1989.

231 Stern, N., *The Economics of Climate Change: The Stern Review*, Cambridge University Press, Cambridge, 2007.

232 Mudelsee, M. 'The phase relations among atmospheric CO_2 content, temperature and global ice volume over the past 420ka', *Quaternary Science Reviews* 20, 2001, p. 587. Also see Fischer, H. et al., 'Ice Core record of atmospheric CO_2 around the last three glacial terminations', *Science* 283, 1999, pp. 1712–14, and Callion, N. et al. 'Timing of atmospheric CO_2 and Antarctic temperature changes across Termination III', *Science* 299, 2003, pp. 1728–31.

233 See the paper by Princeton university physicist William Harper, 'The Truth about Greenhouse Gases', www.thegwpf.org.

234 See Shaviv, N. and Veizer, J., 'Celestial driver of phanerozoic climate?' *Geological Society of America Today* 13, 2003, pp. 4–10; Veizer, J., 'Celestial Climate Driver', *Geoscience Canada* 32, 2005, p. 1; Svensmark, H., 'Cosmoclimatology', *Astronomy and Geophysics* 48, February 2007, 1.18–1.24; and Svensmark, H. and Calder, N., *The Chilling Stars: A new theory of climate change*, Icon Books, London, 2007.

235 For a lucid account of the formation of the IPCC and its takeover by scientists with an a priori belief in anthropogenic global warming see Booker, C., *The Real Global Warming Disaster*, Continuum, London, 2009.

236 See www.cei.org.

237 Also see Scafetta and West, who show how the short-term fluctuations in the sun's irradiance are also linked to the Earth's average surface temperature along with the longer-term solar cycles. They show that the IPCC's erroneously ignores these fluctuations as noise, assuming their distribution is Gaussian, when in fact it is not. They then show how fluctuations in solar irradiance are linked to those on Earth's surface temperature in addition to the longer-term solar cycles (Scafetta, N. and West, B., 'Is climate sensitive to solar variability?', *Physics Today*, March, 2008, pp. 50–51).

238 Gregory, K., *Climate Change Science*, 2009, available at www.friendsofscience.org/assets/documents/FOS%20Essay/Climate_Change_Science.html.

239 Kirby et al., *Nature* 476, 2011, pp. 429–433.

240 Svensmark, H., 'The cosmic ray/Cloud seeding hypothesis is converging with reality', www.thegwpf.org.

241 Montford, A., 'CLOUD experiment media links', www.thegwpf.org.

242 Garnaut, R., *The Garnaut Climate Change Review: Final Report*, Cambridge University Press, Australia, 2008; Stern (2007).

243 See Nordhaus, W. D., 'The 'Stern Review' of the Economics of Climate Change', NBER WP. 12741, December 2006 and *The challenge of Global Warming: economic models and environmental policy*, Yale University Press, New Haven, 2007.

244 Nordhaus, W. D., *Managing the Global Commons*, MIT Press, Cambridge, Mass, 1994 and Nordhaus, W. D. and Boyer, J., *Warming the World*, MIT Press, Cambridge, Mass, 2000.

245 Lal, D., *Prices for Planning: Toward the reform of Indian planning*, Heinemann Educational Books, London, 1980.

246 For a more wide-ranging critique of economist shortcomings in their treatment of climate change see Henderson, P. D., 'Economists and Climate Science: A Critique', *World Economics* 10 (1), 2009, pp. 59–90.

247 Murthy et al., 'CO_2 emission reduction strategies and economic development of India', *Margin*, 2007.

248 See Booker, *The Real Global Warming Disaster*, p.11.

249 Though it has now (July 2011) been revived by Rudd's successor Julia Gillard to pacify her Green coalition partners.

250 A forensic account of this saga and how a 'hockey team' is still active in global warmist scientific circles to resurrect this statistical artifact is provided in Montford, A. W., *The Hockey Stick Illusion: Climategate and the Corruption of Science*, Stacey International, London, 2010.

251 In Lal (2006), I had used a diagram from Houghton (1994) to show this well-known pattern in its Fig. 8.1 (p. 216). See

Houghton, J., *Global Warming: the complete briefing*, Lion Hudson, Oxford, 1994.

252   See Mann, M., Bradley, E. R. S., and Hughes, M. K., 'Global scale temperature patterns and climate forcing over the past six centuries', *Nature* 392, 1998, pp. 779–787, and 'Northern hemisphere temperatures during the past millennium: Inferences, uncertainties and limitations', *Geophysical Research Letters* 26, 1999, 759–762.

253   See McIntyre, S. and McKitrick, R., 'Corrections to the Mann et al. (1998) proxy database and northern hemispheric average temperature series', *Energy and Environment* 14, 2003, pp. 752–771 and 'The M & M critique of the MBH98 Northern Hemisphere climate index, Update and applications', *Energy and Environment* 16, 2005, pp. 69–99.

254   Wegman Report, 'Ad hoc Committee Report on the 'Hockey Stick' Global Climatic Reconstruction', 2006, available at gochttp://www.cimateaudit.org/pdf/others/07142006_ Wegman_Report.pdf; also see NRC Report, *Surface Temperature Reconstructions for the Last 2,000 years*, National Academic Press, Washington D.C., 2006.

255   See Booker, C., *The Real Global Warming Disaster*, pp. 239–242, and Mclean, J., *Prejudiced authors, prejudiced findings*, Science and Public Policy Institute, Haymarket, VA, 2008.

256   This account is based on Booker, C., 'Climate change: this is the worst scientific scandal of our generation', *Daily Telegraph*, 28 November 2009. Also see Singer, F. S., 'Junkscience: Climate gate Distortion of Climate Data', SEPP Science Editorial 4, 23 January 2010, available at www.SEPP.org.

257   Booker, C. and North, R., 'Climate change guru and a question over business deals', the *Sunday Telegraph*, Special Report, 20 December 2009.

258   These are available at www.montpelerin.org.

259   Lal, D., 'The Great Crash 2008: Causes and Consequences', *Cato Journal* 30 (2), 2010.

260 Like the *Financial Times* star economics commentator Martin
    Wolf.
261 Like the Chairman of the US Federal Reserve, Ben Bernanke.
262 Lal, D., *The Limits of International Cooperation*, twentieth
    Wincott Memorial lecture, Occasional Paper 83, Institute of
    Economic Affairs, London, 1990.
263 Also see Cooper, R., 'Living with global imbalances', *Brookings
    Papers on Economic Activity* 2, 2007, pp. 91–107 and Corden,
    W. M., 'Those current account imbalances: A sceptical view',
    The World Economy 30, 2007, pp. 363–382, which also
    support this view expressed in my February 2006 *Business
    Standard* article 'Global Imbalances?'
264 These are statistical measures of different definitions of 'broad
    money'.
265 See Calomiris, C. W., *US Bank Deregulation in Historical
    Perspective*, Cambridge University Press, Cambridge, 2000
    and Meltzer, A., *A History of the Federal Reserve*, Chicago
    University Press, Chicago, 2009.
266 Meltzer, A., *A History of the Federal Reserve*, referencing
    Benston, G. J., *The Separation of Commercial and Investment
    Banking: The Glass-Steagall Act Revisited and Reconsidered*,
    Oxford University Press, Oxford, 1990.
267 Calomiris, C. W., *US Bank Deregulation in Historical
    Perspective*, p. xiv and xvii.
268 Calomiris also seems very enamored of the German universal
    banks (see his Chapter 4), and this is the direction in which
    he hopes the US banking system will evolve. But this 'rela-
    tionship banking' based on corporatism is the direct antithesis
    of the free market Anglo-Saxon capitalist model. See Rajan,
    R.G. and Zingales, L., *Saving Capitalism from the Capitalists:
    Unleashing the power of financial markets to create wealth and
    spread opportunity*, Random House, London, (trad. it. *Salvare
    il capitalismo dai capitalisti*, Einaudi, Torino 2004) and Lal,
    D., *Reviving the Invisible Hand*, Princeton University Press,
    Princeton, NJ, 2006, pp. 195–203).
269 The following section has benefited from a paper by my

UCLA colleague Axel Leijunhufvud: Leijunhufvud, A., 'Wicksell, Hayek, Keynes, Friedman: Whom Should We Follow?', Paper presented at the special meeting of the Mont Pelerin Society on 'The End of Globalizing Capitalism?', New York, March 2009. Available at www.montpelerin.org.

270 Taylor, J. B., *Getting Off Track: How Government Actions and Interventions Caused, Prolonged and Worsened the Financials Crisis*, Hoover Institution Press, Stanford, CA, 2009.

271 Haberler, G., 'Reflections on Hayek's Business Cycle Theory', *Cato Journal* 6 (2), 1986, p.422.

272 Keynes, J. M., *Collected Writings of John Maynard Keynes*, vol. 27: *Activities 1940-46: Shaping the Postwar World*, edited by Moggridge, D. E., Cambridge University Press, Cambridge, 1942, p. 122.

273 Fisher, I., 'The Debt-Deflation Theory of Great Depressions', *Econometrica* 1 (4), 1933, pp. 337–357.

274 This was also my diagnosis of the Japanese slump in Lal, D., 'The Japanese Slump', 2003. In Lal, D., 'Notes on Money, Debt and Alternative Monetary Regimes for Brazil', *Revista de Economica Politica* 15 (4), pp. 99–111, I had also used the Wicksell framework to analyse the macroeconomic outcomes in Brazil in the early 1990s.

275 Congdon, T., *Central Banking in a Free Society*, Institute of Economic Affairs, London, 2009, provides a succinct account of the evolution of central banking.

276 See Congdon, *Central Banking in a Free Society*.

277 Meltzer, A., *A History of the Federal Reserve*, p. 1233.

278 Meltzer, A., *A History of the Federal Reserve*.

279 Congdon distinguishes between two types of liquidity traps, one a narrow liquidity trap which applies to narrow money (M0 or M1), i.e. the monetary base, and a broad liquidity trap based on broad money (M2 or M4) which includes bank deposits. He shows that the first one can occur when the Central Bank confines itself to money market operations to influence the monetary base, but the second will not if it co-ordinates with the fiscal authorities to change the broad

money supply. The classic discussion questioning the existence of liquidity traps during the Great Depression and a
rigorous discussion of the implausible assumptions needed to
generate them. See Congdon, T., 'Monetary Policy at the Zero
Bound', *World Economics* 11 (1), 2010, pp. 11–45; Brunner, K.
and Meltzer, A. H., 'Liquidity Traps for Money, Bank Credit
and Interest Rates', *Journal of Political Economy* 76 (1), 1968,
pp. 1–37. In a series of papers in the 1960s they also integrated
credit markets into monetarist theory.

280 Meltzer bases his monetarist argument on narrow money –
the monetary base (M0 or M1). Whether the Central Bank
controls this monetary aggregate, or broad money (M2 or
M4) has been part of a dispute amongst monetarists. Congdon
(2005) argues cogently that it is broad money which is the
correct variable for the Central Bank to control. As it is the
real balance effect of broad money, not narrow money, which
leads to the transmission from money, to nominal output,
and prices.

281 Congdon, T., *Money and Asset Prices in Boom and Bust*,
Institute of Economic Affairs, London: 2005, and 'Monetary
Policy at the Zero Bound'.

282 Unlike the 1930s, governments in developed countries have
much more leeway to do this, as the share of general government revenue (their tax cut) as a share of GDP had increased
from about 20 per cent in the United States and Great Britain
to about 32 per cent in the United States and 38 per cent in
Britain in 1997 (Tanzi, V. and Schuknecht, L., *Public Spending
in the 20th Century*, Cambridge University Press, Cambridge,
2000, p. 52).

283 Guha, K., 'White House hit in skirmishes over spending',
Financial Times, 9 July 2009.

284 The theoretical worry that temporary tax cuts will be saved
rather than raising consumption and aggregate demand is
irrelevant to this case, as the purpose of the temporary tax
cuts is to allow economic agents to raise their savings without
reducing their previous consumption.

285 See Authers, J., *The Fearful Rise of Markets*, Prentice Hall, Harlow, 2010; Rajan, R. G., *Fault Lines*, Princeton University Press, Princeton, NJ, 2010 and Tett, G., *Fool's Gold*, Little, Brown, London, 2009 for incisive accounts.

286 Wallison, P. J., *The Dodd–Frank Act: Creative Destruction, Destroyed*, Financial Services Outlook July–August 2010, American Enterprise Institute, Washington DC.

287 Reinhart and Rogoff, in their empirical historical survey of past crises around the world, have shown they were no different from the current crisis (Reinhart, C. M. and Rogoff, K. S., *This Time is Different*, Princeton University Press, Princeton NJ, 2009). See also Lal, D., 'The Political Economy of Economic Liberalization', *World Bank Economic Review* 1 (2), pp. 273–299, and Lal, D. and Myint, H., *The Political Economy of Poverty, Equity and Growth*, for the anatomy of crises.

288 Walker, D. M., 'Long-Term Budget Outlook: Deficits Matter – Saving Our Future Requires Tough Choices Today', United States Government Accountability Office, Testimony before the Committee on the Budget, House of Representatives, 2007, GAO-07-389T. Available at www.gao.gov/new.items/d07389t.pdf.

289 This remains controversial even amongst American conservative economists. See Calomiris, C. W., *US Bank Deregulation in Historical Perspective* and Meltzer, A. H., *A History of the Federal* Reserve, p. 1245.

SELECT BIBLIOGRAPHY

Bauer, P., *Dissent on Development, Studies and Debates in Development Economics*, Harvard University Press, Cambridge, 1976.

Becker, G., and Murphy, K., 'A theory of rational addiction', *Journal of Political Economy* 96, 1988, pp. 675–700.

—— —— and Grossman, M., 'An empirical analysis of cigarette addiction', *American Economic Review* 84, 1994, pp. 396–418.

—— —— —— 'The market for illegal goods: the case of drugs', *NBER Working Paper,* no. 10976, NBER, Cambridge, Mass, 2004.

Booker, C., *The Real Global Warming Disaster*, Continuum, London, 2009.

Brennan, G. and Buchanan, J., *The Power to Tax: Analytic Foundations of a Fiscal Constitution*, Cambridge University Press, Cambridge, 1980.

Brunner, K. and Meltzer, A. H., 'Liquidity Traps for Money, Bank Credit and Interest Rates', *Journal of Political Economy*, 76 (1), 1968, pp. 1–37.

Buchanan, J. and Stubblebine, W. C., 'Externality', *Economica* 29, 37184.7, 1962.

Calomiris, C.W., *US Bank Deregulation in Historical Perspective*, Cambridge University Press, Cambridge, 2000.

Caulkins, J. P., Reuter, P., Iguchi, M., Y., and Chiesa, J., *How Goes the 'War on Drugs'?: An Assessment of U.S. Drug Problems and Policy*, Occasional Paper, Rand Corp., Santa Monica, 2005.

Chaloupka, F. J. and Warner, K. E., 'The economics of smoking', *NBER* Working Paper No. 7047, NBER, Cambridge Mass, 1999.

Congdon, T., *Money and Asset Prices in Boom and Bust*, Institute of Economic Affairs, London, 2005.

—— *Central Banking in a Free Society*, Institute of Economic Affairs, London, 2009.

—— 'Monetary Policy at the Zero Bound', *World Economics* 11 (1), 2010, pp. 11–45.

De Jasay, A., *Before Resorting to Politics*, Edward Elgar Publishing, Aldershot, 1996.

Easterly, W., *The Elusive Quest for Growth*, MIT Press, Cambridge, 2001.

Le Fanu, J., *The Rise and Fall of Modern Medicine*, HarperCollins, London, 1998.

Fisher, I., 'The Debt-Deflation Theory of Great Depressions', *Econometrica* 1 (4), 1933, pp. 337–357.

Gori, G. B. and Luik, J. C., *Passive smoke,* Fraser Institute, Vancouver, 1999.

Gregory, K., *Climate Change Science*, 2009, available at www.friendsofscience.org/assets/documents/FOS%20Essay/Climate_Change_Science.html.

Haberler, G., 'Reflections on Hayek's Business Cycle Theory', *Cato Journal* 6 (2), 1986, p.422.

Hayek, F. A., *The Constitution of Liberty*, Routledge and Paul, London, 1960, p. 402.

Hecksher, E., *Mercantilism, Allen* and Unwin, London, 1955.

Henderson, P. D., *Misguided Virtue*, Institute of Economic Affairs, London, 2001.

Keynes, J. M., *Collected Writings of John Maynard Keynes*, vol. 27: *Activities 1940-46: Shaping the Postwar World*, edited by Moggridge, D. E., Cambridge University Press, Cambridge, 1942, p. 122.

Krueger, A. and Aturupane, C. E., 'International Trade in "Bads"', in Giersch, H. (ed.), *Merits and Limits of Markets*, Springer, Berlin, 1998.

Lal, D., *The Hindu Equilibrium,* Clarendon Press, Oxford, 1998.

—— 'Notes on Money, Debt and Alternative Monetary Regimes for Brazil', *Revista de Economica Politica* 15 (4), pp. 99–111.

—— 'The Japanese Slump', in Pethig, R. and Rauscher, M. (eds), *Challenges to the World Economy*, Berlin: Springer, 2003.

—— *Reviving the Invisible Hand,* Princeton University Press, Princeton, NJ, 2006.

—— 'The Great Crash 2008: Causes and Consequences', Cato Journal 30 (2), 2010.

—— *The Poverty of Development Economics,* Hobart Paperback No. 16, Institute of Economic Affairs, London, 1983.

—— 'Unintended Consequences: the impact of factor endowments, culture and politics on long run economic performance', *The Ohlin lectures*, MIT Press, 1998.

—— *Unfinished Business,* Oxford University Press, Oxford, 1999.

—— 'Free trade and laissez-faire – has the wheel come full circle?', *The World Economy* 26 (4), 2003, pp. 471–82.

—— *In Praise of Empires,* Palgrave Macmillan, New York, 2004.

—— *Reviving the Invisible Hand: The case for Classical Liberalism in the Twenty-First Century*, Princeton University Press, Princeton, New Jersey, 2006.

—— *Against Dirigisme*, ICS Press, San Francisco, 1994.

—— *Prices for Planning: Toward the reform of Indian planning*, Heinemann Educational Books, London, 1980.

—— 'The Political Economy of Economic Liberalization', *World Bank Economic Review* 1 (2), 1987, pp. 273–299.

—— and Myint, H., *The Political Economy of Poverty, Equity and Growth: A Comparative Study*, Clarendon Press, Oxford, 1996.

Leijunhufvud, A., 'Wicksell, Hayek, Keynes, Friedman: Whom Should We Follow?', Paper presented at the special meeting of the Mont Pelerin Society on 'The End of Globalizing Capitalism?', New York, March 2009.

Mill, J. S., *On Liberty*, Everyman's Library, London, 1859/1910.

Mosley, P., *Overseas Aid,* Wheatsheaf, Brighton, 1987, p. 232.

Naim, M., *Illicit,* Arrow Books, London, 2005.

Meltzer, A., *A History of the Federal Reserve,* Chicago University Press, Chicago, 2009

Montford, A. W., *The Hockey Stick Illusion: Climategate and the Corruption of Science,* Stacey International, London, 2010.

Mudelsee, M. 'The phase relations among atmospheric CO_2 content, temperature and global ice volume over the past 420ka', *Quaternary Science Reviews* 20, 2001, p. 587.

Nordhaus, W. D., *The challenge of Global Warming: economic models and environmental policy,* Yale University Press, New Haven, 2007.

—— and Boyer, J., *Warming the World,* MIT Press, Cambridge, Mass, 2000.

Rajan, R. G., *Fault Lines,* Princeton University Press, Princeton, NJ, 2010.

Rashid, A., *Taliban,* Yale University Press, New Haven, 2000.

Reinhart, C. M. and Rogoff, K. S., *This Time is Different,* Princeton University Press, Princeton NJ, 2009.

Rydell, C. P. and Everingham, S. S., *Controlling Cocaine: Supply versus Demand programs,* Drug Policy Research Centre, Rand, Santa Monica, CA, 1995.

Shaviv, N. and Veizer, J., 'Celestial driver of phanerozoic climate?' *Geological Society of America Today* 13, 2003, pp. 4–10.

Svensmark, H., 'Cosmoclimatology', *Astronomy and Geophysics* 48, February 2007, 1.18–1.24.

—— and Calder, N., *The Chilling Stars: A new theory of climate change,* Icon Books, London, 2007.

Tanzi, V. and Schuknecht, L., *Public Spending in the 20th Century,* Cambridge University Press, Cambridge, 2000, p. 52.

Taylor, J. B., *Getting Off Track: How Government Actions and Interventions Caused, Prolonged and Worsened the Financials Crisis,* Hoover Institution Press, Stanford, CA, 2009.

Tett, G., *Fool's Gold,* Little, Brown, London, 2009.

Thornton, M. and Bowmaker, S. W., 'Recreational drugs', in Meadowcroft, J. (ed.), *Prohibitions,* Institute of Economic Affairs, Profile Books, London, 2008.

UNODC, *The Opium Economy in Afghanistan*, UN, New York, 2003.

Veizer, J., 'Celestial Climate Driver', *Geoscience Canada* 32, 2005

Viscusi, K., *Smoking,* Oxford University Press, New York, 1992.

World Bank, *Curbing the Epidemic,* World Bank, Washington DC, 1999.

World Health Organisation, *The World Health Report 1999,* Oxford University Press, Oxford, 1999.